National Identity
and
Global Sports Events

SUNY series on Sport, Culture, and Social Relations
CL Cole and Michael A. Messner, editors

National Identity
and
Global Sports Events

Culture, Politics, and Spectacle
in the Olympics and the
Football World Cup

Edited by
Alan Tomlinson and Christopher Young

State University of New York Press

Published by
State University of New York Press, Albany

For information, address State University of New York Press,
194 Washington Avenue, Suite 305, Albany, NY 12210-2384

Production by Michael Haggett
Marketing by Michael Campochiaro

Library of Congress Cataloging-in-Publication Data

National identity and global sports events / culture, politics, and spectacle in the
Olympics and the football World Cup / edited by Alan Tomlinson and Christopher Young.
          p. cm. — (SUNY series on sport, culture, and social relations)
     Includes bibliographical references and index.
     ISBN 0-7914-6615-9 (hardcover : alk. paper) — ISBN 0-7914-6616-7 (pbk. : alk. paper)
1. Nationalism and sports—History. 2. Sports and globalization—History. 3 Sports—
Sociological aspects—Cross-cultural studies. I. Tomlinson, Alan. II. Young, Christopher,
1967–   III. Series.
     GV706.34.N38 2005
     306.4'83—dc22   2004029962
ISBN-13: 978-0-7914-6615-5 (hardcover : alk. paper)
ISBN-13: 978-0-7914-6616-2 (pbk. : alk. paper)

10 9 8 7 6 5 4 3 2 1

Contents

v

Acknowledgments

We wish to thank the bursar and staff of Pembroke College, Cambridge, who made possible the initial workshop of this project in such relaxed and congenial surroundings in July 2003. The Thomas Gray Room provided the perfect ambiance for a collaborative exchange between scholars. The University of Brighton provided essential financial support for the editorial process. John Heath went about the formatting of the manuscript with the unflappability of a Yorkshire batsman. Paul Gilchrist provided valuable organizational support at the Pembroke College event, and compiled the index.

We are very grateful to CL Cole, the series editor at State University of New York Press, for accepting this volume into her series and contributing to the final contours of the project by attending the workshop. Thanks are due in no small measure to Toby Miller who, like Ben Carrington, read our initial project outline with great interest, and also put us in contact with State University of New York Press.

We wish to thank all those who attended the workshop from all around the world and made such critical, yet supportive, responses to everyone's work.

Alan Tomlinson   Christopher Young
Chelsea School   Pembroke College
University of Brighton   University of Cambridge

September 2003

Chapter 1

Culture, Politics, and Spectacle in the Global Sports Event—An Introduction

Alan Tomlinson and Christopher Young

The political exploitation of the global sports spectacle and the cultural and economic ramifications of its staging have been critical indices of the intensifying globalization of both media and sport. Sports events celebrating the body and physical culture have long been driven by political and ideological motives, from the ancient civilizations of Greece and Rome to the societies of early modern Europe, in more modern Western societies as well as less developed and non-Western ones. This is never more so than when such events purport to be spheres of neutrality and embodiments of universalist and idealist principles. Spectacles have been justified on the basis of their potential to realize shared, global modes of identity and interdependence, making real the sense of a global civil society. Understanding this form of spectacle, and the extent to which its claimed goals have been met or compromised, contributes to an understanding of the sources of ethnocentrism, and to debates concerning the possibility of a cultural cosmopolitanism combining rivalry, respect, and reciprocal understanding. Analyzing the global sports spectacle is a way of reviewing the contribution of international sport to the globalization process generally, and to processes and initiatives of global inclusion and exclusion.

The most dramatic and high profile of such spectacles have been the modern Olympic Games and the men's football World Cup (henceforth World Cup). Such sporting encounters and contests have provided a source of and a focus for the staging of spectacle and, in an era of international mass communications, the media event. In any history of globalization, it would be an oversight to omit coverage of the foundation and growth of the International Olympic Committee (IOC) and the Fédération Internationale de Football Association (FIFA), founded in 1894 and 1904 respectively. The growth of these organizations, and of their major events, has provided a platform for national pride and prestige. Greece saw the symbolic potential of staging an international event such as the first modern Olympics in 1896 to both assert its incipient modernity and to deflect domestic tensions. Uruguay, having cultivated double Olympic soccer champions in the 1920s, helped FIFA's aspirations take off by hosting the first football World Cup in 1930. From modest beginnings, each event grew in stature and significance as more nations came to recognize the potential benefits of participation in the events and the international status that might accrue from hosting and staging them.

The growth, consolidation, and expansion of these events have been truly phenomenal. From seven founding members in 1904, FIFA has expanded its membership, over the next century (and depending upon suspensions and the state of applications), to more than 200 national associations. From the first World Cup in 1930 at which only sixteen nations competed, and for which there was no real qualifying stage, the tournament has expanded to include thirty-two teams in its quadrennial final, based upon worldwide qualifying phases in which every national association in the world is entitled to participate. The Olympics, initially a platform for the physical, bodily performance of privileged European and North American male elites, now welcomes every nation in the world to its Summer Games. There may still be male-dominated small teams from brutal patriarchal states marching in the opening ceremony of an Olympic Games, but they carry the flag for the nation on a global media stage. In participatory terms, the World Cup and the Olympics offer a platform to all nations, and most of all to small nations, of the world that is unrivaled by any other cultural or political body, even the United Nations. In a postcolonial period, at different points in the twentieth century, this has allowed small and resurgent nations from Africa, Asia, the Caribbean, and parts of formerly Soviet-dominated Eastern Europe to assert their national autonomy on a global stage (in Olympic terms, see Simson and Jennings 1992; for the football example, see Sugden and Tomlinson 1998). Sport has in this way been a major cultural influence, with an explicitly political dimension. While such cultural and political currents have driven the involvement of the nations of the world in international sports events, the increasingly mediated base of such events has proved irresistible to the multinational and transnational corporate world. Miller et al. (2001) have argued forcefully that global sport can be adequately understood only if the character of the main political and economic dimensions is recognized. These dimensions are interconnected and serve the interests of what they call the New International Division of Cultural Labor (NIDCL), which operates in the context of "five simultaneous, uneven, interconnected processes which characterize the present moment in sport: Globalization, Governmentalization, Americanization, Televisualization, and Commodification (GGATaC)" (Miller et al. 2001, 41). Contributors to this volume may not choose to use all of the contents of such a box of conceptual tools, but each tackles in his or her own way one or another aspect of these elements of the NIDCL. It is impossible to account for the scale in the escalation of the sport spectacle without addressing some, if not necessarily all, of these processes. For instance, though sports forms and practices may vary, as is shown when respective cases in time and space are subjected to careful study and analysis, there is no denying that the logic of sport's political economy has been led more and more by what might be called the "U.S. model." And to study this, a blend of cultural analysis and political economy is essential. Alongside these challenging general theoretical questions, it is also important not to lose sight of the conceptual, definitional dimension of such study. Our working definition of global sport spectacle for this book is of an event that has come to involve the majority of the nations of the world, that is transmitted globally, that foregrounds the sculptured and commodified body and orchestrates a physical display of the body politic, and that attracts large and regular followings of on-site spectators for the live contest or event.

The importance of sports mega-events has been recognized increasingly in a world of cultural and economic globalization (Miller et al. 2001; see too the themed issue of the *International Review for the Sociology of Sport*, September 2000). The cultural-political and economic significance of such events (Roche 2001; Simson and Jennings 1992; Tomlinson 1986, 1994; Sugden and Tomlinson 1998, 1999) has not diminished in the wake of revelations about the corrupt politics at the heart of international sports diplomacy. The Olympics and the World Cup as media events (Dayan and Katz 1992; Puijk 2000; Alabarces, Tomlinson, and Young 2001) have continued to stimulate fierce competition among nations for the right to stage such events and to fuel discourses and narratives of international competition and national rivalry. Yet if sports have become increasingly international, this is not to say that sports culture has homogenized: football's global popularity and impact, for instance, have not eroded the distinctiveness of different sport cultures (Giulianotti 2000).

Seminal scholarship by John MacAloon (1981) has identified the interlocking cultural, political, and commercial interests that were the basis of the formation of the Olympics. These interests became stronger as the twentieth century progressed, so that nations, regions, and cities have become increasingly committed to the prospect of staging sports mega-events (Guttmann 2002; Hill 1992). MacAloon (1984) has also assessed the conceptual frameworks available for analyzing the cultural dimensions of such events, and his reflexive contribution (chapter 2) to this book reviews those frameworks. Comments abound on the symbolism and ideologies characterizing such events (for one relatively recent collection, see Smith and Schaffer 2000). The international profile of the media event has produced recurrent discourses of identity and globalization (Tomlinson 1996, 2000). Local opposition to the rhetoric of civic boosterism has sometimes questioned the value of the cultural spectacle (Lenskyj 2000). But the aspirations to stage such events have continued to drive nations from all parts of the globe. For instance, China sought desperately, with eventual success, to stage the Olympics, while Africa staked and realised its moral claim to stage that continent's first World Cup in 2010.

National sports cultures are not all absorbed into a globalized, homogeneous form, as shown in the case of the national distinctiveness of the mainstream sports of the United States and football's continued marginalization there despite the staging of the most commercially successful World Cup ever (Markovits and Hellerman 2001). And at the Sydney 2000 Olympics, Australia's three top national sports (Australian Rules football, rugby football [in two codes], and cricket) were not Olympic disciplines. Yet the sports mega-event—particularly in the regular internationally inclusive events, and when constituted as a media event and global consumption—has worldwide impact. Such events are produced by alliances of the national state, regional politics, and expansion of the global consumer market. How such alliances have been renegotiated and rebalanced across the century of modernity and emerging globalization, mapped in general terms by Maguire (1999), constitutes a further focus of this book. It is particularly important to review the role of transnational organizations (often called international nongovernmental organizations, or INGOs) in the reconstitution of the global cultural order (Sklair 2001), the shifting role and contribution of the state and national governments, and the contribution that performance sports and high-profile international events have made to the reaffirmation of national civil societies (Allison 1998).

Studying the sport spectacle in its form as a media event is also to engage in a form of cultural history and the analysis of the persisting influence and power of ideas, that is, the use to which particular conceptions, values, and ideologies of sport, as well as the performing sporting body, has been put. The founding philosophies of the events were articulated in the writings of two Frenchmen, Baron Pierre de Coubertin and Jules Rimet, the founders, respectively, of the Olympic Games and the football World Cup. De Coubertin's voluminous writings have received extensive scholarly treatment, and detailed debates have taken place over the precise influence that the Parisian aristocrat did or did not have on the institutional evolution of the Olympics and the IOC. As early as 1896, in the buildup to the first modern Olympic Games in Athens, "one Athenian newspaper reviled him as 'a thief seeking to rob Greece of her inheritance'" (Guttmann 2002, 19). But unperturbed by such slurs, de Coubertin could still, and even after Greece's humiliation by Turkey in the thirty-day Cretan War just months after the patriotic celebrations of the Olympic Games, insist vigorously that "internationalism was a bulwark against ignorance, chauvinism, and war" (MacAloon 1981, 263). De Coubertin's belief that athletic contests between young people could be a force for international harmony and universal peace has framed the rhetoric and ideology of the Olympic Games throughout its turbulent and extraordinary history. For de Coubertin, the Olympic project had philosophical, historical, and educational dimensions and goals: "Everything in the restored and modernized Olympism," he wrote in 1931, "focuses on the ideas of mandatory continuity, interdependence, and solidarity" (2000, 603). De Coubertin puffed up his conception of Olympism consistently for more than forty years, inscribing it in the expanding rituals and protocols of the Olympic event and claiming a remarkable continuity and expansion of impact and importance of the Olympic movement and family. It was a heady mix of lofty ideals and grandiose ambition, yet it represented a set of contradictions underlaying the baron's aristocratic and elitist roots and exposing the ethnocentric and patriarchal nature of his Olympic ideals and associated beliefs (Tomlinson 1984).

Jules Rimet, president of FIFA from 1921 to 1954, was a self-made professional and religious philanthropist who dominated the international growth of football (Tomlinson 1999). Rimet was trained in law. Bearded, bowler-hatted, and thoroughly bourgeois, the elder Rimet was an established figure among the Parisian elite. He was born, though, in humble circumstances, into a rural family in 1873, learning the lessons of the work ethic as a young boy by helping his father in the family's grocer's shop. At age eleven, Rimet followed his father to Paris, where the rural grocer had moved in search of work. The immigrant family lived in the heart of the city, and the young Rimet learned lessons of survival, and football, on the street. He worked his way toward a full legal qualification and was active in encouraging football among the poorer children of the city. Seeing in sport a means of building good character, Christian and patriotic, his love of God and France was combined in his passion for football. He believed in the universality of the church and saw in football the chance to create a worldwide "football family" welded to Christian principles. Like his countryman, de Coubertin, Rimet believed that sport could be a force for national and international good. Sport and football could bring people and nations together in a healthy competitiveness, he thought. Sport could be a powerful means of both physical and moral progress, providing healthy pleasure and fun, and promoting friendship between races (Guillain 1998).

The idealist rhetoric of universal peace and international harmony has, then, underpinned the philosophies underlying the rationale for events such as the Olympics and the World Cup, but the importance of such events in a formative phase of globalization has remained too little remarked upon. These sports mega-events were used by the host nations both to celebrate an historical legacy and to aspire to the expression of their modernity: in Greece in 1896, this was based upon a reclamation of the classical past, and in Uruguay in 1930, upon the centennial celebration of its constitutional independence. This motivational matrix continues to characterize the aspirations of many host nations today.

From a national standpoint, and that of the sporting organization, the rhetoric of universalism is sustained, but equally sports mega-events are seen as global marketing opportunities by multinational corporations. National governments continue to seek the profile provided by the host role. International organizations such as the IOC and FIFA negotiate these rights. The shifting power structures of international sport have matched the emergence, advent, and decline of different configurations of national interest. Northern Europe and the United States dominated the administration of the Olympics for the first three-quarters of the twentieth century, until Brazilian João Havelange, Spaniard/Catalan Juan Antonio Samaranch, and Italian Primo Nebiolo took the reins of power in world football, the Olympics, and international athletics, respectively. In the 1980s, the foundation was laid for a new economic order for international sports events. By the World Cup in Korea and Japan in 2002, FIFA's main corporate partners were Adidas, Avaya, Budweiser, Coca-Cola, Fuji Xerox, Fuji Film, Gillette, Hyundai, JVC, KT-Korea/NTT-Japan, Mastercard, McDonald's, Philips, Toshiba, and Yahoo (fifteen official, general sponsors, more than ever before, paying a total of 290 million pounds for the privilege, ranging from between ten to a little over twenty million pounds each). During the Olympiad leading into the Athens Summer Olympics in 2004, the IOC's ten major sponsors were Coca-Cola, John Hancock, Kodak, McDonald's, Panasonic, Samsung, Sema, *Sports Illustrated*, Visa, and Xerox—a veritable line-up of predominantly U.S. and Japanese global economic power.

Tracing the changes and continuities in the contours of the spectacle, the relation of emergent nations to new forms of the spectacle in the postcolonial period, and the escalating profile of world sports bodies' partner sponsors is an exercise in the analysis of the dynamics of power in international sport. This book traces the shifting balance in the political, cultural, and economic significance of such events, with reference to selected, detailed cases from the Los Angeles 1932 Summer Olympics to the Korea/Japan World Cup of 2002. Primary themes explored across the different chapters are the rhetoric of the body, sport, and spectacle, ceremony and ritual in the staging of the spectacle, and representational convention in the coverage of the spectacle. Tensions such as the following are emphasized: those between ceremony and rhetoric, on the one hand, and economically driven forms of regional and civic boosterism, on the other; between national and universalist discourse in symbol and ritual; and between the aesthetics of corporate culture, myth making, and often gendered ideologies. In this sense it is the relationship between symbolic and cultural capital in sports practice, performance, and mediation that provides the theoretical aperture through which each of the individual cases is considered. The focus of the case studies is on a variety of forms such as television, film, documentary, press, posters, and artifacts (e.g., emblems, medals), as well as aspects of gender, national identity, imperialism, and neocolonialism in the discourses and narratives of the events.

John MacAloon has conducted ethnographic work on the Olympic phenomenon for more than a quarter of a century. This provided him with an extensive experiential and analytical base for conceptualizing the nature of the sports spectacle, and the related elements of ritual and festival. In his contribution to this volume, he has taken the opportunity to review these interpretative frameworks in light of both burgeoning scholarship on the Olympics and comparable sports events and his own particular interest in the Olympic torch relay as a form of public festival. It is in this relay that the Olympic ideal has been experienced by millions of people who may never get close to the Olympic contests or stadium—yet it receives little coverage outside the nations through which it passes. In its own way, the relay provides a platform for reclaiming the Olympics from corporate sponsors and corporate brands such as Coca-Cola. MacAloon's analysis critiques overgeneralized theories of the spectacle by leftist and rightist theorists alike, and it also calls to task those powerful and privileged members of Olympic and international sporting institutions for whom such public festival has no significance.

Robert Gordon and John London explore how Italy staged and won the 1934 World Cup, the second in FIFA's history, a victory that provided a platform, four years later, for a successful defense of the title in Paris. These victories coincided with an important phase in the history of the fascist regime in Italy, taking in its imperial war in Abyssinia, its massive involvement in the Spanish Civil War, its axis with Nazi Germany, and its passing of anti-Semitic racial laws. At the same time, during this period a peak was reached in the regime's totalitarian social policies, including the exploitation of mass media and leisure (embracing sport) to the full as a means of capillary penetration and control of Italian society. The analysis is based on newspaper and radio archives (the 1934 tournament was the first to be broadcast by radio). Examining the 1934 tournament and its staging, Gordon and London place the event in the context of existing work on the fabrication of consensus under fascism and on the construction of a civic, nationalist religion through rituals such as sport and myths of the strong, heroic, "pure" Italian.

The 1936 Olympics is a pivotal case in the study of modern spectacle for two primary reasons. First, the sports mega-event was utilized explicitly for the celebration of a political regime. Second, the Nazis mobilized a propaganda machine of unprecedented sophistication for the documentation of the event. For the first time in history, viewing screens were erected for the Olympic Games, so that throughout the local communities of Germany, the population could be kept abreast of the progress of its Aryan athletes. The magnificence of the scale of provision for the participants in these Olympic Games is evidenced in the brilliant yet ideologically driven cinematic masterpiece by Leni Riefenstahl. Allen Guttmann revisits the history of this extraordinary event, with an emphasis on the nature and motives of the leadership of the Olympic movement, the nature of the spectator response, the racist agenda of the Nazis, and the legacy of Riefenstahl's artistic yet ideologically disputed genius.

The case studies of 1934 and 1936 demonstrate clearly the escalating scale of the sports spectacle, particularly when driven by an explicit and extreme political ideology. In the wake of this, though, the international community after World War II approached such events with caution. The Tokyo Olympics in 1964 and the England World Cup in 1966, however, marked the beginning of the globally mediated sports event. Tony Mason reviews England's victory in the 1966 World Cup. Hosting and winning the tournament spawned an enduring myth of English superiority. The tournament was, after the Olympic Games of 1948, the largest, most international, and spectacular sporting event ever to be held in the United Kingdom. Moreover, unlike 1948, it was not simply a show for London; it was shared by six other regional centers. The power of television brought live coverage of the matches to almost every household in the country at a formative moment in the expansion of the television industry. The chapter examines the media representation of the World Cup before, during, and after the event, the process of organizing and staging the event, and data on the public response. It also assesses the political importance of the 1966 event in a country in the throes of dramatic changes, as Empire was diluted to Commonwealth and the long-established place of Britain as one of the world's leading powers was increasingly called into question. It was a moment when England looked at itself, and the eyes of the world were on it.

Claire and Keith Brewster analyze the domestic and international ramifications of Mexico's hosting of the 1968 Olympic Games. During the 1920s and 1930s, the postrevolutionary state used sport as part of a broader cultural project designed to create a common sense of national unity and identity, sport becoming a metaphor for the country's well-being and potential. Political scientists and historians, though, mark the repression of the Mexican student movement in 1968 as a watershed in Mexican politics, the point at which the carefully constructed framework that had sustained the postrevolutionary regime began to crumble. This chapter pays detailed attention to the battle around the 1968 Olympics over symbols, perceptions, and interpretations of national history. Drawing upon documentary archives, media sources, and interviews with key political figures, the Brewsters reveal much about the ways in which the Mexican state and a nascent civil society fought to win over domestic and international opinion. This involved confronting fundamental issues of Mexican identity and international stereotypes of the "Mexican character," balancing aspirations to modernity with a reaffirmation of a long-established cultural pedigree, and masking tensions in the Mexican social fabric.

Christopher Young analyzes the 1972 Munich Olympics, infamous for the tragic deaths of eleven Israeli athletes but notable in its organization for two prominent aspects. First, the legendary German efficiency surpassed itself. Second, as a response to the Nazi Olympics of 1936, the 1972 Olympic Games were conceived as the *heitere Spiele* (the joyous Games). Due to the complexities of postwar German society and its dealings with the past, this Olympic legacy was both a burden and an opportunity. This made the 1972 Olympic

Games a particularly interesting case of the blend of the political and the aesthetic. The centerpiece was the phenomenally expensive and architecturally daring Olympic stadium, its transparent "tent roof" set into a rolling landscape beneath the Olympic hill, itself remodeled out of war rubble and Alpine pasture. Central to the chapter is a concern with the interaction of ideology and spatial and visual design that underpins any such sporting spectacle. Young draws upon underevaluated archive material to study the divided Germany dimension (these were the first Olympic Games at which East and West German teams appeared as officially recognized separate units), the charismatic personality of organizer Willi Daume, and governmental contributions.

If much of international sport from the 1960s to the 1980s was determined by cold war considerations, then FIFA politics ensured that Central or South America staged every other World Cup, alternating with Europe. Here it was the footballing, not the political, profile of the nation that counted. Under the military Junta, Argentina both hosted and won the World Cup of 1978. Eduardo Archetti's chapter examines the political and ideological context that was dominated by an extreme, bloody, and authoritarian military Junta seeking, as it put it, "to extirpate the cancer of revolutionary guerrilla infiltrated in the body of Argentinean society." The nationalist language of the military, fighting against "the influence of foreign ideas and communism," created a positive atmosphere for the exploitation by the regime of the populist appeal of football that generated a temporary emotional indifference to the political realities of the day. Combining literary, journalistic, and observational sources, Archetti shows that although the discourse of football (a form of "football essentialism") could claim the Argentinean victory as one of a particular politically neutral traditional style, it was instantly incorporated into the regime's celebratory national politics. This process revolved around paradoxes that Argentineans are used to: the victory of style and modes of bodily action was transformed into the victory of the race and a nation against external forces and enemies. This complex and difficult relation is keenly felt in post-Junta Argentina, where, in 2003, the twenty-fifth anniversary of the triumph exhibited a fascinating collective amnesia.

The reciprocally boycotted Olympic Games of Moscow 1980 and Los Angeles 1984, plunged the world sporting spectacle back into the depths of cold war dynamics. Robert Edelman's study of the Moscow Games contextualizes the spectacular opening ceremony and the sports events that followed as a culmination of practices that had been developing since the mid-1920s, when the Soviets decided that competitive sport, as opposed to participatory physical culture, was an appropriate policy priority for a socialist state. The structures, themes, slogans, and tropes on view in 1980 were first seen during the 1930s when immense Physical Culture Day parades were held each summer on Red Square. A comparison of film footage of the Moscow opening with these earlier events reveals many similarities. Yet these continuities mask a very different kind of historical experience. Football was always something quite different—far more popular and the only real oasis of the carnivalesque during the Soviet period. It was the real passion of the working males who comprised the overwhelming bulk of the sporting public. The rituals of football were quite different from those practiced by the organizers of Olympic sport. In this sense, the 1980 Olympic Games were a major intervention in a contest of rituals that characterized Soviet sport from its beginning.

In 1984, the Los Angeles Olympics rewrote the formula for staging the global sports spectacle. Alan Tomlinson reviews the pivotal place of this event in the genealogy of the modern Olympic Games, drawing on comparisons with the staging of these Games half a century earlier in Los Angeles in 1932. After the 1980 Moscow Games, the Olympics was on the verge of its biggest ever crisis. It took 1984's combination of regional posturing, private capital, and national backing to reframe the Olympics. This became the first case of a profit-making modern Olympics, according to the forms of accounting reported after the event. In this case, the opening ceremony celebrated the globally resonant image of U.S. culture: grand pianos, Western genre, jazz, slavery, spaceman. Comparing and contrasting the conditions of the 1932 and 1984 events provides a basis for the analysis of fundamental shifts in the cultural and political meanings and significance of the international sports event. The two Los Angeles events, beyond their superficial similarities, demonstrate the changing relationship between capitalism and public service in the staging of the spectacle.

Arguably, the Barcelona 1992 Olympic Games have been more fully researched than any other comparable sporting event. Christopher Kennet and Miquel de Moragas review the claims widely made for the success and impact of these Olympic Games. The staging of large-scale international cultural events has been important in the post-Franco period of Spain's rapid modernization. This has included events such as the Expo exhibition in Seville, the 1982 World Cup, and the 1992 Olympic Games. The Barcelona Olympics demonstrated Spain's capacity to stage the largest-scale international sports event. Against many stereotypical expectations (which had anticipated the inefficiencies of a mañana culture), the Barcelona Games were a triumph of style, efficiency, and organization. This was a consequence of a creative tension between the central state and the Catalan regional government of which Barcelona is the capital. It also showed positive effects, for a city and a region, of staging events: Barcelona's transport and communications structure was transformed, its waterfront was remodeled, and its civic pride was celebrated in relation to the national capital, Madrid, and the rest of the world.

After the anti-climax at the centennial, so-called "Coca-Cola," Olympic Games in Atlanta, 1996, Sydney 2000, picked up the organizational gauntlet thrown down by Barcelona's excellence. David Rowe and Deborah Stevenson show how, at the Summer 2000 Olympics—hailed by outgoing IOC president Juan Antonio Samaranch as the most perfectly organized Olympic Games ever—Australian national triumphs, particularly in the swimming events and in Cathy Freeman's gold-medal winning performance in the 400 meters, were symbolic highlights for the host city and nation. The opening ceremony emphasized the theme of reconciliation related to the history of the nation's treatment of its Aboriginal peoples. The choice of Aboriginal Freeman to light the Olympic flame was a climax to the theme of reconciliation. She also had run the stadium lap of the torch relay with other celebrated Australian women athletes, thus representing the inclusiveness of the contemporary Olympic ideal on several levels. The Aboriginal theme had been prominent in the arts and cultural festivals during the Olympiad. Rowe and Stevenson analyze the Sydney Olympic Games from the hermeneutical vantage points of the spectators in the stadium and the spectators of the event in the giant-screen live sites and living rooms of the Australian nation. They show how the media transform events into global phenomena that can neither be reduced to embodied experience nor to their representation.

Soon-Hee Whang's study of the 2002 World Cup continues on the theme of spectator and supporter experience by looking at how the spectacle translates into popular celebration in everyday life. At this event, two nations co-hosted the finals of the World Cup for the first time in the tournament's history. Japan and Korea were reluctant co-hosts, forced into this position by the global politics of international sport. Both nations have been fully aware of the benefits of staging sports mega-events. For Japan, the 1964 Summer Olympics was an immensely important expression of its international rehabilitation in the postwar period. It also provided Japan with the opportunity to exhibit its increasingly technological profile on the international stage. For Korea, the 1988 Seoul Olympics was used by the overlapping interests of Korean business and government to catapult the country into the world's industrial and trade elite. Korea also was establishing its profile within Asia itself, in particular, in relation to neighboring Japan, its imperial oppressor until a mere generation before. In such a historical, cultural, and political context, co-hosting would clearly be no simple matter. Whang, a native Korean living and researching in Japan, provides a comparative analysis of the impact of the event in the two hosting nations and also considers how such an event generates forms of popular ritual and cultures of consumption.

This book assembles a unique lineup of international scholars to subject the selected examples to either a reevaluation or their first critical treatment, blending historical and literary scholarship with the theoretical concerns of interpretative social science. The studies are characterized by a methodological eclecticism central to any vibrant multidisciplinary project. The case studies are conceived not just as focused analyses of particular sports events but also, in the accumulated understanding generated by the complementary chapters, as a scholarly contribution to the study of the place of local cultures and politics in a globalized world and to a much overdue analysis of issues surrounding the global governance of sport as this has affected the growth of international sport and borne upon national, regional, and local cultures and institutions.

The case studies reaffirm a set of central issues at the heart of the study of the modern sporting spectacle. First, however much the sport event has developed into a media event, it is still watched and consumed in a variety of ways. As the studies of Sydney, 2000, and Korea and Japan, 2002, demonstrate, sport fans can, in their own ways, reclaim the streets and the public spaces of cities and communities. Second, right through the seventy years that span the case studies covered in this book, high-profile international sporting events have been used to assert particular national ideologies, whether this was the emergent modernity of California 1932, the fascist models of Italy 1934, and Berlin 1936, the Soviet communism of Moscow 1980, the glamourized capitalism of Los Angeles 1984, the authoritarian ruthlessness of Argentina 1978, or the thrusting capitalism of Seoul, South Korea, 1988. Third, some nations have been particularly attracted to hosting events as a means of rehabilitation or regeneration: post-World War II, or in a cold war setting, in Munich 1972, or Barcelona 1992, for instance, the Olympics was seen in this way. Fourth, staging such events has been seized as an opportunity to overturn international stereotypes, from Mexico City 1968, to Sydney 2000, where these cities, on behalf of Mexico and Australia, sought to demonstrate a national maturity and a cultural modernity. Fifth, such events, framed as cosmopolitan and internationalist, can reiterate national, cultural, and racist stereotypes, as was evident in certain controversies and international tensions in England 1966. Sixth, the large-scale event can provide a temporary, transient sense of relief from the troubles and tensions of the day, as tragically captured in the study of Argentina, 1978, in particular. Seventh, the sports event can provide a forum for refusal or contestation, if not outright resistance, as in the case of the negotiations concerning the centrist state and the Catalan region in Barcelona 1992, behind the scenes of the Soviet sport pageants or in its rougher football cultures, in the communities welcoming the torch relay with its accessible and voluntarist version of the Olympic spirit, or on the streets of Seoul in 2002. Three recurrent themes stand out across numerous of the selected cases: the bogus or inaccurate costing of bids and provision, the use of sports events in the reconstitution of public spaces, with the stadium embodying a high-profile articulation of a dynamic of space and power, and the gendered body, persistingly predominantly male, despite real signs of progress toward a more egalitarian gender profile. These ten themes continue to be relevant research questions for the study of the sport spectacle. Other selected case studies may have informed this analytical and research agenda in different ways and with varied emphases—the media innovations of the first Olympics to be relayed live across the world from Tokyo 1964, the politics and economics of a Montreal 1976 Olympic Games boycotted by African nations and soaring through the highest imaginable roof in costs, the glamour of the World Cup in Italy in 1990, or the multicultural optimism of the French triumph when hosting the 1998 World Cup (on France 1998, see the admirable collection edited by Dauncey and Hare 1999). But we have not sought to compile an all-embracing encyclopedic compendium here. Such sources are available elsewhere. Rather, we have developed informed case studies that provide a basis for further agenda-setting and research into the nature of the contemporary sport spectacle. As a coherent, single monograph produced collectively by individual scholars, this book, therefore, aims to provide an enhanced understanding of the place of spectacle in global society, an in-depth understanding of the generation of national identities through sport spectacle and contests, and examples of the value of multidisciplinary and interdisciplinary approaches to analyzing the culture and politics of global sports events.

References

Alabarces, Pablo, Alan Tomlinson, and Christopher Young. 2001. England vs. Argentina at the France '98 World Cup: Narratives of the nation and the mythologizing of the popular. *Media Culture & Society* 23 (5): 547–66.

Allison, Lincoln. 1998. Sport and civil society. *Political Studies* 46 (4): 709–26.

De Coubertin, Pierre. 2000. *Pierre de Coubertin 1863–1937—Olympism: Selected writings*. Edited by Norbert Muller. Lausanne: International Olympic Committee.

Dauncey, Hugh, and Geoff Hare, eds. 1999. *France and the 1998 World Cup: The national impact of a world sporting event*. London: Frank Cass.

Dayan, Daniel, and Elihu Katz. 1992. *Media events: The live broadcasting of history*. Cambridge, MA: Harvard University Press.

Giulianotti, Richard. 2000. *Football: The sociology of the global game*. Cambridge: Polity Press.

Guillain, Jean-Yves. 1998. *La Coupe du Monde de football—L'oeuvre de Jules Rimet*. Paris: Editions Amphora.

Guttmann, Allen. 1994. *Games and empires: Modern sports and cultural imperialism*. New York: Columbia University Press.

———. 2002. *The Olympics—A history of the modern Games*. 2nd. ed. Urbana and Chicago: University of Illinois Press.

Hill, Christopher R. 1992. *Olympic politics*. Manchester: Manchester University Press.

Lenskyj, Helen. 2000. *The Olympics industry*. Albany: State University of New York Press.

MacAloon, John J. 1981. *This great symbol: Pierre de Coubertin and the birth of the modern Olympic Games*. Chicago: University of Chicago Press.

———. 1984. Olympic Games and the theory of spectacle in modern societies. In *Rite, drama, festival, and spectacle: Rehearsal towards a theory of cultural performance*, ed. John J. MacAloon. Philadelphia: Institute for the Study of Human Issues.

Maguire, Joseph. 1999. *Global sport: Identities, societies, civilizations*. Cambridge: Polity Press.

Markovits, Andrei S., and Steven Hellerman. 2001. *Offside—Football and American exceptionalism*. Princeton: Princeton University Press.

Miller, Toby, Geoff Lawrence, Jim McKay, and David Rowe. 2001. *Globalization and sport —Playing the world*. London: Sage.

Puijk, Roel. 2000. A global media event? Coverage of the 1994 Lillehammer Olympic Games. *International Review for the Sociology of Sport* 35 (3): 309–30.

Roche, Maurice. 2001. *Mega-events and modernity—Olympics and expos in the growth of global culture*. London: Routledge.

Simson, Vyv, and Andrew Jennings. 1992. *The Lords of the Rings—Power, money, and drugs in the modern Olympics*. London: Simon and Schuster.

Sklair, Leslie. 2001. *The transnational capitalist class*. Cambridge: Polity Press.

Smith, Sidonie, and Kay Schaffer, eds. 2000. *The Olympics at the millennium: Power, politics, and the Games*. New Jersey: Rutgers University Press.

Sugden, John, and Alan Tomlinson. 1998. *FIFA and the contest for world football: Who rules the peoples' game?* Cambridge: Polity Press.

———. 1999. *Great balls of fire—How big money is hijacking world football*. Edinburgh: Mainstream.

Tomlinson, Alan. 1984. De Coubertin and the modern Olympics. In *Five-ring circus: Money, power, and politics at the Olympic Games*, ed. Alan Tomlinson and Garry Whannel. London: Pluto Press.

———. 1986. Going global: The FIFA story. In *Off the ball: The football World Cup*, ed. Alan Tomlinson and Garry Whannel. London: Pluto Press.

———. 1994. FIFA and the World Cup: The expanding football family. In *Hosts and champions: Football cultures, national identities, and the USA World Cup*, ed. John Sugden and Alan Tomlinson. Aldershot, UK: Ashgate.

———. 1996. Olympic spectacle: Opening ceremonies and some paradoxes of globalization. *Media Culture & Society* 18 (4): 583–602.

———. 1999. FIFA and the men who made it. *Soccer and Society* 1 (1): 55–71.

———. 2000. Carrying the torch for whom? Symbolic power and Olympic ceremony. In *The Olympics at the millennium: Power, politics, and the Games*, ed. Sidonie Smith and Kay Schaffer. New Jersey: Rutgers University Press.

Chapter 2

The Theory of Spectacle

Reviewing Olympic Ethnography

John J. MacAloon

INTRODUCTION

Over two decades ago, I offered a model of complex types of cultural performance, what I called "nested and ramified performance forms," exemplified by the Olympic Games (MacAloon 1984b). Like all social science models, mine was deployed chiefly to organize voluminous ethnographic, interview, and textual data in a less reductive way than had been possible up to that point. I also intended a double intervention with respect to the field of cultural performance theory, as it had come to be known due largely to a senior Chicago colleague, Milton Singer (MacAloon 1984a). First, I tried to show that respecting and charting the differences, and thereby the complex interactions among the master performative genres of game, ritual, and festival, offered the only way forward toward a satisfying account of the distinctive and truly global demographies of attention to and radically dissimilar experiences of the Olympic Games. Second, I insisted that spectacle had to be treated carefully as a performative genre in its own right, engaged in complex dialectical and functional dynamics with the other master genres, and not just as a loose, imperial trope for everything dubious about the contemporary world.

"SPECTACLE": STRICTLY AND SPECTACULARLY SPEAKING

As illustrations of this latter trend, I selected Daniel Boorstin's *The Image: A Guide to Pseudo-Events in America* (1961) and Guy Debord's *The Society of the Spectacle* (1977), because two stranger bedfellows could scarcely have been imagined than the American conservative historian and Librarian of Congress and the French neo-Marxist promoter of *situationisme*. Yet their critiques of contemporary alienation and manipulation were nearly identical in emphasizing the triumph of pseudo-realities and pseudo-events, and—more than Baudrillard was subsequently to do in his closely related *Simulacres et Simulations* (1981)—they both emphasized the role of visual phenomena and symbolic codes in this transformation. Visibility, invisibility, and pseudo-images were taken to be the key modalities of contemporary power and alienation; therefore, spectacle (or one of its cognates) became the encompassing trope for the decaying public sphere. Boorstin and Debord, however, each offered a telling exemption from the general critique, a certain zone of resistance to the overall logic of encroaching pseudo-reality. Boorstin exempted Olympic-style "amateur sport" (together with crime) from his category of pseudo-events,[1] and Debord, in the spirit of Paris, 1968, and the American "yippies!," prescribed street theatre as the best means to turn the political-economic system of the spectacle reflexively back upon itself.

Thus by their own admission, concrete and literal cultural performance forms such as sport and street theater could stand in opposition to "the society of the spectacle," that is, to spectacle used as a general trope for the social and moral maladies of the contemporary Western capitalist world. To develop this critically suggestive position, I tried to distinguish the characteristics of spectacle as one performance genre among others, retaining the critical edge without lapsing into the hyperboles that in the end reveal the critiques of Boorstin, Baudrillard, and Debord (and many derivative others) to be themselves compromised participants in the logic of the spectacle. For what could be more "spectacular"—grandiloquent, grandiose, awesome, and alluring, and morally, intellectually, and politically suspicious (MacAloon 1984b, 243–50, 265–70)—than imperialist "critical theories" claiming that it is all just a big show? Breaking out of this pseudo-critical prison made inquiry into the actual cultural meanings and social functions of concrete spectacles in relation to other performance genres the imperative task at hand. I believe it still is.

Terms such as spectacle continue to be used today as master metaphors for every conceivable manufacturing of power, and critical terms old and new (spectacle, commercialization, alienation, hegemony, mass culture, invention of tradition, simulacra, commodification, mediatization, globalization) are if anything even more conflated in today's "discursive world." Recently, a notion of "mega-events" has been added to this critical vocabulary of the spectacular, in the case of the Olympic Games quite understandably, given their fantastic growth since the 1960s and 1970s (Roche 2000; Tomlinson and Young, chapter 1 of this volume). There is no question that sheer scale, particularly in organizational matters, now touches every aspect of the Olympics. Therefore, it would be a contribution if the "mega" lexicon could be developed from simple descriptors into a real, analytic terminology. But this can never happen if this language functions, like the earlier language of spectacle, merely as a machine for erasing empirical, cultural, and conceptual distinctions.

Just as the consolidation of the Olympic spectacle frame and its transformation from an interrogative to a declarative meta-communication (MacAloon 1984b: 260–69) for more audiences has inflected but not necessarily dominated (much less put an end to) Olympic ritual, festival, and agonal framings and experiences, so too the aggregate "giganticism" of the Games (to use long-standing insider vocabulary) must never conceal the fact that all Olympic encounters for most people around the globe and some Olympic encounters for everyone involved transpire in small-scale, even intimate social settings and according to behavioral logics that are anything but spectacular. Relatively few people performatively experience the mega-spectacle. For all others, it exists solely as discourse—for example, as internalized television, commercial, journalistic, or critical theory discourse—which is hardly the same thing at all. Indeed, as Miquel de Moragas, Nancy Rivenburgh, and their colleagues have shown (1995), spectacularizing rhetoric (in my definition) has not even been predominant in the Olympic broadcasts of some (largely non-Western) national televisions.

In what follows I will, after a brief note on ethnography, provide illustrations of how maintaining distinctions among the performance genres, including spectacle, as demanded by the complex performance systems model, permits recognition, characterization, and correlation of differential experiences among cultures, social segments, and layers of power within the Olympic movement and among its audiences. I wish to suggest that a productive view of the "whole"—to speak ironically, since the Olympic Games are not only "mega" but literally unknowable in their full complexity—can only be built up in this mosaic fashion. Totalizing theoretical deductions may be satisfying, even necessary, for other purposes, but they can never, in my opinion, have any standing as social science. Finally, I will conclude with some observations on the Olympic flame relay. The relay is today's master example of an Olympic performance that to such "theoreticians" (particularly where official texts, media discourse, and one-off visits afford their only data) seems firmly part of the spectacle. There is no doubt that the relay is indeed subject today to interventions by managerial and commercial actors pushing it in that direction. Nevertheless, long-term, multi-site, continuous, and team-based fieldwork in fact shows the flame relay to be in many more respects and for many more persons the Olympic anti-spectacle par excellence.

A NOTE ON ETHNOGRAPHY AND CRITICAL THEORY

Having campaigned for it (MacAloon 1992), I can hardly regard the recent acceptance in sports studies by previously skeptical "critical theorists" of the value, indeed, the necessity, of ethnography as anything but positive (e.g., Sugden and Tomlinson 1998; Hargreaves 2000). Exaggerated oppositions between theory and method are always particularly ironic in this case, since the ancient Greek term from which we derive our "to theorize" literally meant going and seeing for oneself as a matter of principle (Hartog 2001).[2] Furthermore, "ethnography"—minimally, the resolve to try not to write professionally about peoples and events that could have been but were not seen, discussed, and lived with face to face—can be shown to be chartered in the very intellectual genealogy of mainstream critical theory itself.

Underlying many of the vocabularies and arguments I have been indexing, including my own understandings of "empty forms" (discussed later), is Marx's analysis of the commodity form, in particular, his discussion in *Capital* of the "fetishism of commodities." Indeed, these passages have lately been claimed as the fountainhead of all continuing relevance of Marxist analysis of contemporary capitalist societies (Postone 1993). Commercialization of course requires commodification, that is, everything necessary to price something for a market. But Marx went further than the other political economists, recognizing that the fetishized character of commodities, owed to the disguised social relations and human experiences of production, "congealed" into material forms. Therefore, it follows that to defetishize any commodity is always to discover and as much as possible to experience directly for oneself ("species-being") the concrete and particular social relations that went into making it, just as direct experience of the social relations of resistance will be required to explain why and where commodification has been headed off. Ethnography should therefore be seen as a practice of defetishization, including the theoretical commodities of the academic industry.

FROM PROCESSUAL REDUCTIONISM TO COMPLEX PERFORMANCE TYPES

Indeed, it was less a theoretical road to Damascus than the straightforward experience of fieldwork in Montreal, 1976, that finally knocked me off the reductionist horse I had been trying to ride. There is not enough space here to review in detail the conceptual evolution that led me to abandon my teacher Victor Turner's insistence that a single paradigm of the ritual process could serve to interpret very diverse performance genres (Turner 1969). From the ancient Olympia flame lighting and relay to the opening ceremonies and through the victory ceremonies to the closing ceremonies, the Olympic performance system certainly reproduces the classic *rite de passage* paradigm (MacAloon 1978). Indeed, the Olympics now present, from the standpoint of demographic encompassment of attention, the hyperbolic epitome (Berkaak 1999) of this classical paradigm. Alas, the sports contests did not easily fit within it, for they are anything but ritual games in the technical sense of ludic contests whose outcomes are known in advance.[3]

I subsequently tried to derive both games and rites from then an underlying order of play, à la *Homo Ludens* and the existential phenomenologists, but this ended me up in the famous Huizingan dead end, where the concept of the ludic becomes so abstracted as to be nearly indistinguishable from the concept of culture itself, and the most interesting genre differences (particularly ones most vexed or politicized in the multicultural contexts of the Olympics) were pushed completely out of focus.[4]

Lévi-Strauss had famously articulated the oppositional complementarity of the logics of games and rites at a structural level (Lévi-Strauss 1966, 30–33). By collapsing the two genres into one another, one could scarcely hope to understand their mutual attractions and interactions—Olympic contests and Olympic victory ceremonies, for example—or the curious failure of other sports events—the football World Cup, most notably—to bring any novel or evocative ritual forms into being.[5] Finally "getting it" about the conceptual autonomy of ritual and game made it easier for me to pay attention to my own empirical studies and to recognize other genres composing the nested Olympic system. As a poor graduate student with no credential or research funds in Montreal, I spent much more time outside than inside the stadiums.[6] I was simply compelled to discover the vibrant world of popular festival that quite literally encompasses the sports and the main rituals at an Olympic Games. Those who know the Olympics only through mass media have little reason to suspect the existence of this festival genre, given the practices of most national broadcasters and the contradictions of "festival by television" (MacAloon 1989).

With games nested within rites and surrounded by festival, the recognition and characterization of the encompassing spectacle frame, indexed earlier, completed the core model, once, that is, I found a way of characterizing the genres. Because everything else that becomes Olympic does so in the end in relation to these core cultural performances, and because there is no performance without pre-formance, I followed Gregory Bateson (and to a lesser extent Erving Goffman) in stressing the different meta-communicative framings of the different master genres of the Olympic system. That my formulations of the specific frames were culture and history bound I did not doubt (and will repeatedly notice), but they were also general and abstract enough to address at least putatively universal human experiences (such as competitive drama, joy, ritual respect, and awe) and not recognizably tied to any one specific culture or community. This is the technical definition of what I subsequently came to call "empty forms."

GENRES AND CONTEXTS:
THE GLOBAL LOGIC OF EMPTY FORMS

To which culture does "game" or "ritual" properly belong? Maybe or maybe not to every culture but certainly to no culture uniquely. The creation of empty, that is, deracinated and decontextualized forms is an active process, spread unevenly through any culture and across cultures and social segments, but it is a recognizable process and one critical, I believe, to grasping contemporary social structurations and intercultural interactions. Take some sport forms as examples. To whose culture does the 200-meter breaststroke belong? Archery? Team handball? Table tennis? Tae kwon do? In the modern West, there are three main modalities by which to answer: the historicizing, the essentializing, and the dominating. Across these modalities range various social conditions of knowledge. I am sure there are professional sports historians who could give a historicizing answer for each form. I am not one of them, since I have no idea where or when the breaststroke was invented, and, for a different reason, I would not know how to answer the archery question either. Whatever they once were, these are now "empty forms" for me, as I am sure they now are, historically speaking, for most people in the world. Essentializing is not an option for a cultural anthropologist, but I know that there are many who might be tempted to refer to one or another putative water or hunting culture (with predictably humorous results). As to domination, at least today, one would be hard pressed to say whether the 200-meter breaststroke was more Chinese than Australian, Russian, American, or Dutch.

At the other end of the series, tae kwon do is surely less "emptied," as many more social fractions in many more populations would still identify it as "originally" or "essentially" or "competitively" Korean. Yet the mere fact that it is an Olympic sport practiced throughout the world indicates that the process of emptying is well begun. And, indeed, it is by this process of emptying through the agency of conforming to the already emptied and more abstract rules and practices of becoming an Olympic sport that Germans, and Senegalese, and Indians come to be adepts of and competing in Olympic tae kwon do, while simultaneously developing their own specifically German, Senegalese, and Indian tae kwon do communities, organizations, and styles. Deracinated, dehistoricized (if you will), globalized empty forms thus simultaneously become means of interconnection across cultural boundaries. The forgetting or active suppression of history and of cultural context simultaneously generates interconnection and new particularized histories and cultural localizations by which social groups newly define themselves off against one another. Empty forms are thus simultaneously the means of homogenization and heterogenization. This is the dominant cultural logic and cultural economy of the "world system" today (Sahlins 1990), where isolation and strict autonomy are less frequent options.

As illustrated in certain critiques of the spectacle, Western social theories, liberal and Marxist, no less than Western social criticism, left and right, have had a very difficult time seeing past the first process to the second.

GENRES, SOCIAL SEGMENTS, AND POWER FORMATIONS: SAMPLE CORRELATIONS

As with the Euro-American broadcast media, the dominant discourses of the IOC, the National Olympic Committees (NOCs), and the International Federations (IFs), the main institutional actors in the Olympic system, contain little reference to much less concern with the popular festival. These agents live inside, not outside, the arenas, and in restricted backstage and VIP stands even there. As the first Olympic Games after Munich, Montreal introduced security measures that radically segregated credentialed from uncrendentialed participants, and this security effect has been multiplied one-hundredfold since the 1970s. Ever-more complex practical requirements have likewise contributed to the overall segregation of insiders from the general public, as well as to differentiation of space and access among the credentialed. Today, the athletes and team officials have their Olympic Villages, their training halls, and their backstage zones in the venues. The rightsholding broadcasters and credentialed press have their press villages, their international broadcast center and main press center headquarters, and their hierarchy of restricted access positions in the stadiums. The IOC members and staff and the NOC and IF officers have their respective headquarters hotels, closed beyond their lobbies to the public, while in the arenas each group occupies special "Olympic Family zones." While the ever-growing numbers of official guests ("G"-credentialed heads of state, diplomats, government ministers, industrialists, sponsors, celebrities, artists, religious leaders, and even a few professors) generally arrange their own accommodations, they too have their special entrances, stands, and backstage areas in the performance venues, spaces where their own types of work can privately and uninterruptedly get done.

Each of these groups, moreover, makes use of a special transportation system to shuttle between its hotels, workplaces, and arenas. Indeed, it is perfectly possible for top-credentialed persons never to step outside of their own particular *cordons sanitaires*; many, as I have documented ethnographically, do not do so for days at a time. These behaviors are matters of status hierarchy and prestige accumulation, of course, and not just of security, work efficiency, and cost control. Next to the sports events themselves, struggle for and jealous comparison of credentials compose the biggest Olympic game for what across the Samaranch years came to be referred to as "The Olympic Family." Notables tend to feel delinquent if they fail to occupy an inside circle of privilege, once admitted to it, and here is where the networking and politicking must be done to get one deeper inside at the next Olympic Games.[7]

Distinguishing festival from ritual and game thus contributes to characterizing the differential behaviors and experiences of distinct political agents and occupational groups at the Olympics, as well as of trends in these over time. If becoming more elite in Olympic prestige circles is correlated with less and less direct experience of the popular festival, then it is further comprehensible why local Organizing Committees for the Olympic Games (OCOGs) are the only institutional actors who today pay a great deal of attention to this genre of Olympic experience, lately coming into real tension with the other stakeholders on this matter. Under the too-often dissembling slogan of "athletes first," international sports officials press OCOGs to spend all discretionary monies and energies on the sports venues and sports personnel. The IOC members and staff have been pleased after the fact to share in the public happiness created by such OCOG festival innovations as Calgary's downtown medals plaza or the "live sites" in Sydney's or Atlanta's Centennial Park, with its nightly free musical festivals, when the fact is that many of these same officials vigorously opposed these festival plans in the design stage.

Indeed, some IOC and IF officials today do not shrink from asserting publicly that because host cities have become overcrowded and overburdened, ordinary folks ought to stay at home and watch the Games on television. More than generically obnoxious elitism is operative here. Such attitudes toward the popular festival—games, rites, and (if we ever cared to indulge) festival for us elite, "media events" (Dayan and Katz 1992) for all the rest—directly undermine Olympism's key commitment to face to face intercultural interaction and education, a commitment to "popular ethnography" that is central to Coubertin's and to the continuing Olympic Movement's understanding of the social and political ends that sports (and sports by media) were meant to serve only as powerful means (MacAloon 1984b). In yet another way, then, charting the vicissitudes of festival in tension with the other master genres conveys us into the center of questions of the survival of that Olympic ideology and conception of the Olympic Movement that are the main features distinguishing the Olympics from other "mega" productions of the global sports industry (Alabarces, Tomlinson, and Young 2001).

The most important category of emergent actors in the Olympics is unquestionably the volunteers, tens of thousands of whom are now required to stage any Olympics at all (Moragas et al. 2000). Though commentators, whose only sources of information about the Olympic Games are media texts, typically fail to realize it, growth in the numbers, training, and dedication of the volunteers has been the chief means of absorbing the "spectacular" growth of the Olympic Games and of their burden on the host city. The familiar "critical" argument that bigger money, say, increased corporate sponsorships and television rights fees, translates readily and directly into bigger spectacle is simply wrong. Though the calculations are difficult (MacAloon 2000, 20–21; Chalip 2000, 205–15), it is clear that the value of volunteer Olympic labor is equal to a very high percentage of that acquired through commercial sponsorships. Yet the latter have received nearly all the attention of both conservative sport business analysts and left cultural critics of the Games alike, volunteers seeming to offer a particular embarrassment to both analytic agendas.

Volunteers are active in and critical to every Olympic performance space and genre. With respect to the popular festival in its unfocused, carnivalesque aspects, they are (with the police) the most important category of actors in determining whether the tone for a vast public navigating the hurdles of passage among event venues will be good-natured and convivial or stressful and antagonistic. Volunteers placed as Olympic Village drivers, stadium ushers, media runners, ceremonies performers, VIP hostesses, and the like have their own rewards correlated with proximity to sports contests and rituals. But the overwhelming majority of Olympic volunteers are outside, not inside, Olympic performance venues. They deal with masses of ordinary citizens, not celebrities, and in the most banal, not the spectacular, public spaces. Their chief reward—as fieldwork with them consistently reveals—is the very festival experience that they themselves do so much to create.

PERFORMANCE SYSTEMS AND COMPARATIVE STUDIES

Attention to the performative genres likewise offers important comparative possibilities, in turn permitting anthropologists to probe both local cultural logics and concrete local-global-local interactions across time and space. Over the years, our research teams have been composed to try to maximize these comparative opportunities (MacAloon 1999). For example, Montreal was not just any festival venue. French Canadian traditions of carnival and public celebrations of dance and music, combined with Anglophone Canadian traditions of public conversation and debate, set the context for an especially vibrant festival scene in the city. The existence of the old city as an established entertainment quarter, outdoor café culture, ease of transportation from Olympic venues with their own focal plazas to the public quarter, and an easy forbearance of the authorities were the key factors. For some Olympic visitors, the enduring icon of these Games was a late-night conga line of revelers through a police station, not anything that happened on a sports field. I also have written often about the marvelous way in which the truly popular, and truly Olympic, festival was allowed to take over and liberate the stadium space after the formal Closing Ceremonies concluded (1984b, 277), an occurrence that has not subsequently been reproduced in any Summer Games.

Eight years after Montreal, the Olympic Games took place just to the south in another liberal capitalist democracy, and yet, aside from interesting religious and political phenomena in the Coliseum Olympic plaza, there was next to nothing in the way of true popular festival in Los Angeles. The venues were dispersed, there was no central entertainment quarter, public transportation was impossible, no OCOG official took on this mandate, the college campus Olympic Villages were so successful and the entertainment so marvelous therein that the athletes rarely ventured out, and the private party scene was intense enough to keep the elites, lobbyists, and social climbers indoors and preoccupied.

Together with their "Hollywood" opening ceremonies, the financing of these Games has most drawn the attention of commentators. Certainly new marketing and sponsorship practices were destined to transform the Olympic system. However, none of these "spectacularizations" can be tied directly to the absence of festival in Los Angeles. For that, one must turn in my opinion to the urban environmental factors, but only as these were activated by current political conditions and their underlying cultural structures. A preoccupation with security and fears of violence in a highly class and ethnically segregated town, the Soviet boycott in the general context of high cold war, the worldview of the Republican conservatives who led the local organization and dominated the federal government presence from the Reagan administration, and the themes of that president's reelection campaign for which the Olympics were made to stand as metonymy—these factors contributed the most, in our observations, to an overall "the event is over, go home, no hanging about" atmosphere. In stark contrast to Montreal, at the conclusion of the Closing Ceremony the stands were forcibly emptied by the police who had also cordoned off the field, and the organizers did not shrink from even threatening athletes on the public address system with being left in the dark if they did not vacate the ceremony and go to their buses immediately. (So much for the festival joy of Montreal and Olympism.)

In Seoul, four years later, there was again very little in the way of popular festival, in the way I have characterized this empty form. Again, of course, there were security worries, concerns for practicality and efficiency, and so forth, but the most important reason was social and cultural. The core conception of the festival genre in my model is tilted toward the carnivalesque, incorporating voluntary, even spontaneous, participation, vigorous interaction of strangers, expressive/inversive behaviors, and relative absence of supervisory authority and controlled program. All of these experiences are certainly familiar to Koreans, but not in the context of massed crowds of strangers on public occasions. Upon bumping up against an unexpected cultural performance, the first thing an adult Korean of the 1980s typically wants to know is, to paraphrase a Korean expression, "Who is the owner of this festival?" If the answer cannot be determined with clarity, then the result is discomfort, not gaiety, holding in, not acting out. Rather than generic, cosmopolitan forms that release, reverse, or invert normal social positions (as Roberto Da Matta has so richly analyzed in Rio carnival), festival forms in Korea are very particular and come with quite specific social specifications. Indeed, *nori*, the very word used by Koreans to translate "festival" in my model, is a pragmatic neologism generated by Korean scholars so as to be able to communicate with Western counterparts who trade in such abstractions all the time. In Korea, by contrast, there is typically only this *nori* or that one (Kang Shin-pyo 1987, personal communication).[8]

The Olympic Games, of course, are intercultural on a massive scale, and these different models bump into one another in enlightening, creative, and sometimes destructive ways. (That is the whole point of building analytics for them for scholars, and from the standpoint of education the whole point of the Olympics for its founders.) Almost inevitably when we would spot groups of excited Koreans spontaneously congregating on the streets or in the parks during the Seoul Games, it would be to observe and enjoy cavorting foreigners! Were these Koreans then participating subjectively in festival or rather in an inverted tourist show, a species of spectacle, well known in the Far East (Cohen 2002)? To me this remains an open question, but because of the model, we had a new and more highly contextualized research question in the domain of local-global-local intercultural phenomena, moreover, one that helped spot change over time.

In 2002, we were back on Korean boulevards comparing 1988 with the performances of hundreds of thousands of Koreans out in public "Being the Reds," that is, supporting the Korean football team during its World Cup matches. But with far fewer foreigners around to provide an in-person public show, the attention was focused this time on the huge video boards showing the games. Whether in the key of sports fanship or of political demonstrations, these rally-festivals were unprecedented in contemporary Korean history, and many Korean commentators have now strongly linked them to subsequent electoral developments. While hardly unorganized, these rallies were not perceived as "owned by" the state but rather by "civil society" organizations (to use a controversial expression), local institutions and community organizations, or what Robert Oppenheim (2003) has analyzed as "new cultural movement networks."[9] These observations in Korea have encouraged an adjustment to my theory that was already being pressed upon me by Michael Cohen's wonderful performance studies dissertation analyzing the Sydney Olympic rites and festivals from a performer's point of view (Cohen 2002).

In my original formulations in the 1980s, I expressly doubted that there could ever be such a thing as a festival via television or true spectacle experience for that matter. While many analysts speak as if watching a television "spectacular" and directly viewing a public spectacle were the same things, I insist that in key aspects they are not and cannot be. For example, what you see on the little box may impress you, particularly when accompanied with the usual verbal hyperbole and hype (Berkaak 1999), but it rarely renders you awestruck.[10] I still hold to this point of view when it is a question of whether television can ever communicate and transfer to viewers the same festival or spectacle experience of those participants being visually broadcast and verbally reported. However, when the question is changed to whether the televising of games or rites can ever call into being a large group subject to real festival or spectacle experience, I now offer a qualified yes. This is not festival by television, but certainly it is festival with television.

Back in the 1980s, we knew all about festive group viewing of the Olympic Games. Eric Rothenbuhler had documented the phenomenon in American living rooms in 1984, and anthropologists had contributed their observations of village viewing in remote corners of the world to the attempts by communications researchers to provide an accurate estimate of Olympic broadcast audiences.[11] But the groups studied were always small and typically intimates or consocials. What changed is technology. Today's huge video boards and attendant electronic technologies mean that very large groups can congregate to "watch" together, that is, to be assembled into what can become, other distinctive features being present, a festival, and, with the required scale and other genre stipulations, even a spectacular gathering. The Sydney "live sites" were not always as hot as their reputation today suggests, and, as the model would predict, there were often serious tensions between artists, partiers, and sports fans, rather than the easy festival *flanage* among types of activity. But there is no question that the Sydney live sites added a new dimension of specifically Olympic festival. Indeed, it is now possible to hypothesize that for persons actually present in the stadium for the Opening Ceremonies, Olympic ritual is quite likely to be nested in spectacle, whereas for public live site participants, convened, so to speak, by the big screens, it is more likely ritual (though unlikely ritual experience) encompassed by festival. This is not to suggest in some imperious manner that one experience is necessarily superior to another, but only to assert that they must be different and have different social and political valences and entailments in different cultural contexts. These differences are what should interest social scientists.[12]

There is not space here to linger over other surprising and important observations of Cohen's that necessitate adjustments to the model of complex performance types. For example, he shows that performance conditions for actors with respect to the live audience in Olympic Opening Ceremonies (faceless distance, sound conditions, darkness, etc.) are such that performers, particularly experienced theater people, are forced to play to each other (and sometimes to cameras) and hardly to the audience at all. Moreover, practical and secrecy considerations were such that performers in the Sydney Opening Ceremonies had never been shown the whole script and run of show and in rehearsal had seen no more than bits of the acts just prior and subsequent to their own. Cohen describes ceremonies performers racing out to live sites and later searching out video replays to get their first encounter with their "own" ceremony as a whole. Again, there are striking comparisons here. Preoccupation with secrecy and surprise for a one-off performance such as the Opening Ceremonies is typical for producers with Western television backgrounds and is often encouraged by commercial and television sponsors (MacAloon 1992). But culture, in the matter of whether the Opening Ceremonies are master framed as spectacle or ritual, plays the critical role. Japanese and Korean (and probably in 2008, Chinese) Olympic producers with identical professional backgrounds are not in the slightest reticent about showing their entire performance over and over again, not only to the performers but to scores and even hundreds of thousands of volunteers and ordinary citizens at open dress rehearsals.

THE FLAME RELAY AS ANTI-SPECTACLE

I will conclude with a brief note on how twenty further years of Olympic flame relay fieldwork will confirm my original insistences that spectacle be understood as a specific performance genre among others and not be assumed automatically to encompass, dominate, or destroy other kinds of Olympic experience simply because of its scale, its association with state, commercial, and media actors, or the special fears it induces in ideologists on the right and the left. After hundreds of miles of travel with the Olympic flame in seven countries and as many hours observing, interviewing, and cohabiting with every sort of participant, mostly in collaboration with local cultural experts, I conclude that the flame relay is the performance deserving the most attention from Olympic movement partisans opposed to the consolidation of spectacle as the encompassing Olympic performance form and from theorists seeking evidence that this particular genre *paraphrasis* is not inevitable.

Certainly the relay is in aggregate a "mega-event." At moments, it is visually awe-inspiring in the way of true spectacle, and its summoning meta-message for many first-timers is a spectacle-like "Ah, the Olympic flame, maybe it won't be much, but let's go see." (All we skeptical people *have* to do is go see.) Unquestionably there are persons who remain in the spectacle (or a feeble festival) frame after "seeing the show." Yet in other remarkable ways and for the overwhelming majority of persons, in our ethnographic experience, the relay is an anti-spectacle, par excellence. Spectacle not only institutionalizes a radical role separation between actors (or better "the action") and observers, it depends on an imposing, overwhelming, awesome, and perhaps frightening and humiliating distance between them. By some demographic measures, the relay is bigger in terms of direct, non-mass-mediated, person-to-person and person-to-symbol encounter than the Games themselves, and yet out on the relay, the intimacies associated with ritual, festival, and game (for certain kinds of actors) predominate. And for the last three relays at least, top officials and volunteer staff have been engaged in a vigorous, continuous, and highly self-conscious struggle to maintain these values and practices against what they themselves understand to be agents of spectacle, notably representatives of the presenting sponsors perhaps in league with the distant IOC.

For both the Winter and Summer Games, there are now more torchbearers in action than there are athletes. (In 1996, nearly 13,000 runners carried the flame in Greece and the United States.) The numbers are even more dramatic for live spectators. The record for Olympic sports ticket sales was in Atlanta, with over 9 million. If we generously estimate that this represented an audience of 5 million unique individuals, then the live audience for the Atlanta flame relay through the United States was somewhere between five and ten times as many persons. In host countries with smaller populations, such as Australia and Korea, the absolute numbers have been smaller, but the percentage figures may well have been higher. So for those who believe that live, face to face encounters with Olympic symbols (characteristics of ritual and festival) are more powerful than mass-mediated texts, the Olympic flame relay might be more significant than the Opening and Closing Ceremonies or the sports events. Naturally, the flame relay would not be so attractive, indeed, would not exist without the Games, but this should not blind us to the phenomenal attention that the flame relay today attracts. What draws that attention? In the terms of my model, what conditions make so many so eager to fill in the emptinesses of this simple ritual form?[13]

If you happen to be in Greece or the Olympic host country, how much does it cost to witness the Olympic flame? The answer is nothing. It is not ticketed; it is free. You only have to get yourself to where the flame is passing by. (In 1996, the flame came within a two-hour drive of 90 percent of the U.S. population.) While of course there are a few special places the flame goes in any country where access is restricted, 98 percent of the time the flame is on ordinary streets passing through ordinary communities. That is, the flame lives mostly in banal human social settings, made newly lively by its passage.[14] Only upon its arrival at the stadium in the Opening Ceremonies is it taken away from ordinary human hands and virtually entombed in a sports mausoleum behind checkpoints and razor wire.[15]

Of course, the Olympic flame is these days accompanied by security on its journey, and the relay is no longer possible, outside of Greece at least, without a staff of 200 or 300 uniformed OCOG personnel. (And Greece, in 2004, had that too, the caravan itself having become something of a spectacle.) But compared with the Olympic Games themselves, the security presence is unobtrusive, relatively proportionate, and reasonably relaxed, in part, because, as I can say with some authority, the Olympic flame has never proved to be a terrorist target, and even pranks against it are remarkably rare. Thus if you have come out to see the flame, you will see it very close up, often just next to you.

And what sort of motivation and preparation is required to go see the flame? Nothing beyond "Hey let's go see it, it might be cool." Of course, many people have more complex initial motivations, but my point is that the spectacle frame may serve here as elsewhere as a recruiting device into other genres of experience in a way that conforms to expectations of individual autonomy and freedom of action in liberal democratic cultures (MacAloon 1984b).

And just as you have come out voluntarily to participate, 90 percent of the staff are volunteers themselves. As a result of their service, most become devoted to the Olympic flame, and through it to their version of the Olympic idea. I have collected cases of flame relay volunteers who have not been able to go back to their previous lives. Countless other staff members pronounce their lives changed in less dramatic ways by the experience. I also must report that I have rarely experienced, in all my years of observing Olympic organizations and events, such dedicated, compassionate, and effective leadership as that shown on the flame relay by directors such as Han Guang-soo, Nassos Kritsinelis, Di Henry, and Steven McCarthy. Of course, they have been very carefully selected, but each asserts that something about the flame relay itself demands this leadership style.

The relay is an ordeal, even, we might say, an athletic event, for its staff. It is physically and emotionally demanding in a way that compels leaders to take careful account of their team's medical and moral well-being, and of team members to take care of one another. Members of the ACOG flame relay team, for example, developed an admonitory saying for themselves, which they repeated regularly to each other: "If you do not weep at least twice a day, it is time for you to leave the relay and go home." What they meant is that if you do not vent the emotions generated by the powerful things you witness along the relay, then you can be overwhelmed and even emotionally harmed. During the Salt Lake relay, director Steve McCarthy said the slogan had been revised: "More times a day than that."[16]

The staff is dedicated to supporting the experience of each torchbearer, and before long it becomes clear to each volunteer that the overwhelming majority of torchbearers will be thrilled by that experience. I am sure that there have been flame bearers who have been disappointed by the experience, but I have never met one. (To be sure, many wish that they could have carried the flame a longer time and distance, or in a different location.) As a result, a kind of "contact high," or what Durkheim called in more academic language "the contagion of the sacred," develops among torchbearers and staff and between torchbearers and audiences. I have long since stopped counting instances of strangers asking surprised torchbearers for their autographs. Carrying the flame for a leg of the relay is an athletic event, and not only for the elderly, the infirm, or the physically and mentally challenged torchbearers. In a kind of inversion of the main game genre of the Olympics, torchbearers frequently compare themselves to Olympian athletes. "I won't win a gold medal in the stadium, but I ran my leg of the relay." Most, once their selection has been confirmed, put themselves into training.

Even the Olympians, celebrities, politicians, and sponsor torchbearers feel this contagious power, and it is a key part of the powerful collaborative symbolism of the relay that the legs and hearts of the big shots are no more important in getting the flame where it is going than those of the humblest torchbearer.

Indeed, since 1996, this symbolism has been given a new dimension. Billy Payne, the Atlanta OCOG chief, decided that the majority of Atlanta torchbearers should be "community heroes," nominated by ordinary citizens and community groups for their services to others and selected in collaboration with major civic charities. If it is to be a real social movement and not just an athletic and a commercial extravaganza, Payne reasoned, the Olympic movement should be able to honor not only sports heroes and administrators with Olympic medals and Olympic Orders but also ordinary heroes who have sacrificed greatly for the well-being of others. What better way than to give them the honor of carrying the Olympic flame. This exceptional innovation, which has brought to the relay greater diversity, even more moving stories, and yet stronger ties to local communities, has been repeated in Sydney and Salt Lake, and the current intention is to try to find a way to do it again in the very different and difficult cultural contexts of Athens and Torino. For those of us who judge that the main source of creativity in the Olympic movement (as opposed to the Olympic sports industry) is today the OCOGs, not the IOC, the NOCs, and certainly not the IFs, the flame relay offers compelling evidence.

These latter sorts of officials are rarely seen out on the relay, perhaps making a brief appearance at a particularly photogenic or prestigious stop, showing up to run a leg if they wish to, but otherwise uninvolved. Even at the flame lighting in Olympia, the IOC members in Greece and often (but not always) in the host country are the only ones ever present.[17]

The contrast with OCOG presidents such as Park Seh-jik, Pascal Maragall, Gerhard Heiberg, and Billy Payne could not be more striking. They not only fulfilled their ritual roles at Olympia (IOC members are not asked to speak), but they also became immediate adepts of the flame relay, sneaking out whenever they could to rejoin it. In part, this is due to the especially uplifting effect that the relay rituals can have on long-suffering OCOG officials. A. D. Frazier Jr., the chief operating officer of ACOG (Atlanta Committee for the Olympic Games) and the person chiefly responsible for raising over U.S. $1 billion in corporate and private capital for these Olympic Games (and, thereby, an automatic epitome of "commercial spectacle" for those "theorists" who have never actually seen anything nor met anyone) has repeatedly insisted to me that being in Greece for the flame-lighting ceremony and out on the relay were "the only moments I was ever sure the whole Olympic thing was worth it." Video clips from the relay intended to inspire ACOG operational meetings on the eve of the Olympic Games instead became their centerpiece.

The simple, readily abstracted, and "universalizable" requirements of this ritual—light a flame, relay it from hand to hand to the stadium, light the cauldron in the opening ceremony—make it especially open to local meaning making, not only among different cultures but also in the hearts of different persons. The flame is fragile; without human support and care, it dies. Therefore, though inorganic, it takes on a life and a personality. Because it depends upon so many thousands of individuals across the relay, those individuals cannot help but feel related and experience a special solidarity when the flame arrives at its destination.

Every culture known to us makes symbolic meaning out of fire. At the same time, these meanings are highly differentiated, context dependent, and not reducible to some common denominator. Just so, beyond the empty basics, the Olympic flame is open to free interpretation. No one can force anyone to interpret it one way or another. Precisely because it is such an open signifier, it presents itself so powerfully to diverse and frequently antagonistic interpreting communities, even communities within the same national culture.[18] This factor contributes mightily to the difficulty that elite agents are having in homogenizing, capturing, and redirecting the meaning of the relay to their own ends.

Commercial sponsorships do not in and of themselves necessarily promote spectacle values, but the marketing of those sponsorships almost inevitably does. Marketers want big shows, simplified and consistent messages, and a passive audience content to be wowed. Because of the unparalleled goodwill that it generates, the flame relay is particularly attractive to sponsors. Coca-Cola has been particularly aggressive not only in securing relay sponsorships but in marketing itself out on the relay, so much so that Atlanta flame relay director Hilary Hanson estimates that she spent over half her time dealing with the demands and practices of the Coca-Cola "partners" (personal communication, 1997).

Coke sends out its own caravan of vehicles manned by scores of young marketers, publicists, customer relations people, and salespeople. Audiences who arrive early on the flame route encounter these sponsor teams first and are bombarded with advertising trinkets, noisy music, and audio commentaries trying to link the Coke and Olympic "brands." Sponsor agents purposely try to disguise the difference between themselves and the OCOG torch relay staff. Not content with the sizable number of torchbearer slots guaranteed in the sponsor contract, Coke officials work tirelessly to try to position "their" torchbearers for maximum exposure, even if that means shouldering Olympian and community torchbearers off to the margins. In 1996, no tactic was too devious in Coke's effort to circumvent the ACOG's policy against sponsor representatives among official speakers at relay celebration points. Sydney observers along the Atlanta relay found Coke so ubiquitous, insatiable, tasteless, and obnoxious and the backstage battles between Olympic officials and sponsor agents so enervating that they resolved against having any retail products company as a flame relay sponsor in 2000.[19] Desperate to crack into Oceania markets where the flame was going for the first time, Coca-Cola was nevertheless rebuffed in Sydney. It was back in Salt Lake where, as a senior relay official explained to me, "We conceded Coke and Chevy the right to speak briefly at celebrations. This distracted them from their other demands and actually made them a little better behaved [than in 1996]. Of course, we tightly monitored the content of those speeches too."

I am certainly critical of the "Olympic industry," but I have nothing in common with critics who cannot seem to imagine (if they do not do fieldwork they could hardly know) that many of the same Olympic officials who sign the sponsorship contracts proceed to battle those sponsors in defense of the values of the Olympic movement. In the flame relay, the values of ritual and festival continue to prevail over those of spectacle, due in great part to the effective political action of such leaders and their volunteer staff. It is to their additional credit that most of these bitter struggles remain backstage, as the OCOG relay officers continue to devise secret practices to check their commercial "partners."[20] Meanwhile, because of the structural and symbolic aspects of the relay previously mentioned and, in my country, at least, the habitual ease with which citizens set aside commercial "clutter," the sponsor presence is mostly ignored by the crowds. Or, said more precisely, it is part of the spectacle hype that serves to attract skeptical people in a reassuring fashion into scenes in which they are subject to recruitment into festival and ritual experiences. And if they are so recruited, nothing, at least in the flame relay, subsequently seems so laughable to them as to suggest that it is all just someone else's big show.

Coca-Cola was back on the relay in Athens, where a stronger threat to the ritual had arisen from the attempted imposition by a new IOC regime of managerial technocrats of a standardized "world-best practices" model for the Greek relay organization. What these Lausanne experts (not one of whom has ever spent any time out on a relay) fail to grasp is that this model, originated by Atlanta and successfully deployed in Sydney and Salt Lake City, remains tied through and through to an Anglo-Saxon cultural base. It is anything but culturally neutral nor yet, in my language, an empty form. It proved hugely disruptive for the veteran Greek relay officials (who called it "the American model"). Moreover, these were on-stage, public conflicts, for nowhere in the world are Olympic flame performances more commonly framed as ritual than in Greece, the Olympic flame being broadly understood and treated—no matter its twentieth-century invention—as a key symbol of Greek national sovereignty and patrimony. In this particular Olympic context, one was confident that the ritual and festival framings would maintain their dominance over that of spectacle. In other Olympic contexts, the reverse is probably true. How could one recognize the differences, let alone compare them over historical time and cultural space, with only a monolithic understanding of "the Olympic mega-event" and an imperialist conception of "the spectacle"? Ethnography remains essential for this interpretive task.

NOTES

1. With amateur sport, according to Boorstin, "We have succeeded to a certain extent in guarding the uncorrupted authenticity of the event." Sport is "one of our few remaining contacts with an uncontrived reality: with people really trying to win and not merely to have their victory reported in the papers" (1962, 254). Of course, Boorstin was writing before the era of widespread doping, the massive growth of sports marketing, and the melodramatization and trivialization of athletes' stories by television. Perhaps he would today restrict his positive judgment to school and community sports contexts. Then again, perhaps not.

2. As my Chicago colleague, James Redfield (1985, 102), has put it, "The Greeks were great tourists, but were not given to participant observation." As Sugden has himself signaled in an anxiously titled article (1997), there needs now to be a serious conversation about the relation between what sport studies practitioners are labeling ethnography and the practices of professional anthropologists and field-working sociologists. For the moment, we can agree that we are all grappling with some similar problems, notably that of the scale and mobility of "mega" phenomena. Multilingual, multicultural, and multidisciplinary research teams have centered my approach to these difficult questions (MacAloon 1999).

3. I think I persisted as long as I did in trying to account for Olympic-level athletic contests in ritual terms because to a former athlete, at least in my sport in my context of the 1960s and 1970s, these terms seemed experientially appropriate. But as total social facts in Mauss's sense, games simply are not rituals.

4. Reacting to my explorations of the play concept and to parallel ones by Barbara Babcock on reflexivity and reversibility and Richard Schechner on the rehearsal process, Turner, too, near the end of his life, was experimenting with a near equivalence of the terms play, performance, and liminality, prepared to subsume even the category of ritual, at least in the context of pluralistic industrial society, into some new ludic Ur-process (Turner 1974). Trouble was, Turner's moral and literary gifts notwithstanding, this move actually resolved itself to a structure/anti-structure bipolar dynamic even more abstract and undifferentiated than the generic "ritual process" had been.

5. World Cup researcher-partisans tend toward a negative kneejerk reaction to this observation, until you ask them to honestly evaluate the World Cup opening and

closing and victory ceremonies. Inevitably they then agree that these are silly, derivative, insignificant performances in contrast to the Olympic ritual system, and these
days much more a matter of spectacle than ritual anyway. Some of these authorities will
proceed then to assert that the football matches themselves are ritual forms, with these
writers ending up in the same conceptual confusion I am describing. Instead, they
should devote their expertise, in my opinion, to answering this very interesting question of difference that from my point of view is correlated with the presence or absence
of developed ideology. Whatever one may think of "Olympism," "footballism" and
much less "World Cupism" are hardly equivalent if they can be said to exist at all as
self-conscious ideological projects.

6. Though I did manage in Montreal to see every moment of my own sport of
track and field, as I would again in Los Angeles, Seoul, and Barcelona. In Atlanta, I
found myself missing some preliminaries, and in Sydney, I finally admitted to myself
that drugs had made Olympic track and field no longer anything I remembered as my
sport, and therefore no longer anything very interesting, much less imperative for me to
attend, except as a duty-doing ethnographer and activist. In the language of my own
model, values, meanings, and practices associated with the spectacle genre had pene-
trated the game frame to a degree that watching on television would suffice. Indeed,
physical proximity with these particular Olympic bodies, in the Olympic Village, locker
rooms, the arena, and on the train—the expected intimacy of games, rites, and festivals—only made matters worse for me. A cynical logic of spectacle—of course, it is all
morally dubious, it is a big, awesome show!—is required to contend with drug-enhanced
bodies which, for experienced track athletes of a certain age, one generally has only to
see to know. The moral entailments of honesty, openness, earnestness, and joy that
should accompany games, rites, and festivals in my cultural contexts as well as in
Olympic ideology are seriously destabilized by out-of-frame pharmaceutical practice. As
the core genre of game ramifies outward, further pushed toward thinking and experi-
encing in a legal framework because of drugs (Kidd 1990; MacAloon 1990), the nested
system is disaggregated.

7. The booklet differentiating the privileges of the dozens of credential categories
in Sydney ran to nearly seventy pages. Most of the nearly 200,000 credentials issued at
those Olympic Games were for volunteers and contracted service workers, functioned
chiefly for security purposes, and offered the holder nothing beyond free public transport and access to their place of service. Perhaps 70,000 credentials brought a measure
of open access to particular special zones as well as a perk or two beyond basic transportation. Fewer than 3,000 credentials bore the "infinity" icon, the object of all desire
for insiders at an Olympic Games because of the general access it permits to nearly
every backstage and on-stage space and scene.

I stress "very nearly" because, as I have elsewhere described, the existence of a very
deep backstage in the most highly restricted Olympic Family zones is what—together
with the "natural" reasons for high-level persons of every nationality to be found in the
Olympic city as "simple sports fans" or state officials "supporting the national team"—
creates an unparalleled setting for international diplomatic activity, noble or nefarious,
and protected more completely from the journalistic gaze—ironic, because there are over

20,000 credentialed journalists at a Summer Games today, twice the number of athletes!—than any other setting of which I am aware. (No journalist should ever even dream of being admitted to these deep Olympic backstages.) Just as the spectacle frame—"You only have to watch and be awed"—sets up ordinary persons to be captured into other kinds of experience (ritual, agonal, festival), so too the "It's all a big show" message of spectacle framing deludes journalists (and often critical theorists) into failing to imagine that there are quite other, less trivial things going on.

8. In another big problem of intercultural ambiguity, *nori* is also used for "game" or ludic contest, as in the famous *ko-nori* battle of the Seoul Opening Ceremony, but not typically for sport of the Olympic kind for which loan words suffice. A partially similar condition obtains in the semantic field of contemporary Japan. Asking native speakers in diverse cultural environments to translate the specifications of my nested performance model and then back-translating their answers is an inevitably revealing methodological procedure.

9. In our own observations of these World Cup rally-fests and those of several Korean social scientists, middle-age women, teenagers, twenty-somethings of both sexes, and children seemed to dominate. Adult men were only scattered through these crowds. This social demography can be correlated with absence of state sponsorship and also with portions of the electorate thought to have put Roh Moo-hyun over the top in subsequent presidential elections (see Soon-Hee Whang, chapter 13, in this volume).

10. To take a classical example, Xerxes had to gaze out with his own eyes over his massed armies at the Hellespont to be overawed and to break down weeping at the spectacle. A report from the front would not have had that effect.

11. The official broadcast audience estimates emanating from bodies such as the IOC and FIFA are compromised by marketing considerations. As a rule of thumb, most experts deflate them by at least 30 percent. (See Moragas, Rivenburgh, and Larson 1995).

12. With Korea, 2002, the nesting of genres in the mass public rally-fests would be televised sport inside festival for actively participating Koreans (following Cohen's elaboration of the model), while encompassed as live spectacle for me as a foreign observer (and perhaps for some of those reticent senior Korean males as well). The live site model, by the way, was subsequently copied in Salt Lake and has even caused IOC planners to take notice and to insist that future bid committees include such measures in their plans. We shall now need to watch the cultural and urban contexts in which host cities accept or resist these recommendations in the future, diagnostic as they are of concern for the experiences and pleasures of uncredentialed, class-diverse publics, as well as of local estimations of and comfort with mass and relatively unregulated public assemblies.

13. The Olympic flame relay offers a particular opportunity to document and explore the processes of an emptying out of a cultural and historical form, and I will present an analysis of this process in a larger work on the performance.

14. Thanks to Arne Martin Klausen and his colleagues (Klausen 1995), we have a brilliant field study of the community festivals mounted throughout Norway to

celebrate the passage of the flame to Lillehammer. One can only hope that the English translation of this important text is published soon.

15. The cauldron lighting is inevitably the dramatic highlight of the Opening Ceremonies, far more decisive than the head-of-state's declaration as the moment when an Olympics actually begins. However, recalling the weeks and months of its former freedom and human intimacy on its passage from Greece, one can feel rather sad for the flame now made captive in the stadium cauldron.

16. I hesitate to mention the suicides of two Atlanta relay staffers not long after the Olympic Games, for, as every clinician knows, suicide is an act overdetermined by several life factors and experiences. Both were Georgia State Patrol troopers on loan to the flame relay, intensely involved in the work, and well-liked by scores of relay staffers. (I spoke several times with each but did not formally interview either.) Today their former relay colleagues to whom I have spoken are cautious about addressing these tragedies. But nearly all wonder, as one put it, "whether something didn't happen to them out there."

17. This fact has always puzzled and slightly offended me, in part because it contributes to a certain culture among the IOC leadership and senior staff in Lausanne. Persons there are prepared to give one a lecture about the torch relay, persons who have no idea whatsoever about it, because, beyond a sponsor contract, or media blurbs, or a few minutes in the host city, they have never actually seen it. (Ironically, in this they closely resemble many "critical theorists" devoted to criticizing the IOC and its commercial spectacle.) Of course, one could argue that it is a good thing for the flame relay that the Olympic bosses stay so far away. I understand the argument, but I also think this distance is unfortunate because it contributes to the impression that Lausanne is not very concerned nor in adequate touch with the Olympic movement anymore. As a result, as a member of the Executive Committee of the IOC 2000 Reform Commission, I introduced a resolution, later passed by the IOC Session, calling on the IOC Executive Board to be present in Olympia for the flame-lighting rituals. (If the board were here, then the senior staff would follow.) This IOC 2000 reform resolution has been ignored for the last two flame lightings.

18. Kang-Shin-pyo and I (1990) have demonstrated how the radical socio-political antagonisms associated with the transition from military regime to an elected presidential system in South Korea were inscribed in and altered the organization and symbolic practices of the 1986 Seoul Asian Games and the 1988 Seoul Olympic Games flame relays, respectively. Elsewhere, I will present a detailed account of the intercultural misunderstandings and leadership failures that nearly led to bloodshed in events surrounding the 1984 Los Angeles Olympic flame relay, as well as the heroically successful efforts by 1996 Atlanta Olympic leaders to return Greek-American flame relay relations to harmony. The main difference between the two American OCOGs? For Peter Ueberroth and his LAOOC (Los Angeles Olympic Organizing Committee) colleagues, the Greek flame ceremonies were understood to be political spectacle and economic bargaining in folkloric drag; for Billy Payne, Charlie Battle, A. D. Frazier, and the rest of the Atlanta core leadership, they were, by the time of their performance, thoroughly framed as ritual nested in festival.

19. Banks, insurance firms, oil companies, and state-owned agencies such as the postal service have been better-behaved sponsors in Calgary, Lillehammer, and Sydney.

20. To honor its role in Olympic history, the University of Chicago was selected for a special celebration during the Atlanta relay, and I was asked to organize it. Despite helping to plan this relay, working closely with all of the leaders, and being out on earlier segments, I was unprepared for the appearance in my university office of a previously unknown ACOG advance person whose mission it was to describe for me all of the things Coke would try to do to make its presence felt in our neighborhood, on campus, and in my ceremony. In careful language repeated in hundreds of venues across the country, she concluded: "ACOG wants you to know so that you can decide for yourself what you wish to permit." And this, so one hears, was "the Coca-Cola Olympics"!

References

Alabarces, Pablo, Alan Tomlinson, and Christopher Young. 2001. England vs. Argentina at the France '98 World Cup: Narratives of the nation and the mythologizing of the popular. *Media, Culture & Society 23* (5): 547–66.

Baudrillard, Jean. 1981. *Simulacres et simulations.* Paris: Éditions Galilée.

Berkaak, Odd Are. 1999. "In the heart of the volcano": The Olympic games as mega drama. In *Olympic games as performance and public event*, ed. Arne Martin Klausen. London: Berghahn.

Boorstin, Daniel. 1961. *The image: A guide to pseudo-events in America.* New York: Vintage.

Chalip, Laurence. 2000. Sydney 2000: Volunteers and the organization of the Olympic Games: Economic and formative aspects. In *Volunteers, global society, and the Olympic Movement*, ed. Miguel de Moragas, Ana Bélen, and Nuria Puig. Lausanne: Olympic Museum Press, 205–20.

Cohen, Michael. 2002. Performance as artifact: Objectification and agency in international spectacle. Ph.D. dissertation, University of Sydney.

Dayan, Daniel, and Elihu Katz. 1992. *Media events: The live broadcasting of history.* Cambridge: Harvard University Press.

Debord, Guy. 1977. *The society of the spectacle.* Detroit: Red and Black Press.

Hargreaves, John. 2000. *Freedom for Catalonia?* Cambridge: Cambridge University Press.

Hartog, François. 2001. *Memories of Odysseus: Frontier tales from ancient Greece.* Chicago: University of Chicago Press.

Kidd, Bruce. 1990. The World to Seoul, Seoul to the world . . . and Ben Johnson. In *One world beyond all boundaries: Seoul Anniversary Olympic Conference*, vol. 1, ed. Koh Byong-ik. Seoul: Poong Nam: 434–54.

Klausen, Arne Martin. 1995. *Fakkelstafetten: En olympisk ouverture*. Oslo: Ad Notam Gyldendal.

———. 1999. The torch relay: Reinvention of tradition and conflict with the Greeks. In *Olympic games as performance and public event*, ed. Arne Martin Klausen. London: Berghahn.

Lévi-Strauss, Claude. 1966. *The savage mind*. Chicago: University of Chicago Press.

MacAloon, John. 1978. Religious themes and structures in the Olympic Movement and the Olympic Games. In *Philosophy, theology, and history of sport*, ed. Fernad Landry and W. Orban. Miami: Symposia Specialists.

———. 1981. *This great symbol: Pierre de Coubertin and the origins of the modern Olympic Games*. Chicago: University of Chicago Press.

———. 1984a. Cultural performances, culture theory. In *Rite, drama, festival, spectacle: Rehearsals toward a theory of cultural performance*, ed. John MacAloon. Philadelphia: Institute for the Study of Human Issues.

———. 1984b. Olympic games and the theory of spectacle in modern societies. In *Rite, drama, festival, spectacle: Rehearsals toward a theory of cultural performance*, ed. John MacAloon. Philadelphia: Institute for the Study of Human Issues.

———. 1989. Festival, ritual, and television. In *The Olympic movement and mass media: Past, present, and future issues*, ed. Roger Jackson and Tom McPhail. Calgary: Hurford.

———. 1990. Steroids and the state: Dubin, melodrama, and the accomplishment of innocence. *Public Culture* 2 (2): 41–64.

———. 1992. The ethnographic imperative in comparative Olympic research. *Sociology of Sport Journal* 9 (2): 104–30.

———. 1999. Anthropology at the Olympic games: An overview. In *Olympic Games as performance and public event*, ed. Arne Martin Klausen. London: Berghahn.

———. 2000. Volunteers, global society, and the Olympic Movement. In *Volunteers, global society, and the Olympic Movement*, ed. Miquel de Moragas, Ana Bélen, and Nuria Puig. Lausanne: Olympic Museum Press.

MacAloon, John, and Shin-pyo Kang. 1990. Uri nara: Korean nationalism, the Seoul Olympics, and contemporary anthropology. In *One world beyond all boundaries: Seoul Anniversary Olympic Conference*, vol. 1, ed. Koh byonk-ik. Seoul: Poong Nam, 117–59.

Moragas, Miquel de, Ana Bélen, and Nuria Puig, eds. 2000. *Volunteers, global society, and the Olympic Movement*. Lausanne: Olympic Museum Press.

Moragas, Miquel de, James Larson, and Nancy Rivenburgh. 1995. *Television and the Olympics*. London: John Libbey.

Oppenheim, Robert. 2003. The place of projects: Remaking locality in Kyongju, South Korea. Ph.D. dissertation, University of Chicago.

Postone, Moishe. 1993. *Time, labor, and social domination: A reinterpretation of Marx's critical theory*. Cambridge: Cambridge University Press.

Redfield, James. 1985. Herodotus the tourist. *Classical Philology* 80 (1): 97–109.

Roche, Maurice. 2000. *Mega-events and modernity—Olympics and expos in the growth of global culture.* London: Routledge.

Rothenbuhler, Eric. 1989. The Olympics in the American living room: Celebration of a media event. In *The Olympic movement and mass media: Past, present, and future issues,* ed. Roger Jackson and Tom McPhail. Calgary: Hurford.

Sahlins, Marshall. 1990. Notes on the "world system." In *One world beyond all boundaries: Seoul Anniversary Olympic Conference,* vol. 1, ed. Koh Byong-ik. Seoul: Poong Nam: 78–96.

Sugden, John. 1997. Fieldworkers rush in (where theorists fear to tread): The perils of ethnography. In *Ethics, sport, and leisure: Crises and critiques,* ed. Alan Tomlinson and Scott Fleming. Aachen: Meyer and Meyer.

Sugden, John, and Alan Tomlinson. 1998. *FIFA and the contest for world football—Who rules the peoples' game?* Cambridge: Polity Press.

Turner, Victor. 1969. *The ritual process.* Chicago: Aldine.

———. 1974. Liminal to liminoid in play, flow, and ritual: An essay in comparative symbology. *Rice University Studies* 60 (3): 53–92.

Chapter 3

Italy 1934

Football and Fascism

Robert S. C. Gordon and John London

INTRODUCTION:
A DECADE OF SPORTING GLORY

The second football World Cup took place in Italy between May 27 and June 10, 1934. Thirty-two teams, including Italy, entered the qualifiers. For the tournament proper, sixteen teams took part, playing seventeen matches (the odd number caused by a replay of the quarter-final between Italy and Spain) in eight different venues (Bologna, Florence, Genoa, Milan, Naples, Rome, Trieste, and Turin). Nearly 400,000 tickets were sold, making for a respectable, but not massive, average attendance of over 23,000 per match. The final, between Italy and Czechoslovakia, was held in the Stadio Flaminio or Fascist National Party Stadium in Rome on June 10. Italy won by two goals to one, after extra time (Inglis 1990, 9; Glanville 1980, 23–42).

The 1934 home victory was one of the high points in an astonishing sequence of successes for Italian football in the 1930s, only challenged in the history of the game by the modern Brazilian teams. Italy won a European football tournament played over the three-year period, 1927–1930. After 1934, it went on to win the Olympic football title in Berlin in 1936 (with a team of student amateurs) and then, against the odds and hostile crowds, to retain its World Cup title in France in 1938. Italy also fought the aloof masters of the game, England, in three highly symbolic friendlies in 1933, 1934, and 1939. The middle of these, the "Battle of Highbury" of November 1934, took on near mythic status in Italian collective memory, as the Italians, playing with ten men for eighty minutes, fought back heroically from 3–0 down to 3–2, with only a whisker denying them an equalizer at the death (Beck 2001). For this entire period, the national team was coached by the extraordinary figure of Vittorio Pozzo, former crack *ardito* soldier in the Great War, father figure, and authoritarian: in nearly a decade in charge (1930–1938), his record reads: played 62; won 45; drew 11; lost 6 (Fabrizio 1976, 62; Foot 2006).

Italian clubs also enjoyed signal success in this period, especially the Bologna team, which won the Mitropa (Central European) Cup in 1932 and 1934 and then beat Chelsea in the Paris Exhibition Tournament in 1937 (Lanfranchi 1991). And football was far from being the only sport at which Italy excelled: the Italian team came second to the home U.S. team in the medals table at the 1932 Los Angeles Olympics; Tazio Nuvolari cut a dash around the grand prix circuits and the Mille Miglia race between 1930 and 1935; Italo Balbo flew across the Atlantic to Brazil in 1931 and Chicago in 1933; and Gino Bartali won the Tour de France in 1938 (McCarthy 2000).

Such successes were presented and perceived, nationally and internationally, as victories, not merely for Italy but more particularly for the Fascist regime (1922–1943). When Primo Carnera became World Heavyweight Boxing Champion, in 1933, Mussolini and Carnera swapped telegrams after his victory, the latter claiming: "My victory was for Italy and for the Duce" (Valentini 2002, 32). Carnera was flown home, feted and decked out in a black shirt. The Italian team at Los Angeles was nicknamed the "Mussolini boys." The Bologna team was very much the plaything of influential local Fascist *ras* (or chief), Leandro Arpinati. Jules Rimet himself could not contain his astonishment at what he took to be the root cause of Italy's triumph in the World Cup, Fascism, "a faith able to perform such miracles" (Ghirelli 1990, 133).

The 1934 World Cup thus appears to be part of an image of Italian sporting prowess encouraged and manipulated by the Fascist regime. It can be seen to anticipate the Nazi achievement of the Berlin Olympics two years later. Indeed, chroniclers of the World Cup concur in describing how the Italians exploited the event for propagandistic purposes (Crouch 2002, 23; Godsell 1990, 32); in the words of one account, the competition "reverberated to the hideous strains of a growing, pervasive Fascist ideology" (Shirley and Wight, 2002, 11). Closer examination reveals a rather more complex jumble of contradictions in which, despite the final result, there were failures as well as successes. To assess the nature of the Fascist impact on this early, international sporting event, it is first necessary to analyze the development and realization of notions of sport under Mussolini's regime before moving on to examine the tournament itself.

Fascist Ideology, the "New Man" and the Organization of Sport

Although Fascism as an ideology has proved notoriously hard to define, certain persistent elements in its makeup drew it ineluctably toward sport from the outset, even if on occasion from contradictory directions. These elements include its nationalism; its militarism, anti-individualism, and pedagogical totalitarianism; its aesthetics and culture of consent; and the myth of Mussolini.

Fascism was a nationalist movement to its core and was constantly alert to means of exalting the nation, restoring the glory of the past (Roman Empire, Renaissance Italy), acquiring the modern trappings of international power (Empire) and emulating the status of rivals in Europe. Sport would come to play a key role in the promotion of the nation's glory abroad, especially in the 1930s. International sport as an arm of diplomacy was beginning to take root throughout Europe in this decade (Teja 1998), and Fascist Italy was alert to its potential. Hence in the 1939 Italy-England game in Milan, weeks before war, the English team's Fascist salute was perceived as a key propaganda coup. Conversely, Italy pulled out of both the 1936 Tour de France and a 1937 football match in France on Mussolini's orders, to signal his hostility to Léon Blum's government, only to return and win the World Cup in Paris in 1938, weeks after the Nazi Anschluss (Murray 1994, 96–101).

Meanwhile, within Italy itself, the prime task of the totalitarian nation was the training of the population to breed and educate fighting soldiers. Both Nazism and Fascism inherited this idea from Victorian and Prussian notions of the education of the body (Pivato 1994). A huge program of mass participation sporting activity, run under the auspices of the web of Fascist child, youth, and student organizations, came into being in the 1920s to sustain this form of education in Italy. The militaristic principle also nourished the Fascist subordination of the individual to the corporate body of the state, achieved through a regimented conformist culture of the uniform, the group (modeled on the army unit and trained to move as one), and public spectacle at mass parades and, on occasion, sporting events.

The promotion of these concepts in an ultranationalist framework was achieved through legislative change and the subsequent formation of new Fascist organizations. Institutional reform occurred on several levels from 1922, and especially after 1925. Fascism reformed physical education in schools (part of the important Gentile reforms of the school system launched in 1923) and transformed sporting institutions (the CONI [Comitato Olimpico Nazionale Italiano], IOC, and FIGC [Federazione Italiana Ginoco del Calcio]) into organs of the Fascist Party and state, dominated by a series of high-ranking party officials, either from the party leadership itself or from the increasingly influential propaganda unit, the Ufficio Stampa, as if to emphasize the importance of this area of policy. Fascism then used those institutions to restructure the organization of sport, most fundamentally with the Carta di Viareggio (1926) for football, which regularized the status of clubs and players, Italianized the language of this Anglo-Saxon sport (Inter became Ambrosiana; Milan Milano, for example), and paved the way for the first national league, launched in 1929, and the Carta dello Sport (December 30, 1928), which regulated all sports from the elite down to the mass level.

Great importance was attached to the sporting aspects of the immense youth and after-work organizations, the Balilla (or ONB, Opera Nazionale Balilla) and the Dopolavoro (or OND, Opera nazionale Dopolavoro), launched in 1925 and 1926, respectively (De Grazia 1981). Around the OND and ONB, local, regional, and national competitive and collective display games were set in place in the 1930s (such as the *littoriali*), and, at ground level, most sections included some form of sporting activity and/or spectatorship as part of a wide range of programs offered. By 1936, the ONB had 5,500,000 members; by 1937, the OND had almost 20,000 local sporting associations and organized 130,000 tournaments or meets (although over half of these were bowls matches), involving tens of millions of players and spectators (Pivato 1994, 101). A mass culture of sport was, then, truly established and rooted in Italy, even if concentrated in the center and north of the country and among men rather than women (Dogliani 2000).

From the lowest to the highest levels, the Fascist regime also invested heavily—using tax breaks, subsidies, programs of public construction, and the input of local figures of influence—in sporting infrastructure. By 1930, over 2,000 new local stadia or tracks had been built (500 new stadia were inaugurated simultaneously on one day in 1929), and eighty-three out of a total of ninety-four official provincial centers in Italy had their own regional sports grounds (Pennacchia 1999, vol. 1, 160; Martin 2004, 79–171; Rossi 2002). This capillary infrastructural program had a direct impact on the 1934 World Cup: a series of major architectural projects between 1926 and 1933 led to the construction or modernization of all the stadia used as venues in the tournament (1926, Stadio San Siro, Milan; 1927, Stadio Littoriale, Bologna; 1928, Stadio Flaminio/PNF, Rome; 1930, Stadio Ascarelli, Naples; 1932, Stadio Littorio, Trieste; 1932, Stadio G. Berta, Florence; 1933, Stadio L. Ferraris, Genoa; 1933, Stadio B. Mussolini, Turin). The Bologna and the Florence stadia are commonly taken as the most interesting and telling as innovative Fascist architecture, employing styles both modern (concrete and glass materials in nontraditional forms) and neoclassical (Marathon Towers, porticos, friezes, and sculptures) (Inglis 1990, 10–57).

Much of the mass participation in sporting activity mentioned was low level, often non-competitive, and formed by an aesthetics of display as much as by the virtues of physical exertion (e.g., gymnastics); and for this reason it was able to perform a second, perhaps more immediately effective function beyond its long-term prospect as a primary trainer for the military. Sport also became a form of mass leisure and thus a manufacturer of consent (Cannistraro 1975), although there was an inevitable conceptual tension between the active participant and the passive spectator. Furthermore, the idea of mass leisure was at odds with the notion of an individual sporting hero. Two contrasting and even contradictory principles underlay the nationalist and militarist impulses within Fascist sport: the harmonized, non-competitive, and homogenizing principle symbolized by mass gymnastics, and the competitive, aggressive heroism epitomized in sportsmen such as Carnera or Pozzo's star player, Giuseppe Meazza. Within the Fascist conception of the body and the individual there was a possible way out of this contradiction: even the gymnasts were ultimately intended as subunits of mass aggression in war, and the sporting heroes were not so much heroes qua individuals as embodiments of a core Fascist myth, that of the "New Man," the perfected Fascist individual wholly imbued, in body and in spirit, with a near-mystical devotion to the state. Of course, the highest exemplar of the Fascist New Man was Mussolini himself, who literally embodied the state and was ever depicted as the fighting and sporting hero in his own right, his body frequently on display as physical worker, soldier, pilot, rider, skier, fencer, runner, and swimmer (although rarely, if ever as footballer) (Gori 2000; Mosse 1996).

Several key characteristics of the New Man were echoed in the so-called "metodo" of Pozzo's team: youth (Malvano 1984), love of risk and danger, sacrifice to the nation's cause, and pride in the nation (and, increasingly, in the race). Football's individual heroism in a collective, team cause was in harmony with such forces; and even the crowd attending matches could be seen to represent an ideal, choral collectivity coming together in a single, viscerally felt, faith and cause, much like Fascism itself (Fabrizio 1976, 52). As a radio broadcast just before the start of the 1934 World Cup put it: "Italian crowds will certainly recognize in each athlete the representative of that virtue that twelve years of Fascism have distilled in the collective soul and which is called 'self-esteem' or 'being aware of one's own worth'" (CONI 1936, 49).

THE ROLE OF THE MEDIA

The press was the first medium to exploit sport to the full and the first to exploit the new category (and spending power) of the fan (Panico and Papa 1993, 121–32). *Gazzetta dello Sport*, founded in 1896, came out daily from 1913 and *Il Guerin Sportivo* weekly from 1912. Newspapers began offering daily sports coverage in the 1920s (*Il Popolo d'Italia* from 1923; *Corriere della Sera* from 1927), a crucial stage in sport's infiltration of daily life outside sport (Lanfranchi 1991, 340). Magazines proliferated, including several illustrated ones, such as *Calcio Illustrato*, and Fascist titles such as *Il Littoriale* (from 1927) or *Lo Sport Fascista* (from 1928). To a greater or lesser extent, all adopted the rhetorical, epic style in tune with Fascist public pronouncements (Brera 1975, 77–83; Fabrizio 1976, 149–65). The national press also made efforts to use printed images to enhance its coverage. For the World Cup, between 275 and 400 foreign journalists from twenty-nine countries (the sources disagree) were accredited at the competition (CONI 1936, 57; Murray 1994, 87–93; Panico and Papa 1993, 190), and they found a coordinating press center with regular press conferences in central Rome (Recanatesi 1978, 23–24).

The regime only began to invest heavily in the power of radio from the early 1930s—Mussolini's brother, Arnaldo, ran the state radio company, EIAR (Ente Italiano per le Audizioni Radiofoniche) from 1930—and radio ownership was relatively low compared to other European countries. By 1932, 340,000 licenses had been issued, compared to 4 million in Germany (Richeri 1980, 52), rising to 535,000 in 1935, but collective listening in public places was commonplace, especially for certain key types of broadcast, from major national events to football matches (Forgacs 1990, 63–68). Many sets were owned by organizations such as the OND and schools, as well as, increasingly, bars and cafés. To gauge the maximum reach of collective listening, it is estimated that Mussolini's famous speech declaring his imperial war on Abyssinia on October 2, 1935, drew approximately 10 million listeners (Richeri 1980, 55). Sports broadcasting—featuring, especially, football and cycling—was a staple in both news and live commentary, although it is worth noting that it was not hugely prominent in the scheduling, nor the most popular item: only half of the listening population—probably the male half—listened regularly, compared to 95 percent for news and 80 to 85 percent for entertainment, according to a 1939 questionnaire (Monticone 1978, 66–69). From 1930, the second half of a league match was broadcast live every week, followed by the list of league results, and it swiftly became a public ritual (Panico and Papa 1993, 206).

The rapid acceleration of state initiatives in radio, from the early 1930s, coincided with the build-up to the World Cup, and the role of radio in football was immeasurably enhanced following the debut in 1933 (for a match between Italy and Germany) of legendary commentator Niccolò Carosio, whose florid, creative, and decidedly non-technical broadcasts—Gianni Brera described him as the "unrivalled Homer of a footballing epic" (Brera 1975, 133–34)—would be for decades at the heart of the collective memory of Italian football. Radio sales saw a spurt for the World Cup (Recanatesi 1978, 26) and, for the first time, radio rights were sold internationally: Holland bought exclusive rights, and between nine and fifteen other countries (assessments differ according to sources) took feeds of commentaries in four different languages set up by radio company EIAR, from the quarter finals onward (Vigarello 1990, 10; Panico and Papa 1993, 190).

A parallel story can be told of the Fascist state's investment in newsreels and the position of sport within them. The Istituto LUCE (L'Unione Cinematografica Educativa), founded in 1924, began producing over 100 newsreels a year in 1927, and these were a compulsory part of any cinema screening (Argentieri 1979). This latter point is crucial, since Italians spent far more of their leisure time and money on cinema than they did on sports events—by a ratio of 14 to 1, according to a survey of spending carried out in 1938 (Rossi 2002). All newsreels were previewed by Mussolini himself (Wagstaff 1984, 163–64). Sporting events, whether competitive matches or organized displays, were a stock feature of the newsreels, typically included alongside items of local interest and state ceremonies, as frames for the more tightly news-driven and international segments (Mancini 1985, 121–68; Argentieri 1979). The Istituto LUCE also produced more extended documentary pieces, on a variety of topics, but again, sporting prowess featured here. For the World Cup itself, over 15,000 meters of film were shot (Panico and Papa 1993, 205). As with several other areas under Fascist state management, the period 1933–1935 showed a marked acceleration in control and aggressive propagandizing in newsreels (evinced, for example, in the use of the Fascist calendar in newsreels from 1934), coinciding with the period of the World Cup. In the same year the Fascist salute became a compulsory prelude to all football matches, thus giving an added visual impact to Fascist symbolism.

THE POLITICS, RHETORIC, AND REALITY OF THE WORLD CUP

The World Cup was not the first international sporting competition to be hosted by Fascist Italy. The International University Games were successfully staged in Rome in 1928 and Turin in 1933. (The second event especially was an excuse for much boasting about the achievements of the regime: see Tomlinson 2005, 54–55.) A campaign was launched in 1930 to secure the 1936 Olympics in Rome (which lost out to Berlin). After informal assurances in 1930, at a 1932 meeting of FIFA in Stockholm (and then Zurich), Italy did succeed in securing the 1934 football World Cup, due to the dynamic negotiation of the international secretary of the Italian Football Federation, Giovanni Mauro. Mauro had carefully orchestrated the campaign to claim the hosting of the tournament, backed up by government guarantees to underwrite any losses, a crucial prerequisite for the staging of the modern global sporting event (Ormezzano and Colombero 1978, 22).

Given that Achille Starace, the longest-running Fascist Party secretary (1931–1939), was the figurehead for the 1934 World Cup, one would expect a high degree of fascisticization in the presentation of the competition. It was Starace who did the most to proliferate uniforms and parades and to promote the Fascist (or Roman) salute in Italian society. He was, in the words of one historian, "the high priest of the 'cult of the Duce'" (Gentile 1984, 264). In fact, the functioning of the tournament involved disguising to a certain degree the Fascist potential of the event and its iconography, while simultaneously attempting to present a Fascist image of it to an Italian public.

Take the promotion of the tournament through visual material. In all, 100,000 posters, 300,000 postcards, and 1 million stamps were put into circulation to commemorate the occasion. There was even a new cigarette brand called "Campionato del mondo" (World Championship) (Valentini 2002, 36). As part of the open collectivity, national competitions had been launched, such as that for the design of the tournament posters and other publicity material. It could be argued that designs of a typically Fascist-modernist style were chosen as winners (Vigarello 1990, 9–10; Ormezzano and Colombero, 1978, 170–71; Pinkus 1995). However, the use of the winning entries is telling (Figure 3.1). Luigi Martinati's image of the football with the world in the background seems to emanate from an abstracted form of the *fascio littorio* in the bottom left-hand corner, the rods tied to an axe that was at the heart of the etymology of Fascism and had, in 1926, been officially adopted as the symbol of the Fascist state (Falasca-Zamponi 1997, 95–99). Mario Gros's footballer is giving the Fascist salute. In contrast, Gino Boccasile's player is about to kick a ball, and while the image shares the modernist sans-serif lettering of the other winners, the flags convey the international nature of the competition. Although Martinati's design won first prize, it was Boccasile's design, the one with no overt Fascist symbolism, that became the most familiar and lasting image of the competition, since it was used on the cover of the official tournament program. Morever, even Boccasile's image had been transformed: in the original, published in 1933, a small *fascio littorio* had been present in the bottom right-hand corner, there had been no translations—eventually, on the left-hand side—and "Italia" had followed the main lettering indicating the world championship (Pennacchia 1999, vol. 1, 168). In this sense, extreme nationalism was visually subsumed into an internationalist stance.

FIGURE 3.1   The final form of three of the winning entries in the design competition for the 1934 World Cup. The artists, from left to right, are Gino Boccasile, Mario Gros, and Luigi Martinati. *Source:* Private collection.

A similar lack of uniformity can be observed when the rhetoric of the reporting is compared to what was happening during the matches. It is not difficult to find examples of propagandists wanting to connect the victory of the team to the glory of the nation:

> It is an event which acquires greater importance if it is considered as one of so many expressions of national will set on securing for our Country a position of supremacy in each field of human activity, especially in those chiefly dominated by effort and individual risk and the spirit of organization and collective discipline. (Volontà di primato 1934, 1)

The national glory was in turn related to Mussolini's role. "The Duce's congratulations for the great success of the Italian players" ran one headline to an article assessing the competition (De Martino 1934e, 4). The newspaper founded by Mussolini, *Il Popolo d'Italia*, proudly declared in its headline: "In the name and in the presence of the Duce, the *azzurri* [as the national team was known] win a new world title." The same journalist, Luigi Freddi—a veteran Fascist and a key figure in the press and cinema of the regime—went on to reinforce the link by quoting his master: "We have seen the *azzurri* continuously apply the teaching of the Duce, who wants to make out of our people a 'methodical, tenacious, and persevering' race (*razza*)" (Freddi 1934f, 8).

In practice, the Duce's presence at the games did not imply consistent support. He attended a qualifying match between the United States and Mexico (4–2) and the first game played by Italy in the competition in which it thrashed the United States 7–1 in Rome. He was present to receive personal applause at the final, yet he had sent his sons to the replay between Italy and Spain in Florence (1–0) and did not attend the Italy versus Austria semi-final (1–0), preferring to stay in Rome to see the other semi-final in which Czechoslovakia beat Germany 3–1. Despite accusations of match fixing that favored Italy, one can but wonder how the regime would have dealt with the leader's absence at what could have been the national team's last match. An inkling is given by what actually occurred during the Czech-German semi-final: before the end of the match, news of Italy's victory against Austria was announced through loudspeakers to the spectators of the Stadio Flaminio in Rome. The result was to focus the Roman crowd on events in Milan: having heard the announcement, they stood up and turned toward where Mussolini was sitting, all the time applauding (Freddi 1934e, 8).

In order to highlight the intimate connection between the totalitarian state and sporting success, statements about control and discipline had to be transferred from their civil, pedagogical context to an international sporting event. A radio preview of the competition therefore stressed that the training of the *azzurri* had been "meticulously controlled by the hierarchs of the Italian Football

Federation" (CONI 1936, 49). It was then a logical step for *Il Popolo d'Italia* to cherish the "vision of harmony, discipline, order, and courage" shown by the national team in its eventual victory over Spain. These were "winning" virtues (Freddi 1934d, 8). As was the case for internal politics, such qualities became a preparation for combat, even if the military nature of the struggle remained metaphorical. In the reinforcement of a fiery journalistic style invented during the Fascist regime to describe sport (Castellana 1991, 34–41), each match became a warlike encounter. Italy's 1–1 draw against Spain after extra time (the match that necessitated a replay the following day) provoked heroic rhetoric in *Il Popolo d'Italia*: "It was not a game, but a battle" (Freddi 1934c, 8). The lexicon was not merely journalistic but formed part of the sporting strategy. For the final, Vittorio Pozzo drummed into his players his militaristic vision: they were soldiers, the matches were battles, and the task of the team was like holding the "Piave line," after a famous front in Northern Italy in the First World War (Milza 1990, 55).

The stress on control extended beyond sporting achievement. It was quite clear from the outset that the tournament was going to be a challenge or, as one journalist wrote in a preview, "a testing ground for the organizational capabilities of Italian sport" (Lazotti 1934a, 6). General Vaccaro, the president of the Italian Football Federation, claimed that Italy had shown its "perfect [. . .] cordial hospitality, discipline, and organization" to the foreigners who had arrived (Freddi 1934a, 8). During the competition, Italian radio lauded "the efficiency of Mussolini's Italy" in relation to the event (CONI 1936, 57). Whereas efficient organization can be viewed as part of the military ethos, the materialist obsession with the profitability of the competition fits less comfortably with an heroic attitude. And yet, by May 29, there were public announcements about what was called the "financial success" of the tournaments, and newspaper reports trumpeted details of the accounts for each match (De Martino 1934b, 4; Il successo 1934, 8). In the end, the competition made a healthy profit of 1 million lire (Ghirelli 1990, 132).

Of course, financial success did not necessarily indicate ideologized mass participation. At every level it is possible to observe almost overt tensions and attempted solutions for papering over the cracks in the enactment of an ideology. The unificatory and simultaneously superior role of leaders is the first, most striking example. Matches were attended by the royal family and Fascist Party leaders, including Mussolini himself, who made a show of buying his tickets for himself and his family, like anyone else. However, the very same accounts that underlined this action of the Duce as a man of people (e.g., Freddi 1934b, 8) went on to report how he then proceeded to settle down in the *tribuna d'onore*, the covered VIP stand with a full view of the pitch from the center (see Figure 3.2, next to letters D and C in the center left of the plan). To counterbalance potential elitism, the media made much of a worker from Milan who could not come to Rome for the final and so sent fifteen lire to a newspaper editor with a letter saying: "I cannot

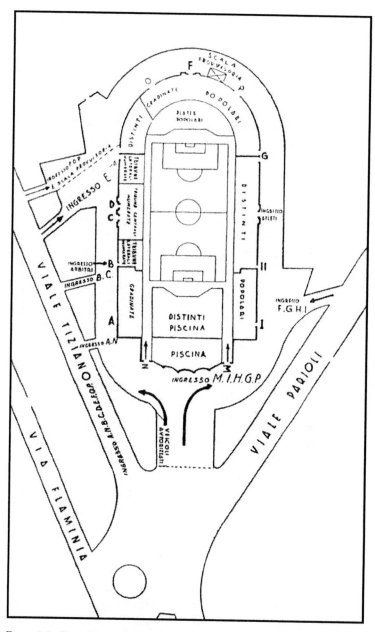

FIGURE 3.2   Plan of the Stadio Flaminio, otherwise called the Fascist National Party Stadium, in Rome, showing the layout of the public areas for the World Cup final. *Source:* La Tribuna, June 10, 1934, p. 8.

go, but I want in some way to be represented. So I ask you to buy a ticket and send a worker in my place" (De Martino 1934e, 4). The request was apparently fulfilled, and whatever the veracity of the incident, it painted a picture of nationwide, cross-class support, especially necessary for this event, since the center for the sport was still perceived as being in the north of the country, and the national team had played in Rome for the first time only six years before the World Cup, in 1928.

A more blatant problem was the discrepancy between expectations and outcome with regard to attendance at matches. Few of the games reached capacity figures, but hopes were high for the final. On the day before the match, June 9, Italian radio confidently announced that 70,000 people would go (CONI 1936, 62). *Il Giornale d'Italia* anticipated a crowd of over 60,000 (Lazotti 1934b, 1), but the headline in the same newspaper introducing the report about the match explained how "fifty thousand people applaud the Duce in the Stadium of the Party" (50,000 persone 1934, 1). Another Roman daily, *La Tribuna*, gave a detailed description of the stadium, pointing out how empty spaces could be seen. (In fact, the Milan semi-final, in which Italy defeated Austria, was more intensely followed and better attended; see Cante 1996). Anybody present at the final could have seen the gaps, many of which were at the curved end of the pitch, near the goal, on the side of the Viale Tiziano (see Figures 3.2 and 3.3). *La Tribuna* argued that the sun and ticket prices had been responsible (Giottoli 1934d, 9), thereby raising, right at the end of the competition, a controversial point: to some degree, ticket prices were aimed as much at the relatively wealthy and the traveling fans as at home crowds, for whom the price in the "popular" terraces was a relatively expensive six lire, while the covered stands went up to sixty lire (Mannucci 2002, 38). An Italian factory worker could expect to earn between 300 and 400 lire per month in the 1930s (Milza 1999, 606). Perhaps it was the socio-political sensitivity to such causes that forced *Il Popolo d'Italia* into denying the truth: its report of the match boasted that an "immense crowd" had submerged every structure of the "immense stadium," so that the pitch was the only unoccupied area (Freddi 1934f, 8). This was mendacious on another account: as international observers were keenly aware, the Stadio Flaminio could hardly be called "immense," since it did not conform to international standards of size (Inglis 1990, 50).

Spectators were, however, measured not just by numbers. As a reflection of the regime's concern about the potential ideological contradiction between passive spectators and active participants, the two categories were consciously blurred. Spectators became active participants in the sporting struggle. Before the semi-finals, the radio was proclaiming that, in supporting the Italian players, spurring them on and making them proud, the public would be the "leading actor in tomorrow's encounter" (CONI 1936, 59). Italian fans were engaged in the same militaristic activity as their team, so they played their part in the first battle against Spain: "The shouting of twenty thousand people hurls the *azzurri* into the attack" (Freddi 1934c, 8). By the end of the whole competition, congratulations were in order for Italian crowds who had participated "more often as actors than as spectators" and had shown through their behavior "a demonstration of ethical maturity second to none" (Freddi 1934f, 8). Their role was not simply to be active in relation to the players on the field, but to take part in something beyond the realm of sport. A radio broadcast on the day before the first games of the competition made this clear by pointing out that what was going to take place on the following day, "more than a spectacle of great proportions, is a ceremony of profound significance" (CONI 1936, 54). The journalistic depiction of the events just after the final elevated the experience to new heights: the joyful applause and the austere music of the Royal March "gave the characteristics of a religious rite to the consecratory ceremony of the success" (Giottoli 1934c, 1). Of course, this can simply be viewed as relabeling existing actions, and one can be cynical as to how many fans felt they were either actively or ritualistically involved. Nevertheless, it is relevant that such vocabulary should have been used in 1934, precisely the year in which fascist public ceremonies and rituals took on a more aggressive, militaristic cast (Berezin 1997, 116–19).

FIGURE 3.3   The final of the 1934 World Cup, played between Italy and Czechoslovakia. Clearly visible at this, the curved end of the stadium, are signifcant gaps in the crowd.
Source: Private collection.

Alongside this increasingly nationalist categorization, several events and rhetorical ploys combined to place Italians in a markedly internationalist context (just as we have seen the visual imagery fluctuate between the two extremes). The press quoted from the telegrams the Duce received from the competing countries at the beginning of the tournament, thus seeming to give his regime added legitimacy. General Vaccaro was proud to declare, in a florid, rhetorical style, that one of the decisions agreed at FIFA's Twenty-second Congress was to

> multiply yet further on the . . . playing fields international contacts, striving to contribute, with our sensibility of sportsmen at the vanguard of every realistic ideal, to the tightening between Nations of those ties of respect and reciprocity whose moral value is in the conscience of each of us. (Freddi 1934a, 8)

Such goals would be achieved from the Italian standpoint with a mixture of arrogance and manipulative diplomacy. Foreign fans arrived from abroad in unprecedented numbers, by tens of thousands (7,000 from Holland, 10,000 each from Switzerland and Austria; see Vigarello 1990, 8), with special trains (including four from Czechoslovakia for the final alone) and tourist packages laid on to facilitate their journey. The new stadia were shown off to groups of international journalists as engineering and architectural triumphs. But an element of nationalism was introduced through geographical choice: matches were placed in cities of cultural and/or political prestige, or to make a political point—Trieste, for example, for Italy's on-going irredentist claims (Dogliani 2000, 334).

Italy's first game of the tournament, against the United States, is a good illustration of the way Fascist diplomacy would function. Mussolini sat in the VIP stand with his sons, Bruno and Vittorio, members of the Italian royal family and the U.S. ambassador. The players from both teams gave the Fascist Party salute to the stand, and the Duce replied. Before the start of the game, the Americans gave the Italian team a pennant and a statue of a cowboy (Freddi 1934b, 8). It was a potent exchange of national symbolism.

There is no evidence that Fascists did anything during the World Cup to publicize another international feature within the Italian team itself. Four of its players who were active in the competition—Attilio De Maria, Enrico Guaita, Luisito Monti, and Raimundo Orsi—were of Argentinean origin (and this, in a tournament in which Argentina played in the first round). Their Italian family roots were used as a loophole in the Fascist law of the Carta di Viareggio against the importation of foreign players (Ghirelli 1990, 99). (In fact, the regime had previously flirted with the residual patriotism of the large Italian emigrant populations in the Americas.) In the 1934 final, Orsi scored the first goal, and it was Guaita who set up the ball for Schiavio to score the winner.

Another element intrinsic to the ambivalent nationalism of Italian football was language. A radio broadcast just before the 1934 final boasted that football had originated in Italy in the sixteenth century (CONI 1936, 62). Nevertheless, such nationalist reappropriation of the sport sounded awkward when juxtaposed with the preponderance of anglicisms in the press. Newspapers referred to "goals," a totally unidiomatic plural in Italian, and "corner" instead of the indigenous equivalents (e.g., Bevilacqua 1934, 1; De Martino 1934c, 5). Most interesting in this respect is the name of the game itself. As the winning designs show clearly (Figure 3.1) the Italian invention for football is "calcio." This did not stop some dailies from using the English word. Most striking is the appearance in the illustrated magazine *Gente Nostra*, which was described in its subtitle as *Illustrazione fascista*: the issue released on the day of the final called the championship the "Campionati del mondo di Foot-ball" (June 10, 1934, 13). All of these terms contradicted Fascist decrees to de-anglicize football terminology and gave a perhaps involuntary non-Italian gloss to the game.

In terms of sporting achievement, the celebration of nationalist triumph in an internationalist context was even more problematic, for this second World Cup was patently not a competition including all the best teams in the world. The defenders of the title, Uruguay, plagued by internal problems and still offended by the refusal of many Europeans to come in 1930, did not participate. The only Latin Americans in the tournament, Argentina and Brazil, did not send their best teams and were therefore eliminated in the first round. (Mexico had traveled to Italy only to be knocked out in a qualifier.) Coupling these defeats with the fate of the United States at the hands of Italy, *Il Giornale d'Italia* was able to announce in a headline: "All the American teams have been eliminated" (Tutte 1934, 6). It was not so easy to dismiss the absence of the English team, and so intricate tirades evolved. This is how *Corriere della Sera* put it on the day before the start of the competition:

> For years and years England has not been sending its teams to official tournaments. It was not at Antwerp or Paris or Amsterdam. But the results achieved by the English team recently are decisive and significant. The national team of England, defeated in Budapest, beaten in Prague, will have to bow to the winner of the World Cup. The "splendid isolation," as the withdrawal of the British was called, is no longer valid. Times have changed. (De Martino 1934a, 6)

To anticipate the universal value of ultimate victory, *Il Popolo d'Italia* pointed out on the day before the final that Czechoslovakia had recently beaten England 2–1 (La finale 1934, 8).

Whereas these arguments drew attention to a significant absentee, in Britain the splendid isolation was genuine. None of the British newsreel companies appear to have bought footage of the competition, and no journalists from the major newspapers were sent to cover the event. In *The Times*, the only information about the World Cup was the reproduction of an Italian postage stamp issued to commemorate the tournament (June 5, 1934, 18). Despite considerable interest in Italian politics, newspapers such as the *Daily Mail* (June 11, 1934, 18) and the *Daily Express* (June 11, 1934, 21) gave just the result of the final, in tiny notices copied from a news agency release. Although there was interest in countries such as Germany (whose team reached the semi-finals), in France the general coverage was patchy and inaccurate, especially since the national team was eliminated in the first round. (*Le Figaro* [June 11, 1934, 8], for example, limited itself to an undetailed report of the final in little over 100 words.) The propaganda value of the Italian World Cup was thus considerably reduced outside Italy.

The teams that made it through to the later stages deserved more nuanced consideration. This was necessary above all for the Spaniards, who forced Italy into a replay after a 1–1 draw in the quarter-finals. The representational strategy here was twofold: on the one hand, the Italian players were viewed as not being in top form, while on the other, Spain became a heroic combatant, a worthy adversary (e.g., Giottoli 1934a, 2). The comments after the match of the Spanish captain, Ricardo Zamora, were extensively quoted. According to Zamora, the legendary goalkeeper, nicknamed *El Divino*, "The battle in Florence was one of the most exciting sporting battles at which I have ever been present. We should have met for the final. The final in Rome will certainly not be so fine, so interesting, or so well fought" (L'omaggio 1934, 2). It also was a rather violent game, and it is relevant that Zamora, after what some consider a foul against him that led to the Italian goal (Ghirelli 1990, 136), could not return for the replay the following day, won by Italy 1–0. Even after their defeat (in another violent encounter), the Spaniards still apparently considered their foes in a fraternal light: at the train station in Florence, a fond farewell took place between Zamora and the Italian captain-goalkeeper, Giampiero Combi, who shook hands, the Spaniard declaring that his team would go and support Italy in its next match against Austria (De Martino 1934d, 6). Considering the violent nature of the two games—the first was apparently among the most savage in the history of the tournament (Martin 2004, 162)—it is difficult to believe in the authenticity of these sentiments. By the time the final was over, the "extremely fierce contest" between Italy and Spain was still being evoked (De Martino 1934e, 4).

Treatment of the Czechs followed the ploy of lauding an opposing team to enhance Italian prestige, but there also were signs of a more denigratory approach. (This was perhaps stimulated by the infamously violent encounters between Juventus and Slavia Prague in 1932 [Martin 2004, 177–79]). The free kick that resulted in the goal putting Czechoslovakia into a 2–1 lead against

Germany in the semi-final was seen as uncertain, and at least one report actually claimed that it was a mistaken decision made by the Italian referee, Rinaldo Barlassina (Giottoli 1934b, 9). The Czechs moved ahead to win by 3–1, but maybe Barlassina, one of the best-known referees in Italian history, was helping to force the weaker squad into the final against Italy (where a non-Italian referee would have to preside). Off the field, there were other insinuations about a country whose politics can hardly have been seen as sympathetic to the Fascist cause. A rather cruel caricature of the Czech president, Tomáš Masaryk, appeared on the front page of *Il Popolo d'Italia* two days before the final (June 8, 1934) and on the day of the match itself came the prominent news that Czechoslovakia was resuming "diplomatic relations with Moscow" (Praga 1934, 10). It was just as well that an adversary with such communist connections was defeated (although it was at this juncture convenient to forget the pact of friendship Mussolini had signed with the Soviet Union one year earlier).

The presentation of Nazi Germany, in contrast, involved no such problems. After the semi-final against the Czechs, Germany beat Austria 3–2 in the play-off to win third place, which granted the Germans a prominent position along with the Czechs and Italians in the closing ceremony just after the final. Their flag was one of the three flying in the stadium, and the German national anthem was heard third after that of the others. Germans in the crowd sang along and raised their arm in the Nazi salute. The German captain went up to the VIP stand to receive the corresponding prize for his team, given by Mussolini himself (Lazotti 1934c, 7; Giottoli 1934d, 9). The diplomatic approximation between Germany and Italy would be maginfied four days later, when Hitler came to meet the Duce for the first time, near Venice.

The ceremonies following the Italian victory possessed other features that mixed Fascist appropriation with the veneer of international approval. When the captains of the three teams went down onto the playing field to join their fellow players, the Fascist anthem, "Giovinezza," was played, and the crowd stood up and faced Mussolini, who acknowledged the gesture and smiled. This personal touch was continued in the reward for Combi's squad: as well as the Jules Rimet trophy of FIFA, the winning team received a specially designed Duce cup six times the size of the FIFA trophy, a signed photograph of Mussolini and a gold medal in recognition of their conquest of the football world in the name of Mussolini and Fascism (Martin 2004, 189). Advantage was taken of a good photo opportunity in Mussolini's personal headquarters, the Palazzo Venezia in Rome, where he posed with the team just after the match, the presence of the Swedish referee for the game—Ivan Eklind—seemingly objectifying the sporting achievement (Cascioli 1982 , 112).[1] No wonder *Il Popolo d'Italia* confidently heralded the excellent impression that had been made on foreign visitors by Fascist efficiency, which would all serve for the foreigners who would come to Italy for the 1940 Olympics (Freddi 1934f, 8). (This proved over-optimistic, although Italy was later promised the 1944 games.)

A SUBDUED SUCCESS

It is legitimate to ask whether there was any opposition to the use made by the regime of the tournament and the ultimate victory within it. The evidence is necessarily anecdotal, but one fan has since claimed that he was against the national team in 1934 because, as he put it, "I was against the regime." Trusted friends would express satisfaction to each other when opposing teams scored (Mannucci 2002, 40), yet this could never have been extensively organized as an opposition movement. The clandestine Communist Party newspaper, *L'Unità*, devoted no attention to sport at the time, but contained the following instructions in an issue published during the year of the World Cup: "Every comrade should be registered in a mass organization (union, Dopolavoro, etc.), because this is the only way the party has of linking up with these organizations" (*L'Unità*, 1934, 11, no. 14). Indeed, since 1931, it had been Communist Party policy not to boycott Fascist mass organizations, but to infiltrate them and win their members over to anti-Fascist positions (Forgacs 1986, 45). Since 1934 had been the year in which 99.8 percent of the population voted for the Fascist regime in a plebiscite, it is extremely difficult to see how such positions could be articulated, especially in the realm of spectator sport. More research needs to be undertaken into the crowd dynamics of the time and the songs, slogans, and chants that may have served as vehicles of opposition.

However, there still remains the question of the extent to which the 1934 World Cup was a Fascist event, beyond simply being labeled one because it took place under the aegis of the Fascist regime. Despite military glosses and the trip of the Argentine squad to the tomb of Mussolini's family (Martin 2004, 187), the competition had few of the visits and rituals that took place eight years later, when a Spanish team (representing the Fascist sympathies of the new dictatorship in their homeland) played Italy in Milan: the Spaniards were toured to sites that were important in the early stages of the Fascist movement, and they placed wreaths at memorials to the dead. The match itself was interrupted for a minute of silence for those who had died in military combat (London 1996, 241–42).

Nor could the World Cup compare with the mass events within Italy that were national (not international) in nature. Four months after the conclusion of the World Cup, ideology and athleticism converged in Rome on October 28, 1934, when the twelfth anniversary of the March on Rome—a hugely important date in the "liturgical" calendar of the Fascist civic religion (Gentile 1996)—was celebrated with a choreographed, mass parade in the Circus Maximus, in the Duce's presence, of 12,000 athletes, including footballers and Olympic heroes. In a speech, Mussolini made overt connections between the virility of a new Italian race, its role in "every battle," and the duty of Italian athletes "beyond our borders" (Pennacchia 1999, vol. 1, 172; Fabrizio 1976, 150–51). This kind of grandeur and direct (rather than journalistic) rhetoric had not had a central place in the events of the World Cup.

A few foreign visitors combined their match attendance with visits to the Exhibition of the Fascist Revolution (*La Tribuna*, June 9, 1934, 1), although there seems to have been no mass-scale, concerted effort to coordinate such activities. Even in the realm of sport, football did not dominate public interest on every day of the tournament: the cycling competition—the Giro d'Italia—and the Davis Cup were given plenty of space in the sports pages of newspapers. In the weekly *Gente Nostra*, published on the day of the World Cup final (June 10, 1934, 13), out of ten sports photographs only three were from the football tournament. One was on boxing, and six detailed the first Italian car rally. More striking still is the fact that Fascist Party Secretary Starace is shown in the boxing and car rally photographs but is absent from the soccer images.

Maybe the World Cup did not fit comfortably with the popular participatory notions of the OND, which was prohibited from promoting competitive soccer (the realm of the CONI). Maybe it was at this stage simply too difficult to fascisticize an international competition which, in contrast to the Olympic Games, relied so heavily on the playing of the sport in question and the results of each match. In any case, the undeniable propaganda successes of the 1934 World Cup have remained strangely subdued. Despite the insistence by football specialists (cited at the beginning of this chapter) on the Fascist nature of the event, it has stayed out of historical accounts of Fascism, even those concerned with the influence of the regime on popular culture and social ritual (De Grazia 1981; Falasca-Zamponi 1997; Forgacs 1990; Gentile 1996; Thompson 1991).[2] Although further analysis is needed to define the precise political character of the event, it undoubtedly provides a fascinating example of the way Fascist Italy was portrayed, both in an international and a domestic environment. The very uncertainties that emerge from an analysis of the tournament make it a symptomatic moment in the history of the regime.

NOTES

1. In fact eyewitness accounts accuse Eklind of taking bribes from Mussolini to favor Italy in both the semi-final (against Austria) and the final. In the semi-final he apparently moved the ball in the direction of the Italians at one point and, in the final, he ignored Italian foul play (Hughes 2003).

2. The one well-known study that does devote a sentence to the subject explains how the national team won the "World Championship in both 1937 [*sic*] and 1938" (Tannenbaum 1973, 145).

REFERENCES

(All unauthored references are listed under their titles according to the alphabetical order of the first word.)

Argentieri, Mino. 1979. *L'occhio del regime: Informazione e propaganda nel cinema del fascismo*. Florence: Vallecchi.

Beck, Peter J. 2001. For world footballing honors: England versus Italy, 1933, 1934, and 1939. In *Europe, Sport, World: Shaping Global Societies*, ed. J. A. Mangan. London: Frank Cass.

Berezin, Mabel. 1997. *Making the Fascist self: The political culture of Interwar Italy*. Ithaca, NY: Cornell University Press.

Bevilacqua, Giuseppe. 1934. Le semifinali del campionato mondiale di calcio: Italia batte Austria per 1 a 0 e si qualifica per la finalissima della coppa del mondo. *La Tribuna*, June 5, p. 1.

Brera, Gianni. 1975. *Storia critica del calcio italiano*. Milan: Bompiani.

Cannistraro, Philip V. 1975. *La fabbrica del consenso: Fascismo e mass-media*. Bari: Laterza.

Cante, Diego. 1996. Propaganda e sport negli anni 30: Gli incontri di calcio tra Italia e Austria. *Italia contemporanea* 204 (September): 521–44.

Cascioli, Lino. 1982. *Storia fotografica del calcio italiano: Dalle origini al campionato del mondo 1982*. Rome: Newton Compton.

Castellana, Lorenzo. 1991. *La lingua dello sport in Italia è ancora fascista*. Manduria: Piero Lacaita.

CONI, ed. 1936. *Cronache radiofoniche dello sport*. Rome: CONI-EIAR.

Crouch, Terry. 2002. *The World Cup: The complete history*. London: Aurum.

De Grazia, Victoria. 1981. *The culture of consent: Mass organization of leisure in Fascist Italy*. Cambridge: Cambridge University Press.

De Martino, Emilio. 1934a. Si accende domani su otto fronti diversi la battaglia per il campionato del mondo. *Corriere della Sera*, May 26, p. 6.

———. 1934b. Il campionato del mondo di calcio: Primi bilanci. *Corriere della Sera*, May 29, p. 4.

———. 1934c. Cento minuti di attacco. *Corriere della Sera*, June 1, p. 5.

———. 1934d. Penultima tappa. *Corriere della Sera*, June 3, p. 6.

———. 1934e. Il compiacimento del Duce per il grandioso successo dei calciatori italiani. *Corriere della Sera*, June 12, p. 4.

Dogliani, Patrizia. 2000. Sport and Fascism. *Journal of Modern Italian Studies* 5: 326–43.

Fabrizio, Felice. 1976. *Sport e fascismo: La politica sportiva del regime 1924–1936*. Rimini: Guaraldi.

Falasca-Zamponi, Simonetta. 1997. *Fascist spectacle: The aesthetics of power in Mussolini's Italy*. Berkeley: University of California Press.

Foot, John. 2006. *Calcio: A cultural history of Italian football*. London: Fourth Estate.

Forgacs, David. 1986. The Left and Fascism: Problems of definition and strategy. In *Rethinking Italian Fascism: Capitalism, populism, and culture*, ed. David Forgacs. London: Lawrence and Wishart.

———. 1990. *Italian culture in the industrial era*. Manchester: Manchester University Press.

Freddi, Luigi. 1934a. Il campionato mondiale di calcio: L'organizzazione del grande avvenimento in un'intervista con il generale Vaccaro. *Il Popolo d'Italia*, May 26, p. 8.

———. 1934b. Trentamila persone assistono alla strepitosa vittoria degli azzurri nel primo ottavo di finale. *Il Popolo d'Italia*, May 29, p. 8.

———. 1934c. La lotta tra azzurri e granata: Filo da torcere. *Il Popolo d'Italia*, June 1, p. 8.

———. 1934d. L'Italia vince la Spagna per 1–0. *Il Popolo d'Italia*, June 2, p. 8.

———. 1934e. Alla presenza del Duce la Cecoslovacchia, battendo la Germania per 3 a 1, si qualifica avversaria degli azzurri per la finale. *Il Popolo d'Italia*, June 5, p. 8.

———. 1934f. Nel nome e alla presenza del Duce i calciatori azzurri conquistano un nuovo primato mondiale. *Il Popolo d'Italia*, June 12, p. 8.

Gentile, Emilio. 1984. The problem of the party in Italian Fascism. *Journal of Contemporary History* 19: 251–74.

———. 1996. *The sacralization of politics in Fascist Italy*. Translated by Keith Botsford. Cambridge, MA: Harvard University Press.

Ghirelli, Antonio. 1990. *Storia del calcio in Italia*. Rev. ed. Turin: Einaudi.

Giottoli, Agostino. 1934a. I "quarti di finale" del campionato di calcio: L'incontro ad oltranza tra l'Italia e la Spagna per l'ammissione alle semifinali di domenica. *La Tribuna*, June 2, pp. 1–2.

———. 1934b. La "Coppa del mondo" allo Stadio del P.N.F.: Alla presenza del Duce la Cecoslovacchia batte la Germania per 3 a 1 ed acquista il diritto di disputare la finale con l'Italia. *La Tribuna*, June 5, p. 9.

———. 1934c. Impresa degna di combattenti di razza. *La Tribuna*, June 12, p. 1.

———. 1934d. La cronaca dei centoventi minuti dell'appassionante "finalissima" del campionato mondiale. *La Tribuna*, June 12, p. 9.

Glanville, Brian. 1980. *The history of the World Cup*. London: Faber and Faber.

Godsell, Andrew. 1990. *The World Cup*. Alton: Nimrod.

Gori, Gigliola. 2000. The model of masculinity: Mussolini, the "New Italian" of the Fascist era. In *Superman supreme: Fascist body as political icon, global fascism*, ed. J. A. Mangan. London: Frank Cass.

Hughes, Séan, dir. 2003. *Football and fascism* (documentary television program). Great Britain: BBC4.

Il successo finanziario del torneo e la maturità sportiva delle folle italiane. 1934. *Il Popolo d'Italia*, May 30, p. 8.

Inglis, Simon. 1990. *The football grounds of Europe*. London: Willow Books.

La finale del campionato mondiale di calcio: La grande attesa per l'incontro Italia-Cecoslovacchia. 1934. *Il Popolo d'Italia*, June 9, p. 8.

Lanfranchi, Pierre. 1991. Bologna: "The team that shook the world." *The International Journal of the History of Sport* 8: 336–46.

Lazotti, Umberto. 1934a. Il prologo delle finali del campionato calcistico del mondo. *Il Giornale d'Italia*, May 26, p. 6.

———. 1934b. Con la "finalissima" di domani fra l'Italia ed la Cecoslovacchia si concluderà a Roma, nello Stadio del Partito, il campionato mondiale di calcio. *Il Giornale d'Italia*, June 10, pp. 1, 8.

———. 1934c. L'appassionante contesa allo stadio. *Il Giornale d'Italia*, June 12, p. 7.

L'omaggio di Zamora agli azzurri. 1934. *La Tribuna*, June 2, p. 2.

London, John. 1996. Competing together in fascist Europe: Sport in early Francoism. In *Fascism and theatre: Comparative studies on the aesthetics and politics of performance in Europe, 1925–1945*, ed. Günter Berghaus. Oxford: Berghahn.

Malvano, Laura. 1984. Il mito della giovinezza attraverso l'immagine: Il fascismo italiano. In *Storia dei giovani: II: L'età contemporanea*, ed. G. Levi and J.-C. Schmitt. Bari: Laterza.

Mancini, Elaine. 1985. *Struggles of the Italian film industry during fascism, 1930–1935*. Ann Arbor: UMI Research Press.

Mannucci, Enrico. 2002. Quei calci a villa Torlonia: Intervista a Manlio Cancogni. *L'Europeo* (April–June): 38–40.

Martin, Simon. 2004. *Football and Fascism: The national game under Mussolini*. Oxford: Berg.

McCarthy, Patrick. 2000. Two Fascist champions. *Journal of Modern Italian Studies* 5: 343–45.

Milza, Pierre. 1990. Le Football italien: Une histoire à l'échelle du siècle. *Vingtième siècle* (April–June): 49–58.

———. 1999. *Mussolini*. Paris: Fayard.

Monticone, Alberto. 1978. *Il fascismo al microfono: Radio e politica in Italia (1924–1945)*. Rome: Studium.

Mosse, George L. 1996. *The image of man: The creation of modern masculinity*. Oxford: Oxford University Press.

Murray, William J. 1994. *Football: A history of the world game*. Aldershot: Scolar Press.

Ormezzano, Gian Paolo, and B. Colombero. 1978. *Il calcio e la coppa del mondo*. Milan: Longanesi.

Panico, Guido, and Antonio Papa. 1993–2000. *Storia sociale del calcio in Italia*. 2 vols. Bologna: Il Mulino.

Pennacchia, Mario. 1999. *Il calcio in Italia*. 2 vols. Turin: UTET.

50,000 persone acclamano il Duce nello Stadio del Partito consacrando la conquista italiana del campionato mondiale di calcio. 1934. *Il Giornale d'Italia*, June 12, p. 1.

Pinkus, Karen. 1995. *Bodily regimes: Italian advertising under Fascism*. Minneapolis: University of Minnesota Press.

Pivato, Stefano. 1994. *L'era dello sport*. Florence: Giunti.

Praga e Bucarest riallacciano le relazioni diplomatiche con Mosca. 1934. *Il Popolo d'Italia*, June 10, p. 10.

Recanatesi, Franco. 1978. *Il mondo è un pallone: Storia e attualità dei campionati mondiali di calcio*. Milan: Mazzotta.

Richeri, Giuseppe. 1980. Italian broadcasting and Fascism 1924–1937. *Media, Culture, and Society* 2: 49–56.

Rossi, Lauro. 2002. Un fisico bestiale. *Il manifesto*, April 25, http://www.ilmanifesto.it/25aprile/02_25Aprile/9502rs28.01.htm (accessed May 3, 2005).

Shirley, Simon, and Susannah Wight, eds. 2002. *The World Cup: A definitive history and guide*. London: Janus.

Tannenbaum, Edward. 1973. *Fascism in Italian society and culture 1922–1945*. London: Allen Lane.

Teja, Angela. 1998. Italian sport and international relations. In *Sport and international politics*, ed. P. Arnaud and J. Riordan. London: E & FN Spon.

Thompson, Doug. 1991. *State control in Fascist Italy: Culture and conformity 1925–1943*. Manchester: Manchester University Press.

Tomlinson, Alan. 2005. Olympic survivals: The Olympic Games as a global phenomenon. In *The global politics of sport: The role of global institutions in sport*, ed. Lincoln Allison. London: Routledge.

Tutte le squadre americane sono state eliminate. 1934. *Il Giornale d'Italia*, May 29, p. 6.

Valentini, Sergio. 2002. Vittorio Pozzo, lo strano leader. *L'Europeo* (April–June): 32–3.

Vigarello, G. 1990. Les Premières Coupes du monde, ou l'installation du sport moderne. *Vingtième siècle* (April–June): 5–10.

Volontà di primato. 1934. *La Tribuna*, June 12, p. 1.

Wagstaff, Chris. 1984. The Italian cinema during the Fascist régime. *The Italianist* 4: 160–74.

Chapter 4

Berlin 1936

The Most Controversial Olympics

Allen Guttmann

The 1936 Olympics were the most controversial in the history of the modern Games. They were intensely controversial before they took place. From January 1933 to December 1935, there was an international boycott movement on the part of those who felt that it was morally wrong to celebrate the Games in Nazi Germany. Adolf Hitler's insincere (and eventually broken) promise to accept the Olympic Charter and to allow Jews to compete on the German team blunted the boycott movement, and the Games themselves took place with a minimum of political conflict, but controversy flared again after the athletes departed from Berlin. Historians have for decades debated the political significance of the "Nazi Olympics." The debate has focused on two related questions. Were the Games a propaganda triumph for the Nazis, or were they an occasion for Jesse Owens and other black athletes implicitly to refute Nazi racial doctrines? Was Leni Riefenstahl's two-part documentary film, *Olympia*, politically biased to favor the Nazi cause, or was it—as Riefenstahl continued to claim up until her death—merely an evocation of the intrinsic beauty of sports?

A Sketch of the Boycott Controversy[1]

At its twenty-ninth session in Barcelona in April 1931, the International Olympic Committee had been unable to select the site for the 1936 games, but a subsequent mail ballot produced forty-three votes for Berlin and only sixteen for Barcelona. The choice ratified the full reintegration of Germany within the world of international sports from which it had been expelled in the wake of World War I. When the IOC's decision was announced on May 13, 1931, Heinrich Brüning was Germany's chancellor, and a shaky centrist coalition was in power. On January 30, 1933, six days after the creation of the *Organisationskomitee*, Adolf Hitler became chancellor of the Weimar Republic, which he promptly destroyed.

Although Hitler thought that German boys should learn to box in order to prepare themselves for their role as natural rulers, neither he nor his followers were advocates of modern sports, which they rightly perceived as implicitly universalistic. On August 19, 1932, *Der völkische Beobachter*, which faithfully represented Hitler's views, demanded that the Olympic Games be restricted to white athletes. The following year, after the Nazi seizure of power, Bruno Malitz sneered at modern sports as an egalitarian phenomenon "infested" with "Frenchmen, Belgians, Pollacks, and Jew-Niggers" who had been allowed "to start on the tracks, to play on the soccer fields, and to swim in the pools. . . . Whatever Jews praise is poison for us" (Malitz 1982, 218–19).

Malitz may well have had Theodor Lewald in mind. The son of a Prussian civil servant who had converted from Judaism to Christianity, Lewald served as a German representative on the IOC and as the president of the organizing committee (Krüger 1975). The secretary of the committee, Carl Diem was not stigmatized by Jewish forebears, but his wife was, and the school that Diem had founded a decade earlier, the *Deutsche Hochschule für Leibesübungen* (German College of Physical Exercise), had several Jews on its faculty (Diem 1976). Given their endangered personal positions and the shrill hostility of many Nazis to the Olympics, neither Lewald nor Diem was optimistic about the 1936 games, and both were understandably apprehensive when they were summoned, on March 16, 1933, to meet with Hitler at the chancellery. To their astonishment and relief, Hitler did not order an immediate cessation of preparations. On the contrary, he gave them his tentative approval. The obvious reason for Hitler's change of mind was that he and Joseph Goebbels, who was present at the meeting, realized that the games were an unparalleled opportunity for a propaganda coup.

Hitler's enthusiasm allayed Lewald's anxieties and aroused those of Henri Baillet-Latour, Pierre de Coubertin's successor as president of the IOC. The contradiction between the Olympic Charter and the racist principles of the Nazi regime was too glaringly obvious to be ignored. At the next IOC session (Vienna, June 1933), the discrepancy between Nazi doctrine and the Olympic rulebook was the central issue. The three German IOC members—Lewald, Karl Ritter von Halt, and Adolf Friedrich von Mecklenburg—were asked about Jewish participation. The crux of the matter was not the acceptance of Jewish athletes on foreign teams but rather the right of *German* Jews to try out for *their* national team. To the amazement of their IOC colleagues, the three German members managed to obtain an unambiguous written commitment from their government to abide by the rules: "As a principle German Jews shall not be excluded from German Teams at the Games of the XIth Olympiad" (IOC 1933, 9).

Unfortunately, the credibility of Nazi guarantees, written or oral, was immediately called into question by reliable reports of widespread discrimination against Jewish athletes whom Germany's private sports clubs had rushed to expel (even before the regime denied Jews the use of public facilities). At the convention of the American Olympic Committee (AOC), November 22, 1933, Gustavus Kirby moved that there be an American boycott unless German Jews were allowed in fact as well as in theory to "train, prepare for, and participate in the Olympic Games of 1936."[2] The AOC passed a slightly modified version of Kirby's strong resolution. Although *Reichssportführer* Hans von Tschammer und Osten responded with a statement that Jews were not barred from sports clubs by any *official* decree, Avery Brundage, the head of the AOC, wrote to Baillet-Latour, "The German authorities have displayed a singular lack of astuteness in all of their publicity. On this subject, every news dispatch that has come from Germany seems to indicate that the Hitlerites do not intend to live up to the pledges given to the IOC at Vienna."[3] Lord Aberdare, one of the United Kingdom's representatives on the IOC, shared Brundage's concern. When the IOC convened in Athens on May 15, 1934, he asked his German colleagues point blank if their government's pledges were trustworthy. The Germans assured him that they were.

The IOC was satisfied, but the AOC was not. Brundage was sent to investigate. His German friends, Diem and von Halt, told him that there was no discrimination. The Jews with whom Brundage spoke were monitored by Nazi officials. Brundage met *Reichssportführer* von Tschammer und Osten and "liked him very much."[4] The outcome of the investigation was preordained. Brundage returned home and urged the AOC to accept the invitation to Berlin, which it did by a unanimous vote.

The Amateur Athletic Union (AAU) of the United States was more skeptical about Nazi promises. In December, at its annual convention, it voted to postpone acceptance of the German invitation. By mid-1935, an intensive boycott campaign was in full swing, not only in the United States but also in Canada, Great Britain, and France. Everyone realized that the American campaign was the most important, and that the embattled Brundage was the key figure. He set forth his view of the matter in a sixteen-page pamphlet published by the AOC, "Fair Play for American Athletes" (1935). In it he argued, like a typical liberal, that politics and sports were wholly separate spheres. American athletes should not become involved in "the present Jew-Nazi altercation." In private, Brundage claimed that every call for a boycott was "obviously written by a Jew or someone who has succumbed to Jewish propaganda."[5] Writing to Baillet-Latour, he referred to the "Jewish proposal to boycott the Games" as if Jews were the only opponents of Nazism.[6]

Although American Jews *were* prominent in the boycott movement, it was led by Roman Catholics. The Catholic War Veterans of the United States and the Catholic journal, *Commonweal*, were very much in favor of a boycott. A number of politically prominent Catholics, including Governor James

Curley of Massachusetts and Governor Alfred Smith of New York, joined the call for a boycott. In response to Brundage's unfounded assertions of Nazi innocence, the Roman Catholic president of the AAU, Judge Jeremiah T. Mahoney, published a pamphlet, "Germany Has Violated the Olympic Code" (1935). Writing in the form of an open letter to Lewald, Mahoney cited specific cases such as the expulsion of Jews from sports clubs and public facilities, the ban on competition between Jews and other Germans, and the exclusion of world-class high-jumper Gretel Bergmann from Germany's Olympic team. Brundage ignored the evidence and continued to characterize the boycotters as Jews (aided and comforted by Communists), whose "altercation" with Hitler was unrelated to the Olympics.[7]

The boycott movement gained ground. The Gallup Poll reported in the summer of 1935 that 43 percent of all Americans wanted the United States to boycott the Berlin Olympics, but Brundage continued obstinately to see the opposition as nothing but a conspiracy of Jews and Communists. Having been assured by his German friends that their government accepted the Olympic rules, believing as he did that the games were the most important international institution of the century, a force for peace and reconciliation among peoples, he was unable to imagine honest opposition and attributed it to ethnic prejudice or political ideology.

In November 1935, Mahoney acquired an unexpected ally: Ernest Lee Jahncke, a staunch Republican who had served as President Herbert Hoover's assistant secretary of the navy. In his role as an American member of the IOC, Jahncke sent an open letter to Baillet-Latour in the *New York Times* on November 7, 1935: "The Nazis have consistently and persistently violated their pledges . . . it is plainly your duty to hold the Nazi sports authorities accountable for the violation of their pledges. . . . Let me beseech you to seize your opportunity to take your rightful place in the history of the Olympics alongside of de Coubertin instead of Hitler." Baillet-Latour, who had previously promised Brundage that he was ready to come to the United States to combat the "Jewish" boycott campaign, was furious. He asked Jahncke to resign from the IOC. Jahncke refused. At the next IOC session in Berlin, Jahncke was expelled (and Avery Brundage was elected "en remplacement de M. Lee Jahncke").[8]

That same November, George Messersmith, the American consul in Berlin, reported that Lewald had confessed to him, in tears, that he—Lewald—had lied when he assured Brundage and the AOC that there was no discrimination against Jewish athletes. The message was not made public (Eisen 1984).

The climax came in December 1935 at the annual meeting of the AAU. By a vote of 58 1/4 to 55 3/4, the AAU accepted the German organizing committee's invitation to the Winter Games at Garmisch-Partenkirchen and the Summer Games in Berlin. After the AAU's decision, the National Collegiate Athletic Association gave its approval, which had never really been in doubt.

Brundage's baseless allegations about a boycott movement limited to Jews and Communists might have been true for the *Canadian* opposition to the games. In Canada, "the campaign leadership never really broadened beyond the ranks of the Communist Party" (Kidd 1978, 40). While P. J. Mulqueen and other officials of the Canadian Olympic Committee indicated their satisfaction with the assurances that they had received from the IOC, Eva Dawes, one of the stars of the track-and-field team, clashed with officialdom. Already barred from AAU meets because she had competed in the Soviet Union, Dawes and five other Canadian athletes went to Barcelona in the summer of 1936 to participate in Communist-sponsored alternative games. In fact, this *Olimpiada* never took place, because it was interrupted by the outbreak of the Spanish Civil War (1936–1939).

European opponents of Nazi sports policy also mounted a boycott campaign. The British camaign was undercut by the vocal stand taken by one of Britain's most popular and influential athletes, Harold Abrahams, a nonobservant Jew who had won the 100-meter sprint at the 1924 Olympics. He argued successfully for participation and attended the Berlin games as a radio broadcaster (Murray 1992).

French opposition to the "Nazi Olympics" was much stronger. Jules Rimet, head of the *Fédération Internationale de Football Association* (FIFA), was among those pleading for strong action. He was joined by the French presidents of the international federations for swimming (FINA) and ice hockey (LIHG) and by Bernard Lévy, head of the prestigious *Racing-Club de France*. Late in 1935, a socialist deputy, Jean Longuet, asked the Chambre des Deputés to terminate the government's program for training Olympic athletes. The motion lost by 410–151. Early in 1936, however, Léon Blum led the French Left to victory in national elections. Blum's "Popular Front" government tried to satisfy both quarreling camps by appropriating 1.1 million francs for the Berlin Games and 600,000 francs for the *Olimpiada* in Barcelona. The compromise failed to calm the storm. The Communists' newspaper, *L'Humanité*, was unhappy that government funds were sending 189 male and eleven female athletes to Berlin. The right-wing newspaper, *Le Figaro*, expressed its disgust at the government's support for 1,300 Barcelona-bound athletes, officials, and conference delegates (Kidd 1980).

Although the boycott campaign was a failure, a number of individual athletes refused to join their country's teams. Nearly all of them were Jews.[9] Ironically, Jewish athletes did try out for the German team and would have joined it if they had been invited to compete. The German team for the Summer Games included no Jewish athletes. Although Gretel Bergmann's jump of 1.60 centimeters was, in fact, four centimeters higher than that of her closest rival, *Reichssportführer* von Tschammer und Osten informed her that her performance had been inadequate (Pfister 2001). Other Jews who might have won places on the team were intimidated or lacked the facilities to train and failed to achieve their potential. The "half-Jewish" fencer, Hélène Mayer, is sometimes cited as an exception. Mayer, who lived in the United States, had won an Olympic gold medal in 1928 and had been the American champion from 1933 to 1935. She was, however, an ironic choice. She did not consider herself a Jew. She was a statuesque blonde who looked "like an advertisement for German womanhood" (Eisen 1984, 70). When she stood on the victory stand to receive her silver medal, she raised her arm in the Nazi salute (Pfister 2001b).

With all of the advantages of hindsight, we confront a simple question. Were the National Olympic Committees of liberal-democratic states right to accept the invitation to the 1936 Olympics? Although the Nazi regime was already known in 1936 to be brutally repressive, that *in itself* was not enough to answer the question. When Moscow and Beijing were chosen to host the games, the USSR and the People's Republic of China had committed much greater violations of human rights than the Nazis had in their first three years of rule. The NOCs of liberal-democratic states should not have sent teams to Berlin because the Nazi regime violated the Olympic Charter. To assert *after the Games* that the charter had not been violated—which Avery Brundage did until the day of his death—was inexcusable.

A PROPAGANDA TRIUMPH?[10]

Hitler had told Diem and Lewald that he wanted to impress the world with the magnificence of the Games. The world was impressed. The facilities were monumental. The magnificent *Deutsches Stadion*, designed by Werner March and built from German stone at a cost of 77 million marks, accommodated over 100,000 spectators. At the open-air Olympic pool, 18,000 spectators followed the swimming and diving events. The sites were decorated with statues by Arno Breker and Josef Wackerle. Historians have ridiculed the gigantic nude figures as muscle-bound parodies of "Aryan" athleticism, but German and foreign visitors seem to have been awed by them (Adam 1992, 189–90, 250–53).

At the Olympic Village, every effort was made to secure the athletes' comfort. There were over 100 buildings to house them. Their national cuisines were served in thirty-eight separate dining halls. While in the village, runners were able to train on a 400-meter track, while swimmers and oarsmen utilized a specially constructed artificial lake.

The cultural program that accompanied the Games was truly extraordinary. Among Diem's inspired innovations was an enormous iron bell inscribed with the words *Ich rufe die Jugend der Welt* ("I summon the youth of the world"). It was also Diem's idea that a torch be lit at Olympia and carried by a relay of thousands of runners from there to the stadium in Berlin, where it was used to ignite the Olympic flame. Spiridon Louys, the Greek peasant who had won the first marathon in 1896, was invited to Berlin, where—in one of history's ironies—he presented Hitler with an olive branch.[11]

The most ambitious of Diem's many artistic contributions was *Olympische Jugend* ("Olympic Youth"), a series of dances choreographed by Mary Wigman to music composed by Carl Orff and Werner Egk. The performers of *Olympische Jugend* included a chorus of 1,000, sixty male dancers, and eighty female dancers. The fourth part of this paean to youthful idealism was prophetically entitled *Heldenkampf und Todesklage* ("Heroes' Struggle and Lament for the Dead"). Whether those who watched and listened to the performance were more impressed by the theme of patriotic sacrifice or by the universalistic theme of the fourth movement of Beethoven's Ninth Symphony, which ended the performance, is anyone's guess (Alkemeyer and Richartz 1993).

For these Games, the IOC wanted to use the music performed in Los Angeles, but Lewald had Richard Strauss set to music a poem by Robert Lubahn. The text was altered to make it more rather than less nationalistic.

Visiting dignitaries were invited to performances of the Berlin opera and to a concert held in the Pergamon Museum, which exhibited, then as now, a stunning collection of Hellenstic art and architecture from Pergamon and other ancient cities. Goebbels entertained 2,000 guests at a magnificent country estate recently confiscated from a Jewish family. Small wonder that thousands of visitors left Berlin with a sense of aesthetic fulfillment and a vague impression that National Socialism was not as dreadful as they had thought.

The swastika was much in evidence throughout the Games, but Hitler's role was minimized. Baillet-Latour told him that his duty as host was to utter a single sentence, which Baillet-Latour had typed up for him: "I declare the games of the Eleventh Olympiad of the modern era to be open." Intentionally or not, Hitler's response to Baillet-Latour's instructions was comic. The dictator who was accustomed to delivering four-hour harangues replied to Baillet-Latour, "Count, I'll take the trouble to learn it by heart" (Mayer 1960, 142).

The strongest evidence for the claim that the Games were not a propaganda triumph is the fact that Jesse Owens was unquestionably the star of the Games. Setting a world record of 10.3 seconds for 100 meters and an Olympic record of 20.7 seconds for 200 meters, he went on to jump an astonishing 8.06 meters and to help set still another world record in the 400-meter relay. In photographs published in the German press during and after the Games, Owens appears in a favorable light. *The Spectator* (London) on August 7, 1936, admitted, "The German spectators, like all others, have fallen under the spell of the American Negro Jesse Owens, who is already the hero of these Games." The popular picture-and-text book published by the cigarette firm, Reemtsma, called Owens *ein Wunderathlet* and contained no fewer than seven photographs of him, all of them positive.[12] Ironically, no photographs of Owens (or of any of the other black athletes) appeared in the Atlanta *Constitution*, the most liberal of Southern newspapers.

The unexpected display of apparently unbiased treatment was actually part of a concentrated effort at shaping a favorable image of the new regime. The ministry of propaganda ordered the press to avoid remarks offensive to black athletes. When the editors of the rabidly racist *Der Angriff* were unable to restrain themselves from a much-publicized sneer at American's "black auxiliaries," they were reprimanded by the ministry. There was, in this sense, a "temporary suspension of a core part of National Socialist ideology" (Teichler 1976, 285).

African-American athletes were not the only ones to undermine notions of "Aryan" superiority. Sohn Kee-chung of Korea, competing under his imposed Japanese name (Kitei Son), won the marathon, and the Japanese swimmers did almost as well as they had in 1932. The most annoying outcome for the Nazi hosts was probably the women's high jump. Having barred Bergmann from the German team, they watched Ibolya Czak, a Hungarian Jew, win that event with a leap of 1.6 meters—exactly the height that Bergmann had cleared shortly before the Games. Ironically, in light of the boycott controversy, the most serious allegations of anti-Semitism at the Games concerned the American team. Marty Glickman and Sam Stoller, the only Jews in the American track-and-field squad, had been selected for the 4-×-100-meter relay. At the last minute, they were replaced by Owens and another black sprinter, Ralph Metcalfe. The reason for the last-minute cut may have been anti-Semitism. It also may have been Dean Cromwell's preferential treatment of runners whom he had coached at the University of Southern California. Glickman, for one, remained convinced until his death that he and Stoller were cut because they were Jews. In a poem he cursed Brundage, Cromwell, and head track-and-field coach Lawson Robertson as "Those dirty bastards / Evil Nazis / American Nazis" (Glickman 1996, 1).[13]

The Nazi propaganda apparatus made much of the overwhelmingly favorable press coverage of the Games and exploited to the utmost the aged, infirm Coubertin's last public pronouncement. The baron, who had been assiduously wooed by the Nazis in the run-up to the Games, asserted in an interview published in *Le Journal* (August 27, 1936) that these "grandiose" Games, organized with "Hitlerian strength and discipline," had "brilliantly served the Olympic ideal" (Teichler 1982, 35–36).

To call the Nazi instrumentalization a misuse of sports, as Hajo Bernett and many others have done, is too easy (Bernett 1986, 1995–1996). In a curious way, the accusation—that the Nazis misused sports—repeats Avery Brundage's myopic liberal view that sports have nothing to do with politics. Institutionalized sports are always political, explicitly or implicitly, and every Olympic country instrumentalizes the Games in order to create a positive impression. The main difference—in 1936—was that the gap between the positive impression and the tyrannical reality was a chasm.

There seems little doubt that the Games *were* a propaganda coup for the Nazis. They were indeed magnificently organized. They were, in every sense of the word, spectacular. Although the American athletes dominated the track-and-field events, the German team led in the overall medal count, winning thirty-three gold, twenty-six silver, and thirty bronze medals. And, most importantly, the fact that the Nazis had *not* emphasized nationalism or racial doctrine (*Rassenkunde*) gave the world a benign and an utterly false impression of their regime.

Most historians, whatever their original impressions, have come around to this view. In two comprehensive and influential postwar accounts of the Games, published in 1971 and 1972, Richard Mandell and Arnd Krüger argued that the Games had not been especially successful as vehicles for Nazi propaganda. Mandell, however, backed away from that position when *The Nazi Olympics* was republished in 1987 (Mandell 1987). Krüger's most recent s tatement appears in the epilogue of a 2003 collection of essays (edited with William Murray). Although some of the contributors to the collection indicate that the Games were not as effective a tool as Hitler hoped, Krüger describes them as "a perfect vehicle for Nazi propaganda" (Krüger and Murray 2003, 238). Thomas Alkemeyer, in a long and nuanced analysis of Pierre de Coubertin's ideals as they were "staged" (*inszeniert*) and distorted in the form of the 1936 Olympics, concluded that the Games were relatively free of overt propaganda, and that Goebbels had an important insight: "The best propaganda . . . is that which is not perceived as propaganda."[14]

The strongest statement of the opposite case—that the 1936 Olympic Games were largely free of Nazi propaganda—has been made by Christiane Eisenberg at the end of her massive study *"English Sports" und deutsche Bürger*. Considering the 1936 Olympics in the context of German sports policy during the Weimar Republic as well as during the Nazi period, Eisenberg concluded that one might as well speak about the "sportification of the Nazis as about the Nazification of the athletes." Of Carl Diem's *Festspiel*, which Alkemeyer described as the epitome of Nazi ideology, she wrote, "The *Festspiel* was a success because—like the torch relay—it vividly, sensually presented Coubertin's interpretation of the Olympic Games as 'the springtime of humanity'" (Eisenberg 1999, 411, 426). The Games were propaganda, but they did more to further Coubertin's vision than Hitler's. Eisenberg is probably among the minority in her assessment of Nazi sports policy in general and of the 1936 Olympic Games in particular, but her interpretation should be taken seriously, not as an attempt to exculpate the Nazis but rather as an attempt to understand them and their complicated relationships to Olympic ideology.

ART OR PROPAGANDA?[15]

It is difficult if not impossible to discuss Leni Riefenstahl's *Olympia* (1938) simply on its merits as a documentary film. Quite apart from Riefenstahl's friendship with Hitler, which she acknowledges, her earlier documentary, *Triumph des Willens* (1934), casts a dark shadow over *Olympia*. Although her homage to Hitler in the first film inevitably influences our perception of the second, what follows is a venture in a *textimminent* criticism of *Olympia*. It must be emphasized, however, that the "text" discussed is the one released, in censored form, in 1958. Nine minutes of footage depicting Hitler and other Nazi leaders were cut from part 1 and one minute of footage was excised from part 2 (Trimborn 2002, 272).

The prologue to part 1 is an intensely romantic evocation of ancient Greek culture. Accompanied by Wagnerian music composed by Herbert Windt, the camera moves through Riefenstahl's trademark mists to a series of images of iconic art and architecture. Myron's statue of a discus thrower is transformed into the German athlete, Erwin Huber. He hurls the discus, and we move into a sequence of nearly nude male athletes and nearly nude female dancers (one of whom was Leni Riefenstahl). As Michael Mackenzie has recently noted, the rhythmic motion of the athletes and the dancers is a form of *Ausdruckstanz* ("expressive dance"), a manifestation of the romantic vision Riefenstahl had embodied in her earlier career as a dancer (Mackenzie 2003).

The prologue moves on to the ignition of the Olympic torch, one of Carl Diem's many innovations. The first runner—selected by Riefenstahl for his physical beauty—lights the torch and is on his way through rocky landscape and along the shores of the Aegean.[16] A map of Europe and a series of inserted photographs plot the transit of the torch from Olympia to Berlin, a powerful statement of Germany's putative role as the heir of ancient Greece.

Hitler appears at the opening ceremony, but his presence is not emphasized. The swastika appears, but it is less prominent than the Olympic rings.

Part 1 is devoted to track-and-field sports. Many athletes are identified by name and nationality. Others appear anonymously. Quantified results are sometimes mentioned, but they are clearly less important than the movements of the athletes, who seem at moments to be involved in a modern dance rather than in a sports contest. The women's javelin competition, for example, is a kind of ballet in the course of which the javelin sails from the athlete's hand to its destination in the stadium's turf. German winners are mentioned, but the two men who receive the most attention are Jesse Owens, on whose body the camera lingers lovingly, and Sohn Kee-chung, the Korean winner of the marathon, whose emotionless face contrasts starkly with the contorted visage of the British silver medalist.[17] It is an overstatement to assert, as Mackenzie does, that the "documentary purpose of the film is consistently sacrificed to the principle of eros" (Mackenzie 2003, 325), but Riefenstahl's treatment of Owens can certainly be read as a declaration of love.

There are many images of the spectators, including some remarkably enthusiastic Japanese. Hitler appears several times not as the absolute ruler of the Nazi state but rather as an ordinary spectator. He smiles when German athletes win, and he slaps his knee in a gesture of all-too-human disappointment when a dropped baton deprives the women's relay team of a gold medal. *Triumph des Willens* magnifies the dictator's deadly charisma. *Olympia*—the uncensored as well as the censored version—tends to dispel it.

Riefenstahl's enormously influential cinematographic innovations are more evident in part 2 than in part 1. The prologue takes us through the Olympic Village. Through the mists of dawn—Riefenstahl's trademark once again—ghostly runners appear. They jog through woods and along a lake. When they dive into the lake and then relax—entirely nude—in a sauna, we realize that they are probably Scandinavians. Other athletes—of all races—are shown training or relaxing. There is one comic moment that suggests the Nazi denigration of "inferior" races. After an Asian athlete hops about to strengthen his legs, an incongruous kangaroo appears and disappears into the woods.

Riefenstahl attempts, in part 2, an impossible task—to do justice to all of the events other than track and field. Except for the section on the military pentathlon, there is even less individualization than in part 1. Fencers appear as shadows on the floor, as if they were Javanese puppets. Yachts appear, one after another, sails billowing, prows cutting the waves, in a generic race that might as well have taken place in Homeric times or in the era of the Vikings. In the film's most famous sequence, anonymous male divers follow one another from the platform into the pool (where they are filmed by an underwater camera). As daylight fades, the divers' bodies, filmed from the ground, become silhouettes against the sky. The sequence accelerates until two or three divers at a time seem to inscribe a single arc from platform to pool.

If there is any bias toward German athletes, it comes in the coverage of the equestrian segment of the military pentathlon. The equestrians' names and nationalities are given. German uniforms clearly display the swastika. As they attempt to clear and hurdle and splash through a shallow pool just below it, French and Italian cavalry officers come a cropper. They tumble into the water, struggle wetly to remount, and chase after their runaway horses. In contrast to these comic figures, the German riders clear the hurdle and gallop on to victory—one of them in brave disregard of a broken collarbone.

Art or propaganda? The question implies that art and propaganda are mutually exclusive categories, but they are not. If propaganda is defined as a "scheme or concentrated movement for the propagation of a particular doctrine or practice," which is how the *OED* (Oxford English Dictionary) defines it, then works of art can be—and often are—propaganda. The question should be restated. Is *Olympia* bad art? Are the values celebrated in the film values that we want to celebrate?

The jury at the Venice *Biannale* awarded *Olympia* its first prize. At the film's Parisian premiere, the French press was enthusiastic. Gerard de Houville, reviewing *Olympia* for the *Revue de Deux Mondes*, raved about the film's artistry and marveled at the depictions of Jesse Owens, whom he saw as "*beau comme une statue de bronze animée*" (de Houville 1938, 935). Jürgen Trimborn's highly critical biography of Riefenstahl acknowledges that the international reception of the original, uncensored version of the film was overwhelmingly positive. "Quite unlike the postwar reception of the film, foreign newspapers spoke of the film's international character and characterized it as 'a masterpiece,' as 'a first-rank work of art,' as 'the most wonderful sportfilm ever made,' and as 'the most beautiful declaration of love that film has ever made to sports'" (Trimborn 2002, 267).[18] Robert Sklar and most other film historians agree: *Olympia* succeeds as a work of art.

And its aesthetic success is what damns the film, irrevocably, in the eyes of its most astute critics. Hilmar Hoffmann's *Mythos Olympia* claims that the film "instrumentalizes sports for the political goals of the Third Reich" (Hoffmann 1993, 136). This occurs, according to Hoffmann, because unattractive bodies are eliminated from the film in order for Riefenstahl to focus, relentlessly, on attractive—mainly "Aryan"—bodies. Graham McFee and Alan Tomlinson are less polemical and rather more persuasive when they assert that "the adulation of the perfect human body" is among the aspects of the film that mobilize "a bodily aesthetic in the service of the power interests of the political body" (McFee and Tomlinson 1999, 103). The most extreme (and influential) version of this argument appeared in Susan Sontag's famous essay, "Fascinating Fascism," in which she damns Riefenstahl's films (and photography) as an all-too-successful celebration of Fascism. To idealize Olympic athletes and to celebrate—as Riefenstahl clearly does—the strength and beauty of their bodies is implicitly to devalue all of those other bodies—yours and mine—that fall short of the ideal. And devaluation leads to discrimination, which leads, ultimately, to annihilation. Begin with the slender muscularity of the youth who lights the torch at Olympia, and you end with the emaciated corpses discovered at Auschwitz.

Is this a fair critique? I think not. To praise physical superiority is, by definition, to imply the existence of physical inferiority. The same is true, however, of every form of human excellence. To praise intellectual superiority—like Susan Sontag's—is to acknowledge that most people are—shall I put it bluntly?—not as bright as she is. Of course, one can argue that intellectual excellence is more praiseworthy than physical excellence—philosophers have done that since Plato's time—but *Olympia* should not be labeled "fascist" simply because it celebrates Jesse Owens and Sohn Kee-chung rather than Albert

Einstein and Max Planck. To decry physical excellence because the Nazis celebrated it is foolish. All Nazis admire athletic achievement, ergo, all who admire
athletic achievement are Nazis? The logical error ought to be obvious.

To her dying day, Riefenstahl denied that *Triumph des Willens* contributed
to the Nazi revolution and to all of the horrors done in the name of that revolution. For her absolute denial of complicity, she deserves condemnation.
Throughout her life, Riefenstahl insisted that *Olympia* was nonpolitical. She
was wrong about that, but the politics of the film—even in the original, uncensored version—are much closer to Coubertin's than to Hitler's. Of course, Coubertin's politics can be criticized, but that is another topic.

Notes

1. In addition to the Avery Brundage Collection at the University of Illinois (hereafter ABC), the main sources for this section are Mandell (1971), Krüger (1972),
Bohlen (1979), Guttmann (1984, 62–81), and Hart-Davis (1986).

2. ABC, Box 28.

3. Avery Brundage to Henri Baillet-Latour, December 28, 1933 (ABC, Box 42).

4. Avery Brundage to Karl Ritter von Halt, October 22, 1934 (ABC, Box 57).

5. Avery Brundage to B. Hallbach, March 17, 1936 (ABC, Box 153); see also
Krüger (1978).

6. Avery Brundage to Henri Baillet-Latour, September 24, 1935 (ABC, Box
42). Throughout the boycott controversy, Brundage had the support of Dietrich
Wortmann, president of New York's German-American Athletic Club. See Gray and
Barney (1990).

7. American Communists did call for a boycott, but they were a politically insignificant group. Despite Hitler's stridently proclaimed ideology of "Aryan" racial su-
premacy, African Americans did not join Jews and Catholics in calling for a boycott of
the Games. The *Amsterdam News* supported a boycott, but the *Pittsburgh Courier-Jour-
nal* and most of the other black newspapers were outspoken about their desire not to
deny the athletes the chance of a lifetime. African-American athletes were clearly anxious to go. Sprinter Ralph Metcalfe told the *Chicago Defender* that he and other black
athletes had been treated well during a 1933 tour of Germany; he was ready to return.
Regrettably, there was another side to the controversy. Historian David K. Wiggins, the
closest student of Afro-American responses to the boycott, has indicated that some
blacks were anti-Semitic. "They frequently stereotyped Jews and blamed them for
everything from economic exploitation to murder"; see Wiggins (1983, 282).

8. "Procès-Verbale de la 35ième Session du Comité International Olympique"
(IOC Archives).

9. After a stellar performance at the 1936 Harvard-Yale track-and-field meet,
Milton Green and Norman Cahners qualified for the Olympic trials at Randall's

Island in New York. Shortly after the meet, the two were summoned to meet with Rabbi Harry Levy and members of the executive board of Brooklin's Temple Israel. They were informed of the Nazi persecution of German Jews, and they were asked to boycott the trials, which they did. Herman Neugass, who had tied the world record for the 100-yard dash, refused the chance to compete in Berlin, despite a letter from Lawson Richardson, head coach of the track-and-field team. Among the others who boycotted as a matter of conscience were discus thrower Lillian Copeland, who had won the event at the 1932 Olympics, featherweight boxer Louis Gevinson, and four members of the Long Island basketball team: Jules Bender, Benjamin Kramer, Leo Merson, and William Schwartz. In Canada, the track-and-field star Eva Dawes, the water polo team, and a pair of boxers—Sammy Luftspring and Norman Yack— refused the opportunity to compete in Berlin. Australian boxer Harry Cohen and French fencer Albert Wolff did the same. Three Austrian swimmers—Judith Deutsch, Ruth Langer, and Lucy Goldner—decided not to compete (and were suspended for two years by their national swimming federation). In Denmark's tiny Jewish population, two former Olympic medalists—wrestler Abraham Kurland and fencer Ivan Osiier—forfeited the chance to repeat their triumphs. See Guttmann, Kestner, and Eisen (2000).

10. In addition to Mandell's *The Nazi Olympics*, the main sources for this section are Hoffmann (1993) and Alkemeyer (1996).

11. In retrospect, the symbolism becomes a tragic irony. Other victors from 1896, such as the German gymnast, Alfred Flatow, and his cousin, Gustav, were murdered in the course of Hitler's monstrous "final solution of the Jewish problem."

12. *Die Olympischen Spiele 1936*, vol 2, 17, 23, 26-27, 46-47. Owens figured in a story whose fog of error historians cannot dispel. Hitler, we are told, refused to shake hands with Owens. In fact, when the Games began, Hitler personally congratulated a number of athletes, including the first German victors, Hans Woelcke (shot put), Gerhard Stock (javelin), and Tilly Fleischer (javelin), all of whom he invited to his private box. Two Afro-Americans, Cornelius Johnson and David Albritten, were first and second in the high jump, but Hitler left the stadium before the event concluded. The following day, Baillet-Latour, accompanied by the German IOC member, von Halt, cautioned Hitler and told him to invite *all* of the victors to his box or none of them. Hitler decided to save his felicitations for a post-Games celebration limited to the German athletes. If anyone was insulted, it was Johnson, not Owens. The latter told the *New York Times* (August 25), "There was absolutely no discrimination at all," but the story of the snub was (and is) too good to sacrifice at the altar of historical truth.

13. A number of American Jews did compete in other sports; see Guttmann, Kestner, and Eisen (2000, 57–59).

14. Goebbels, quoted in Alkemeyer (1996, 13).

15. For this section, my main sources—other than the film itself—are Infield (1976), Graham (1986), and Riefenstahl (1990–1992).

16. In fact, Riefenstahl had to film this scene in Delphi, because Olympia was a chaos of officials and journalists.

17. In most histories of the Olympic Games, including my own, Sohn Kee-chung's name is given in its Japanese form, Kitei Son, which Sohn hated.

18. Trimborn's quotations, in order, are from *Marianne* (Paris), *Helsingin Sanomat* (Helsinki), *The Observer* (London), and *L'Intransigeant* (Paris).

REFERENCES

Adam, Peter. 1992. *Art of the Third Reich*. New York: Harry N. Abrams.

Alkemeyer, Thomas, and Alfred Richartz. 1993. The Olympic Games: From ceremony to show. *Olympika* 2: 79–89.

Alkemeyer, Thomas. 1996. *Körper, Kult, und Politik*. Frankfurt: Campus.

Avery Brundage Collection.University of Illinois. Urbana, Illinois.

Bernett, Hajo. 1986. Symbolik und Zeremonial der XI: Olympischen Spiele in Berlin 1936. *Sportwissenschaft* 16 (4): 357–97.

———. 1995–1996. Die Olympischen Spiele 1936 in der Retrospektive. *Stadion* 21–22: 228–50.

Bohlen, Friedrich. 1979. *Die XI: Olympischen Spiele Berlin 1936*. Cologne: Pahl-Rugenstein.

Christensen, Karen, Allen Guttmann, and Gertrud Pfister, eds. 2001. *International encyclopedia of women and sport*. New York: Macmillan.

Die Olympischen Spiele 1936. 1936. 2 vols. Altona–Bahrenfeld: Reemtsma.

Diem, Carl. 1976. *Ein Leben für den Sport*. Rattingen: A. Henn.

Eisen, George. 1984. The voices of sanity: American diplomatic reports from the 1936 Berlin Olympiad. *Journal of Sport History* 11 (3): 56–78.

Eisenberg, Christiane. 1999. *"English sports" und deutsche Bürger*. Paderborn: Ferdinand Schöningh.

Glickman, Marty. 1996. *The fastest kid on the block*. Syracuse, NY: Syracuse University Press.

Graham, Cooper C. 1986. *Leni Riefenstahl and Olympia*. Metuchen: Scarecrow Press.

Gray, Wendy, and Robert Knight Barney. 1990. Devotion to whom? German-American loyalty on the issue of participation in the 1936 Olympic Games. *Journal of Sport History* 17 (2): 214–31.

Guttmann, Allen. 1984. *The Games must go on: Avery Brundage and the Olympic Movement*. New York: Columbia University Press.

Guttmann, Allen, Heather Kestner, and George Eisen. 2000. Jewish athletes and the "Nazi Olympics." In *The Olympics at the millennium: Power, politics and the Games*, ed. Kay Schaffer and Sidonie Smith. New Brunswick: Rutgers University Press.

Hart-Davis, Duff. 1986. *Hitler's Games: The 1936 Olympics*. New York: Harper & Row.

Hoffmann, Hilmar. 1993. *Mythos Olympia*. Berlin: Aufbau Verlag.

de Houville, Gerard. 1938. Les Dieux du stade. *Revue de Deux Mondes* 46: 935.

Infield, Glenn. 1976. *Leni Riefenstahl*. New York: Crowell.

International Olympic Committee (IOC). 1933. *Bulletin du C.I.O.* (September 1933).

———. Procès-verbale de la 35ième session du Comité International Olympique (IOC archives).

Kidd, Bruce. 1978. Canadian opposition to the 1936 Olympics in Germany. *Canadian Journal of History of Sport and Physical Education* 9 (2): 20–40.

———. 1980. The Popular Front and the 1936 Olympics. *Canadian Journal of History of Sport and Physical Education* 11 (1): 1–18.

Krüger, Arnd. 1972. *Die Olympischen Spiele 1936 und die Weltmeinung*. Berlin: Bartels und Wernitz.

———. 1975. *Theodor Lewald*. Berlin: Bartels und Werntiz.

———. 1978. Fair play for American athletes: A study in anti-Semitism. *Canadian Journal of History of Sport and Physical Education* 9 (1): 42–57.

Krüger, Arnd, and William Murray, eds. 2003. *The Nazi Olympics*. Urbana: University of Illinois Press.

Mackenzie, Michael. 2003. From Athens to Berlin: The 1936 Olympics and Leni Riefenstahl's *Olympia*. *Critical Inquiry* 29: 302–36.

Malitz, Bruno. 1982. Die Kritik der Nationalsozialisten am "unpolitischen" Sport. In *Der Sport im Kreuzfeuer der Kritik*, ed. Hajo Bernett. Schondorf: Karl Hofmann.

Mandell, Richard. 1987. *The Nazi Olympics*. 2nd ed. Urbana: University of Illinois Press.

Mandell, Richard D. 1971. *The Nazi Olympics*. New York: Macmillan.

Mangan, J. A., ed. 1999. *Shaping the superman*. London: Frank Cass.

Mayer, Otto. 1960. *À travers les anneaux olympiques*. Geneva: P. Cailler.

McFee, Graham, and Alan Tomlinson. 1999. Riefenstahl's *Olympia*: Ideology and aesthetics in the shaping of the Aryan athletic body. In *Shaping the superman*, ed. J. A. Mangan. London: Frank Cass.

Murray, Bill. 1992. Berlin in 1936. *International Journal of the History of Sport* 9 (1): 29–49.

Pfister, Gertrud. 2001a. Bergmann, Gretel. In *International encyclopedia of women and sport*, ed. Karen Christensen, Allen Guttmann, and Gertrud Pfister. New York: Macmillan.

———. 2001b. Mayer, Helene. In *International encyclopedia of women and sport*, ed. Karen Christensen, Allen Guttmann, and Gertrud Pfister. New York: Macmillan.

Riefenstahl, Leni. 1990–1992. *Memoiren*. 2 vols. Frankfurt: Ullstein.

Schaffer, Kay, and Sidonie Smith, eds. 2000. *The Olympics at the millennium: Power, politics and the Games*. New Brunswick, NJ: Rutgers University Press.

The Spectator. August 7, 1936, p. 230.

Teichler, Hans-Joachim. 1976. Berlin 1936—Ein Sieg der NS-propaganda? *Stadion* 2 (2): 285.

———. 1982. Coubertin und das Dritte Reich. *Sportwissenschaft* 12 (1): 35–36.

Trimborn, Jürgen. 2002. *Leni Riefenstahl*. Berlin: Aufbau Verlag.

Wiggins, David K. 1983. The 1936 Olympic Games in Berlin. *Research Quarterly* 54 (3): 278–92.

Chapter 5

England 1966

Traditional and Modern?

Tony Mason

Perhaps most great sporting events have something in them of both the past and the future. The thirty-two matches of the Eighth World Cup, played in England between July 11 and July 30, 1966, certainly owed much to tradition. The host nation had invented modern football in the nineteenth century but had never before put on its world championship. It had not "put in a bid" to FIFA to stage the event but had merely "put forward a case," and as FIFA policy was to hold World Cups alternately in the European and South American heartlands of football and the Jules Rimet trophy had been played for in Chile in 1962, the decision to choose England was attractively uncomplicated. Neither the Football Association (FA), nor FIFA had much money in the 1960s to provide a modern setting for the tournament. Nor would the organizers have been impressed had they been told that they were staging a "mega-event". What the FA wanted the World Cup to be was a festival of football, the best exposition of the game that it was possible to see.[1]

Most people who saw anything of the World Cup saw it on television. It was the breadth and the sophistication of the coverage that distinguished the 1966 World Cup from previous ones[2] and pointed to its modern future as a live television event. FIFA had not been slow in seeing the value of television and the new money it could provide from selling the rights to show live World Cup matches. It also saw that such exposure would be good publicity for a tournament that was not yet so popular worldwide. The first live television transmission of a match in the World Cup Finals had been the opening game of the 1954 finals in Switzerland from Lausanne when France lost to Yugoslavia. The BBC showed four other matches and three second halves, all live and thirteen hours altogether. In 1958, the European Broadcasting Union (EBU) paid 5,000 American dollars for the rights to broadcast the Sixth World Cup from Sweden. The pictures were not particularly good, and many households in Europe still had no TV sets, but about one-third of households in Britain did, and the BBC televised over twenty hours, most of it live.[3] For the next two World Cups, the FIFA and the EBU signed a combined contract. In 1962 it was not possible to transmit live from Chile to Europe, so FIFA thought that the EBU would be likely to pay more if the tournaments in Chile and England were linked. Together they had worked out that the rights to 1966 in England were worth $800,000, but only $75,000 in Chile. Even without live transmission, the BBC televised eighteen hours of recorded highlights, mostly in prime time. The televising of the 1966 World Cup proved very successful. Thirty-six countries relayed the final match live, and seventy-five broadcast at least one live match. It was estimated that 400 million people watched the finals worldwide, the largest audience for a television broadcast in the world up to that time.

It was British television and especially coverage by the BBC that made the 1966 World Cup the sizeable shared national experience that it became. In the 1960s the close relationship between football and television, commonplace today, had hardly begun. The weekly program of highlights in England, *Match of the Day*, only began in 1964. The rise of the celebrity player was hinted at by the coverage given to George Best, and the behavior of some crowds, such as the Liverpool Kop and Manchester United's Stretford End, was becoming familiar to viewers. But only a few important games were shown live: the FA Cup Final, the European Cup Final, and an occasional England international.

There were two televised innovations, one available only to those who watched in the United Kingdom, the other seen worldwide. The former was the bringing together of a group of football experts to form a panel to comment on and interpret what the viewers had seen. Former England captains Johnny Haynes and Billy Wright, previous England manager Walter Winterbottom, and a clutch of club managers, including Tommy Docherty, Ron Greenwood, Jimmy Hill, Joe Mercer, and Don Revie, was used before and immediately after the matches in the highlight shows.[4] Usually one such guru also supported the match commentators. The BBC journal, *The Listener*, thought this coverage a milestone in the presentation of sport comparable to the time and sophistication spent on general election night. The BBC actually showed fifty hours of World Cup broadcasting, whereas the commercial channel, ITV (independent television), showed only twenty-three hours.[5] The World Cup had never had such coverage.

The second innovation was even more spectacular. "In every soccer competition there is always something which happens so quickly that not even the sharpest and most experienced observers can be absolutely sure of what exactly took place."[6] How wonderful to be able to interfere with time and show the incident again (and again!) not only at the real speed but more slowly so that, in theory at least, the viewer could see what exactly had happened. The BBC engineers had invented a videotape recording machine that could feed the portion of tape to be reshown into a magnetic disc that could make four images of each picture, thus providing the slow-motion effect. Many viewers were astonished by this piece of technological wizardry. Today it is commonplace and is employed even inside many stadiums: in 1966 it was an exciting novelty.

The British TV audience for the World Cup was very large. Well over half of the population of the United Kingdom over age five watched the final, 30,500,000 divided very unequally with 26,500,000 on the public service BBC and only 4,000,000 on the commercial ITV. This was 5 million more than for the funeral of Sir Winston Churchill in November 1965 and the same distance ahead of the most popular BBC comedy program, *Steptoe and Son*. Normally in July the average British household watched 11 hours and 20 minutes of television per week. During the World Cup, viewing figures increased to 13 hours and 35 minutes.[7]

Interestingly there was already a sign that there would be a further price to pay for such startling statistics. The television consortium insisted on some changes to the schedule of matches. The opening game was bought forward by a day. The kick-off of the England-Mexico game was changed from an afternoon to an evening, and that of the relatively unattractive Mexico-Uruguay encounter was brought forward from 7:30 P.M. to 4:30 P.M. so that an extra evening match could be shown. But all of the quarter finals were played at the same time.[8]

If television coverage was the most obvious sign of modernity in the preparations for and coverage of the Eighth World Cup, then the other new influence was the role played by the British government. Of course this was not entirely without precedent. The Foreign Office had kept an eye on the potential for political fallout from the inter-war expansion of international sport.[9] The 1948 Olympic Games could not have been held in a London pockmarked with bomb damage and riddled with shortages without some support from the state.[10] But the idea that a professional sport such as football might be helped by money from the taxpayer was definitely new.

In fact, there was one requirement that was in need of funding before the tournament could start. Although English football could boast of many large stadiums, at least eighteen with a capacity of 50,000 or more, most of them were old and badly in need of refurbishment. Even Wembley, host to the 1948 Olympic Games, venue of the FA Cup Final, and for most England home internationals, was over forty years old. But in 1963 it underwent something of a facelift. Half a million pounds was spent re-roofing the two grandstands and covering both the ends for the first time. It could accommodate almost 100,000 spectators, of whom 44,000 were seated. Most other English grounds offered standing accommodation versus seating in the ratio of 4:1. The members of the Organizing Committee were anxious that most visitors from overseas would be used to seats. Other necessary work on the grounds involved expanding the facilities for press, radio, and television. All of this required money. The FA had asked a Conservative government in 1963 if it would help, but all it offered was a police escort for each of the competing teams. This was not entirely surprising, because although it had recently appointed Lord Hailsham as minister responsible for "coordination in the development of sporting and recreational facilities," he was also responsible for the problems of the northeast and the Minister of Science, seriously higher priorities.[11] But a modernizing Labor government was elected in October 1964, with its leader, Harold Wilson, a self-professed supporter of the Huddersfield Town Football Club, a three-time English champion during his childhood. Moreover, he appointed a former Football League referee, Mr. Denis Howell, Under Secretary of State in the Department of Education and Science, with a special responsibility for sport. Howell had just been told of his appointment, when, according to him, he asked the prime minister for government help to stage the coming world championship. "How much do you want?" asked Wilson. "Half a million pounds," replied Howell (about £8 million in today's money). "Done," said Wilson.[12] It is doubtful if the decision was quite so spectacularly spontaneous. In fact, an FA report claimed that a month after this exchange, in November 1964, Howell was telling them that government help was unlikely. But by February 1965, the government had changed its mind. It would provide money to improve the stadiums in which World Cup matches were to be played.[13]

The treasury grumbled and emphasized that the money would be paid directly to the FA and not to the clubs, because otherwise it might "prompt an unwelcome flood of applications from other clubs or sporting bodies for similar assistance."[14] Its spokesman also asked why the FA did not seek financial support from the football public as a whole and suggested a levy on the price of admission to league games in 1965–1966. Such action would help reduce criticism in parliament and in the country, when it became known that professional football was having to be assisted from public funds. The reluctance of the state to support professional sport could hardly be more clearly expressed.

Yet the government did provide crucial funding and also offered essential diplomatic assistance when a positively tricky problem of international relations suddenly appeared. Most African and Asian football associations boycotted the 1966 World Cup in protest at the award of only one place to the three confederations, which covered the two continents and Oceania. But two football authorities refused the boycott, Australia and the Democratic People's Republic of Korea (North Korea). They played off in Phnom Penh, capital of Cambodia, for the right to fill the sixteenth and final place in the 1966 World Cup Finals, and the Koreans won both games, 6–1 and 3–1, in November 1965.

The cold war was close to its peak in the mid-1960s. The British government, as part of the North Atlantic Treaty Organization (NATO), did not recognize the Democratic People's Republic of Korea. Clearly international sporting occasions were publicly symbolic events. But the non-recognition of North Korea could not be allowed to disrupt the World Cup at so late a stage. However, it was also clear that something had to be done about the flags and anthems. Part of the government grant to those clubs hosting matches had included payments for flag poles that would display the flags of all sixteen competing nations during every match. The Foreign Office accepted that the flags should stay on the flagpoles but did insist that one of the commemorative stamps that depicted all of them had to be withdrawn.

The problem of the anthems was also disposed of with some diplomatic aplomb. It was agreed that national anthems would be played only at the opening match and before the final. It was perhaps made easier by the fact that both Denis Howell and FIFA President Sir Stanley Rous disliked the excessive display of national fervor that they thought sometimes accompanied them.[15] The Foreign Office also insisted that the Korean team play under the name of North Korea, emphasizing the geographical division of what was considered in the West a single country. Most of this had been agreed upon by February 1966 and interestingly was kept out of the newspapers and prevented from becoming one of those media-inspired crises. Some people even thought that it showed the ability of government and sport to work together, even though they rarely had the same agendas. There was to be no public charge that the government was politicizing sport. As it turned out, the North Koreans were one of the stars of the show. Their three group matches at unfashionable Middlesbrough began predictably with a three-goal defeat by the Soviet Union, but after a draw with Chile the North Koreans delighted a crowd of almost 19,000 by knocking out Italy. Enough enthusiasm was generated among the normally taciturn Tees-siders to encourage a thousand of them to travel to Liverpool four days later to support the surprise packet from Asia in what turned out to be one of the most exciting matches of the tournament in their quarter final against Portugal.[16] Over 52,000 saw that match, and many more would see the highlights later in the evening on television.

If the growth and sophistication of the television coverage and the supporting role of the government both pointed to the future, then it has to be emphasized that the 1966 World Cup in England looked to the past in many respects, not the least in the organizers' uncomfortable relationship with commercial interests. Of course, it was a commercial sporting event from which the promoters hoped to make rather than lose money, but the business world was kept at a discreet distance.

There were anxieties over advertising and merchandising, for example, neither of which the FA's Organizing Committee was particularly comfortable. There was certainly no money to spend on an advertising campaign, but British Rail, several airlines, and leading football clubs did allow World Cup posters to be displayed

without charge, for up to a year in some cases. Of course, newspapers also provided
a lot of free publicity. But there was a clear need for a symbol that could be used for
both publicity and commercial activities. A firm had been appointed by the Organizing Committee to sell licenses to use the official World Cup insignia, and one of
its employees came up with the idea of using a small, square-shouldered lion wearing a union jack football shirt as the symbol of the whole occasion. World Cup
Willie was launched initially in 1965, a year before the tournament began, and it
became quickly, and some might think, surprisingly, popular, becoming a regular
feature in newspaper coverage of the England team and other World Cup news.[17]
There would soon be a World Cup Willie song and a World Cup march.[18]

Almost 100,000 licensees eventually applied to use the official insignia or
World Cup Willie or both for some form of merchandizing. A long list of sou-
venirs from clothes and jigsaw puzzles, playing cards and pottery, braces and
belts, scarves and handkerchiefs, T-shirts, diaries, calendars and confectionery,
footballs, crisps, bedspreads, towels, key rings, and much more was sold, although the financial return to the Organizing Committee was considered small

'World Cup Willie, the England "mascot"'
Source: Private collection.

in the context of the whole World Cup operation, with royalties never more than 5 percent of the net selling price.[19] The aim seems to have been not so much to maximize profits but to secure more publicity. As long as money was not lost, then the point of the exercise was achieved.[20] As for sponsorship, there was not very much, although the British Motor Corporation did loan 200 cars to the World Cup Organization. Each traveled about 4,000 miles in the nineteen days of the tournament.

When it came to the opening ceremony, it eschewed the spectacular with schoolboys standing in for the players of the sixteen competing nations. Volunteers remained a crucial part of the organization. Almost 900 volunteered for the 250 steward jobs required for Wembley, coming from county football associations in many parts of the country. A team of local casuals cleaned up Wembley after the games had finished there.

Nor did the event have a major impact on tourism. Local liaison committees were established in each of the towns where World Cup matches were played. Their main purpose was to welcome overseas visitors, to offer information and entertainment, and generally to help solve any small problems that might arise. Four matches were played in the north-eastern city of Sunderland. Chile, Italy, and the Soviet Union each appeared there twice, but they were accompanied by far fewer than the 10,000 supporters who had been forecast. Only 400 Italians stayed in the town, although almost 5,000 came on the two match days. The Russians, Chileans, and North Koreans numbered fewer than 300 between them. After the first week of the tournament, it looked as though the Sunderland quarter-final would be between Italy and Brazil, but both were surprisingly knocked out at the first stage, which meant it was actually between the USSR and Hungary, neither of whom had many traveling followers.

There was a whiff of austerity about some of Sunderland's facilities. Two huts, normally used as temporary polling stations during local and general elections, were used as information centers. Nineteen factories offered tours for visitors, and 350 were interested or desperate enough to accept. An Overseas Visitors Club failed to attract many members, with the Russians particularly reluctant to enroll because it involved giving their names. When the Town Council arranged a reception for the visiting teams on July 14 it was disappointed that the respective team managers refused to allow their players to attend. There was, though, at least one resounding success. The Arts Council, Town Council, and Sunderland Football Club provided financial guarantees so that the theatre committee could engage the Georgian State Dance Company for two weeks, which turned out to be the most popular entertainment ever booked at Sunderland's Empire Theatre. Twenty-two thousand saw the show, stimulating some local people to believe that the town could become an arts center for the region.

As befitted a country that had won two successive World Cups, Brazil brought the largest number of supporters to the 1966 World Cup, 5,000. Unfortunately most of them had bought packages for the whole two and a half weeks, expecting the champions to reach the finals. Most wanted to return home after July 20, which meant buying expensive, one-way air tickets.[21]

There was a large press and television corps, the largest up to that time at a major sporting event, something over 2,000, according to the FA's *World Cup Report* (p. 51), but this represented only sixty-two countries, and both their facilities and access to the players and managers were not only controlled but strictly limited. Each World Cup venue had a press center, but the one in Middlesbrough, for example, was in the Town Hall Crypt.[22] More pertinent is the way in which the post-match interviews were organized. They were carried out "by television commentators, and a journalist representing each of the competing countries and one on behalf of the British press. These were relayed by a closed circuit link to the press working room within the stadium, so that within minutes of the finish of a match, every newspaperman who wished to do so could see and hear the interviews. . . . This eliminated the need for large numbers of journalists to make their way to the dressing rooms."[23]

In spite of the emergence of celebrity in the form of Manchester United and Northern Ireland star George Best and the television exposure on *Match of the Day*, there was less media hyperbole surrounding football in 1966, even World Cup football, although it is probably from this period that the more serious English newspapers began to give more attention and space to football as opposed to rugby union. It was during the build up to 1966, for example, that the *Sunday Times* launched Michael Parkinson's distinctive football column.

Then there were the post-match crowds celebrating the home team's victory, which some people likened to VE day. It is not entirely clear how large these really were, nor how unconfined their behavior was. It was a summer Saturday night in the West End of London, after all, and there were doubtless more people up there than usual, some of whom might be pressing the button of their car horns and/or chanting "Eng-ger-land"! It is worth remembering that pubs did not open in the afternoons in 1966. One man with an invitation to the official banquet at the New Royal Garden Hotel in Kensington, a banquet for all four semi-finalists, never got there, because he was "caught up in the massed crowds a half mile away," but he spent the time instead enjoying being part of a "deliriously happy" crowd.[24] Denis Howell also remembers "thousands of people gathering outside the hotel and the police urging the team to appear on the balcony."[25]

This was the moment when Howell, along with Prime Minister Harold Wilson, appeared on the balcony with the players to take their small share of the glory.[26] Wilson had only returned from the United States shortly before the kick-off of the World Cup Final, where he had been negotiating a large loan from the International Monetary Fund. It is clear that the prime minister was determined to be there. But as we have seen earlier, he was a sort of football fan, if not a particularly obsessive one. And England had not appeared in the World Cup Finals very often. Was there much political capital to be made out of England's World Cup win? It is hard not to be carried away by the excitement sometimes. Richard Crossman was a football hater in the Wilson Cabinet, but even he mused in his diaries whether "the World Cup could be a decisive factor in strengthening sterling. . . . It was a gallant fight that England won. Our men showed real guts, and the banks I suspect, will be influenced by this and the position of the Government correspondingly strengthened."[27] I doubt it!

The World Cup of 1966 was an event of relatively modest commercialism, unsegregated crowds, insignificant tourism, and restrained patriotism. There was no victory parade, and the honors bestowed by the state ignored the elementary fact that football was a team game. Alf Ramsey, the first England manager to be given the time and authority to shape and run the team, was knighted in 1967, and the captain, Bobby Moore, received an OBE (Order of the British Empire). Bobby Charlton received an OBE in 1969, but the rest had to wait thirty years. Most of the players returned to their clubs immediately after the World Cup Final to begin preparing for the 1966–1967 football season. The victory appears to have increased the average attendances at Football League matches, but for only two seasons.[28] It is possible that the satellite pictures of the World Cup Final beamed into the United States increased interest in the sport there, but again it could only have been in a small way.

There are also strong suggestions that the World Cup of 1966 was a moment when more Englishwomen began to take an interest in football. Some actually attended the games, but many more watched on television, much to the surprise of the BBC's Peter Dimmock, who wrote that "housewives" had "begun to appreciate that football was not just 22 chaps kicking a ball about but something involving a great deal of skill."[29] Male viewers had outnumbered females, especially in the early matches, but by the finals the gap between the sexes was closing. The England manager received many letters after the end of the tournament, a surprising number from women saying how much they had enjoyed the performance of the England team, having seen it on TV. Perhaps it helped that the commentators began to probe the more human side of the player. A letter to the *The Listener*, published on August 4, 1966, did not appear to be ironic when asking "was it not fascinating to see last Saturday evening (at the banquet) the mother of the heroic Charltons and the blonde wife of England's triumphant captain?" This trend would continue with the Mexico Olympics of 1968 and strongly suggests the beginnings of the footballer as celebrity. It seems clear that the World Cup of 1966 may also have played a modest part in encouraging younger women and girls to try their feet at playing.

Many contemporaries have said, and many have repeated it since, that the World Cup of 1966 was the first time that football was important to the nation as a whole. They point to the television viewing figures, and to facts such as even Guernsey was deserted on the day of the World Cup Final.[30] The Lancaster and District Cricket League canceled most of its matches on July 30, and England did not play any cricket tests during the World Cup. They also point to the number of Union Jacks in evidence, especially on the World Cup Final day, both inside Wembley and out. Certainly the red-and-white Cross of St. George was hardly anywhere to be seen, but the question of which nation has to be asked. England's victory was greeted by the *Western Mail* of Cardiff and Wales with a supportive editorial.

> England's superb victory against West Germany in the World Cup Final is one which the whole of Britain can be proud of. . . . In a wider sense the triumph of the England team at Wembley belongs to British football as a whole.
>
> [It is hoped] . . . that Saturday's "clean and hard-played" game would mark the end of an unhappy era for the game in this country. The World Cup series and, above all, the final, has shown soccer at its best—as well as its worst. Now is the time for British football to make the most of its well-deserved triumph.[31]

The view was rather different from Scotland. The *Glasgow Herald*, for example, printed a picture of the West German team on its front page as they were given a heroes' welcome on their return to Frankfurt.[32] The *Scotsman* had nothing on its front page on Monday, August 1, when its headline was "Lyceum to change play policy." It also had the photograph of the West German team arriving in Frankfurt, and on the sports page it gave the World Cup Final the same amount of space, two columns, as the university golf tournament at Dalmahoy. John Rafferty, the football correspondent, blamed the English for the poor refereeing and suggested that the crowd at Wembley had approached "the hysteria of the Nuremberg Rallies."

Whatever did he mean? That they were behaving like robotic Germans? Perhaps he was referring to the rhythmical chanting of "Engerland, clap, clap, clap Engerland, clap, clap, clap, Engerland," which was so different to the more traditional and studiously neutral crowds that gathered for England internationals. This more vigorous approach had probably been borrowed and adapted from supporters of Everton and Liverpool and especially those who stood on the large terrace behind the goal. Their chanting and singing had often been shown on television. It must have looked as though, not satisfied with winning the World Cup, English supporters were stealing the traditional fervor of the Scots. Letters to the *Scotsman* tended to support Rafferty, such as the one published on August 5 from a Mr. Read of Haddington who adopted the high moral tone of a Scottish schoolmaster asserting that a proper British pride would be felt in English sporting achievements "when these are once again accomplished with the old spirit of sportsmanship and not as the focal point for a blind emotional nationalism."[33]

Why, then, could Wales and the Welsh rejoice with England and the English while the Scots fumed and glowered? There were several factors at work here. One was that all of the leading Welsh clubs played in the English league.

'Final match of the "World Championship": Cover of Match Program.'
Source: Private collection.

Moreover, their national side was used to being defeated by England. As far as team sports were concerned, the Welsh invested much more of their sporting identity in rugby union, at which they were far more competitive. The Scots meantime were not only bigger than Wales but had a strong, if fuzzy, memory of independence. They were proud of their separate legal and educational systems. Scottish teams did not play in England, but the weaker economy north of the border ensured that many Scottish players did, players who had built a reputation for skill and subtlety. The Scots had beaten England at football many times in the past and had only failed to qualify for the World Cup in a crucial match against Italy, when some English league clubs had refused to release their Scottish players for the game. This was especially frustrating not simply because two of them had Scottish managers, but because Scotland at full strength could be formidable in the mid-1960s. *They* would not have lost to the North Koreans! At the root of all of this chauvinistic posturing was that Scotland had weak nationalist politics and channeled much of its detestation of what it perceived as English arrogance and power into rivalries in other areas of life, especially football, because it had so often provided satisfying victories over the "significant other." Like the French (and presumably the West Germans), the Scottish found no cause for celebration in the English victory. In fact, they were intensely disappointed by it.

The World Cup Finals of 1966, and particularly the final match itself, have become part of the collective memory of the English. Almost everyone over age fifty can tell you where they were on July 30, 1966, and many of those then unborn have heard the stories and seen the final. Indeed, the final has been repeated on nationwide television to mark the various anniversaries of the event. In that sense it has some similarity to the Second World War and Britain's place in it, which remains the subject of, some writers would argue, a perverted media interest.[34] A popular television program, launched by the BBC a third of a century after the triumph, also helped keep the memory alive by taking its title from the words of television commentator, Kenneth Wolstenholme, as he described the events leading up to the fourth England goal: "They think it's all over: it is now!" Wembley Stadium Ltd. helped maintain the vividness of the memory. The company organized tours of the stadium that by the-mid 1990s were attracting 150,000 people a year. Many visitors were from overseas but many were also visitors to London from other parts of the country. The most popular exhibit was the crossbar struck by Geoff Hurst's shot in 1966 and the video showing the ball bouncing down on or over the goal line. Visitors were asked to vote via computer, and most of them thought that it had not crossed the line.[35]

There is also a World Cup (1966) Association whose aim is to keep alive the "true spirit of that year." About ninety people contributed to Norman Shiel's *Voice of 1966*, which is an honest exercise in nostalgia and remembering a past, happy time when the memorialists were young and life was sweet. Many have kept their match tickets, programs, and scrapbooks for which a lively memorabilia market currently exists. In many respects the 1960s were a good time for many people, with the economy growing at an average of 2 percent per year, inflation only averaging 2 percent, and unemployment also at a low 2 percent. And England did win the World Cup, a feat that it had not done before nor been very near to repeating since. Moreover, it was achieved in unsegregated grounds before the blight of "football hooliganism" was to bring the spectacle in England to the brink of disaster and beyond only twenty years later. Many ingredients go into the making of national consciousness; ethnicity, religion, war, and media, but also sport and sporting locations. And as Eric Hobsbawm has reminded us, "the imagined community of millions seems more real as a team of eleven named people. The individual, even the one who only cheers, becomes a symbol of his nation himself."[36] Jeffrey Hill has also pointed out that "if nations are imagined communities, what clearer image of the (English) nation can there be than that of a football crowd at

Wembley?"[37] But the World Cup was not just held at Wembley. Unlike the Olympics, it excited the interest of people in Birmingham and Sheffield, Liverpool, Middlesbrough, Sunderland, and many other places. It was a sporting and cultural moment shared by much of the nation, and because it was a team representing England rather than an individual who won, it became etched more firmly on the collective memory of the nation.

The World Cup of 1966 was a traditional as much as a modern sporting event.[38] The organizers were anxious that they might not sell enough tickets, and that the number of foreign visitors would be embarrassingly small. They sanctioned only a limited commercialism, as they aimed not so much to make money as not to lose it. There was no building of new stadiums, merely modest refurbishment of older ones, and although television was vital to the production of a significant collective experience, the technology allowed neither worldwide live coverage nor the erection of big screens in public places—indeed, there were no large screens even in the stadiums. The celebrations after victory were modest rather than triumphant. Jimmy Greaves, the English star who missed selection for the climactic last three games, looking back on 1966, concluded that it was quite a low-key affair. "If we won it now, the country would come to a stop for a week, and every player would become an immediate superstar: when we won it in '66, everybody cheered, a few thousand came out to say well done, and within a week everybody had disappeared, we'd all gone on our way, and we'd started playing the next season. That was the end of it. Now you get all this aura surrounding '66, but it was never quite like that."[39]

NOTES

1. I thank Neil Carter, Fabio Chisari, Richard Holt, Martin Johnes, and the editors for their help with this chapter.

2. Although two years earlier, in 1964, the new satellite technology had enabled much of the world to see live pictures from the Olympic Games in Tokyo.

3. Chisari (2001, 36–38). Less than one-third of British households had a TV set in 1954, but by 1960 this had risen to almost three-quarters.

4. Greenwood, Mercer, and Revie were to be future managers of the England team.

5. The BBC had already developed a tradition of transmitting sporting events and commentary programs before ITV was created in 1954. It had built up close relations with most national sporting governing bodies, which ITV could not match. The ITV executives were also doubtful about the pulling power of sport on television, especially when put up against popular programs such as its soap opera, *Coronation Street*. This normally was broadcast at 7:30 P.M. on Monday and Wednesday. On Wednesday, July 13, England played France in their first match of the finals. The kick-off was at 7:30 P.M.

ITV did not begin its coverage until 8 P.M. so *Coronation Street's* place in the schedule remained unchanged, but not its place in the popularity league, which fell to number eighteen when it was usually in the top five. See the ongoing research by Fabio Chisari, who is comparing the televising of football in Britain and Italy for research for his Ph.D. at De Montfort University, Leicester, England.

6. *Radio Times*, July 7, 1966, p.12.

7. *The Listener*, August 4, 1966, p.156.

8. Chisari (2004).

9. See Beck (1999) and Polley (1992).

10. See Holt and Mason (2000, 19–35).

11. D. N. Chester, "World Cup Countdown," *Spectator*, July 8, 1966, p.38.

12. See Howell (1990, 142–43).

13. Football Association (1966, 86). Hereafter referred to as *World Cup Report*.

14. See the letter from the treasury dated May 24, 1965, T227/2607. Of the £500,000, £100,000 was in the form of a loan and the remainder a grant. The FA had also loaned £160,000 of its own money to those clubs whose grounds were being used (*World Cup Report*, 89). See also Hansard Parliamentary Debates, vol. 713, May 27, 1965, cols. 117–18.

15. Although both might have been feeling anxious during the quarter final between Portugal and North Korea (as the People's Republic of Korea was called), who at one point led 3–0 before losing 5–3. See Howell (1990, 171–72).

16. The seven surviving members of the North Korean team were brought back to Middlesbrough in 2002 for the documentary film *The Game of Their Lives*, made by Nick Bonner and Dan Gordon and shown on BBC 4.

17. *World Cup Report*, 42–45. The cartoon figure got its name from the nickname given by some of his female staff to the Organizing Committee's administrative officer, E. K. Willson.

18. And some sensational publicity exploded on March 20, 1966, when the Jules Rimet Trophy was stolen from a stamp exhibition at Westminster's Central Hall. It was found in the garden of a house in south east London a week later by a dog named Pickles who was out for a walk and a sniff with his owner. It did not appear in public again until the day of the World Cup Final.

19. *World Cup Report*, 44–45. See also the minutes of the World Cup Organizing Committee, 1965–1966.

20. World Cup stamps did very well. The British fourpenny overprinted with "England winners" after the victory on July 30 sold more than any previous stamp. A limited edition of 12,000,000 sold out in just a few hours. These were the first British stamps to feature sportsmen in action.

21. Shiel (2000, 16); the Sunderland Liaison Committee Report, Appendix VII; *World Cup Report*, 297–99.

22. *World Cup Report*, 58.

23. *World Cup Report*, 55.

24. Shiel (2000, 99). See also Matthew Engel's, "Don't cry for me Wendell Sailor . . ." *Guardian*, p. 4, November 22, 2003.

25. Howell (1990, 174).

26. According to his own account, that is (Howell 1990, 174). Sir Stanley Rous, on the other hand, was alleged to have rebuked Wilson for hogging the limelight. See Tomlinson (1994, 18).

27. Crossman (1975, 594). No one now thinks that England's World Cup performances ever influenced the outcome of general elections. See Butler and Pinto-Duschinsky (1971, 128, 134, 154).

28. Bobby Moore was voted BBC Sportsman of the Year in 1966. Geoff Hurst was placed third. Attendance figures in 1965–1966 had been the lowest since the war up to that moment.

        1965–1966: 27,206,980.
        1966–1967: 28,902,596.
        1967–1968: 30,107,298.
        1968–1969: 29, 382,172.

29. See Chisari (2004, p. 105).

30. Shiel (2000, 106); *Lancaster Guardian*, August 5, 1966, p. 17.

31. *Western Mail*, August 1, 1966, p. 4.. For more on the Britishness of Welsh soccer, see Johnes (2004), from whom I owe this reference.

32. *Glasgow Herald*, August 1, 1966, p. 1.

33. *Scotsman*, August 1, 5, 1966, p. 1.

34. The war was against the same opponents, and this has latterly encouraged tasteless chants among a minority of younger fanatics, like "Two World Wars and one World Cup," whenever England and Germany meet. Interestingly, in 1966, England had never been beaten by Germany, whose first victory did not come until Hannover, 1968. They quickly made up for lost time after that. International Football, Germany has become England's significant other.

35.See *Sportsweek, The Independent on Sunday*, December 14, 2003, p.7.

36. Hobsbawm (1990, 143).

37. Hill (1998, 11).

38. See too Clarke and Critcher (1986, 125–26) on ways in which the victory spoke "simultaneously of modernization and the preservation of tradition." Critcher (1994, 90–91) talks too of the "negative consequences" of the victory, "for the development of the game" in England, "in part because of how it was achieved, in part because of how it was interpreted."

39. *Guardian Sport*, August 25, 2003, p. 19.

REFERENCES

Beck, Peter. 1999. *Scoring for Britain: International football and international politics 1900–1939*. London: Frank Cass.

Butler, David, and Michael Pinto-Duschinsky. 1971. *The British General Election of 1970*. London: Macmillan.

Chisari, Fabio. 2001. *Bringing the World Cup to you: Televising the 1966 Jules Rimet Cup*. Unpublished Master's thesis, De Montfort University, Leicester, England.

———. 2004. Shouting housewives! The 1966 Football World Cup and British television. *Sport in History: The Journal of the British Society of Sports History*, 24(1): 94–108.

Clarke, John, and Chas Critcher. 1986. 1966 and all that: England's World Cup victory. In *Off the ball: The Football World Cup*, ed. Alan Tomlinson and Garry Whannel. London: Pluto Press.

Critcher, Chas. 1994. England and the World Cup: World Cup Willies, English football and the myth of 1966. In *Hosts and champions: Soccer cultures, national identities, and the USA World Cup*, ed. John Sugden and Alan Tomlinson. Aldershot, UK: Ashgatem.

Crossman, Richard. 1975. *The diaries of a Cabinet minister, volume 1*. London: Hamish Hamilton.

Football Association. 1966. *World Cup report*. London: The Football Association.

Hill, Jeffrey. 1998. *Le stade comme lieu mythique: Wembley*. Unpublished paper.

Hobsbawm, Eric. 1990. *Nations and nationalism since 1780: Program, myths, reality*. Cambridge: Cambridge University Press.

Holt, Richard, and Tony Mason. 2000. *Sport in Britain 1945–2000*. Oxford: Blackwell.

Howell, Denis. 1990. *Made in Birmingham: The memoirs of Denis Howell*. London: Queen Anne Press.

Johnes, Martin. 2004. *Sport in Wales 1800–2000*. Cardiff: St. David's Press.

Polley, Martin. 1992. Olympic diplomacy: The British government and the projected 1940 Olympic Games. *The International Journal of the History of Sport* 9 (2): 169–87.

Shiel, Norman, ed. 2000. *Voices of 1966: Memories of England's World Cup*. London: Temple.

Tomlinson, Alan. 1994. FIFA and the World Cup: The expanding football family. In *Hosts and champions: Soccer cultures, national identities, and the USA World Cup*, ed. John Sugden and Alan Tomlinson. Aldershot, UK: Ashgate Publishing.

Chapter 6

Mexico City 1968

Sombreros and Skyscrapers

Claire and Keith Brewster

In April 2001, I (Keith) ended an interview with Pedro Ramírez Vázquez, president of the Organizing Committee of the 1968 Olympic Games, by recalling my own memories of the Games, as a twelve-year-old boy watching the events on a black-and-white television in England.[1] For me, four salient moments stood out: Bob Beaman's record-breaking long jump; Dick Fosbury's revolutionary technique in the high jump; the raised fists of the U.S. black athletes; and, being British, the unforgettable commentary of the BBC's David Coleman, as he saw David Hemery home to victory in the 400-meter hurdles final. Expecting a positive reply, I asked him if he was pleased that these recollections were of great sporting moments. He replied with a blunt "No." Although he understood why I remembered what I had, he said that what the Organizing Committee wanted more than anything else was for the world's audience to remember Mexico. And it is with these parting words from Ramírez Vázquez in mind that this chapter asks what the Mexicans sought to achieve by hosting the Games, what image of Mexico they sought to portray.

In attempting to answer these questions, this chapter differs from the majority of studies covering the 1968 Olympic Games. Understandably, most focus upon the events themselves, whether connected to sporting achievements or the socio-political context of Mexico during the summer of 1968. In the latter, the massacre of up to 500 Mexican students just ten days before the opening ceremony dominates such an analysis[2]: Did the students seek to jeopardize the Games? Who was to blame for the massacre? Was there any chance that the International Olympic Committee would cancel the Games?[3] For this chapter, a discussion of how the Mexican government, the IOC, or the Organizing Committee reacted to the unfolding events of 1968 is of limited use, precisely because they were reactions to developments beyond their control. While not wanting to diminish the importance of such issues, this chapter focuses upon factors that pre-date them, namely, the hopes, desires, and concerns

99

that guided the Organizing Committee's actions from the moment Mexico City was selected to host the Games in 1963.

The main contention of this chapter is that a confused, often contradictory, image of Mexico emerged during the development of these plans, one that revealed fundamental differences concerning how best to portray the nation. We show that such divisions were nothing new and had characterized earlier attempts to project Mexico on the international stage. But we also argue that the protracted debate concerning Mexico's characterization was affected by tensions between a social elite that sought to define Mexico and the vast majority of the Mexican people who, the elite feared, could not fulfill its designs for the nation. In order to test these assertions, we divide our analysis into two sections. First, we draw upon the excellent work of other cultural historians to reveal how the debate concerning Mexican identity was reflected in the ways the nation was represented on the international stage in earlier decades. Second, we follow these patterns through to show how these debates continued into the 1960s to influence the very core of the decision-making processes of the Organizing Committee.

In order to help us understand the historical context of this debate, we begin with the observations of Octavio Paz (1990), one of Mexico's most influential intellectuals of the twentieth century. Long before winning the Nobel Prize for Literature, he published (in 1950) what has become accepted as a classic analysis of the character of the Mexican nation and its people, *The Labyrinth of Solitude*. Among Paz's many observations is that due to the singular nature of its history and geopolitics, Mexico has never developed a truly national identity. Bereft of any real sense of its own origins, he claims, Mexico has all too frequently searched abroad for suitable cultural and societal models. Furthermore, Paz maintains that this lack of identity invades the psyche of individual Mexicans, draining their self-respect and self-confidence. As a defense mechanism they, like their nation, employ diverse masks to hide their true emotions. Only rarely, he continues, do these masks slip to reveal the raw emotions of the Mexican people. At such moments, they get drunk, make love, and fight and kill, all with excessive passion. Yet even as we read these lines, we should not be fooled into thinking that Paz saw himself in such terms. He belonged to a smaller elite group that shared an intellectual background and broader experiences that enabled it to muse on the wider debate concerning the nature of national identity. This group lived in constant fear that, as had happened at distinct moments during the Mexican Revolution (1910–1917), the raw emotions of its compatriots might destroy any façade of civility that the nation builders hoped to sustain.

What vision did the elite hold for the nation? At its most basic, we might see it as an attempt to reconcile the past and present, tradition and modernity. This in itself is no easy thing to achieve. Tom Nairn refers to a Janus-like form of nationalism that accompanies the efforts of a "backward" culture and people to appropriate the powers and benefits of modernity. Even as they do so, they seek comfort, stability, and identity from their own past. As such, a nation looks forward to a bright new future while looking back for reminders of its origins. Nairn develops his theory by suggesting that Janus rarely reveals just two "faces." He offers a tendency toward "internationalism" as an alternative gaze and the heterogeneity of "national" history as another, both conspiring to blur the vision of would-be nation builders (1997, 71–72). As Paz suggests, in the case of Mexico, this process was complicated by those who preferred to view the Mexican past through a foreign lens. So, for example, in late-nineteenth-century Mexico City, Parisenne-style boulevards were adorned with statues of pre-Columbian Aztec warriors, dressed in togas and sculptured in a Romanesque style. As Mauricio Tenorio-Trillo (1996, 181–240) points out, the question of national identity continued throughout the early decades of the twentieth century and is clearly visible from the confused portrayals of Mexico at successive international fairs and exhibitions. At the 1922 Centennial Exhibition in Rio de Janeiro, for example, the Mexican Pavilion openly displayed its Hispanic heritage with a structure clearly resembling the colonial architectural style found in Mexico City. Yet seven years later in Seville, the Mexicans outwardly chose to downplay their Spanish links by erecting a structure that celebrated the Mayan civilization in shape and form. Only when visitors stepped inside could they appreciate the modernist architectural design of the structure and displays emphasizing the strong ties between Mexico and Spain. A decade later, however, Mexico's offering to the 1937 Paris World Fair was bereft of all pre-Columbian and Hispanic symbols. Reflecting the socialist nature of the incumbent government in Mexico, huge figures symbolizing the unity of the worker and peasant dominated the façade, while the modern architectural design had much more in common with the modernism of the German building than anything to be found in Mexico City.

As Tenorio-Trillo makes clear, this seeming confusion regarding how best to project Mexico's image reflected the protracted debate within Mexican intellectual circles concerning the very fabric of Mexican society. It went without saying, however, that irrespective of the sympathies of a given project group, the underlying assumption was to portray an idealized nation. What foreigners saw was a sanitized Mexico, *au fait* with modern technology and at ease with its ethnic diversity. What they did not see in these exhibitions was any hint of discontent within social or ethnic groups, or a display of the raw emotions to which Paz would later refer. Just as, in 1910, Mexico City's authorities cleared the streets of Indians before welcoming foreign dignitaries to help celebrate the country's 100 years of independence, so later designers of Mexican images abroad would also cover what they viewed as the unsightly stains of Mexican society beneath a pure alabaster finish (Tenorio-Trillo 2001, 179–80; Brewster 2004; Ramírez Vázquez 2001).

It is our belief that the interplay between Mexico's lack of self-assuredness and tensions between the different Mexicos that comprised the nation continued into the planning of the 1968 games. In defending our position, we begin with a report presented at the Annual General Meeting of the Mexican Olympic Committee in April 1969, its first meeting after the Mexico Olympic Games. In tones of justifiable self-congratulation, the report listed all of the criticisms that had been leveled at the country prior to the games, among which were the following:

1. Mexico was not a mature country.
2. The installations would not be ready.
3. The expenses would be too much for the country to afford.
4. The organization would be a disaster, and it would be better for Mexico to give up the responsibility of hosting the Games to avoid the inevitable bad publicity.
5. Mexican athletes would be ridiculed in front of the sporting world's crème de la crème.
6. The altitude would cause death and/or permanent damage to the athletes.

The report concluded by observing that "the entire world, including a minority of incredulous Mexicans, witnessed that not one of these dire prophecies was realized. On the contrary, the demonstration of our organizing abilities has projected an image of a modern Mexico that has banished forever the erroneous image held by many that we live in an apathetic, lazy, and backward country."[4] "Apathetic," "lazy," and "backward," all images that had dominated foreign, predominantly U.S., portrayals of Mexico in previous decades, and all images of which Mexicans were acutely sensitive, particularly those with sufficient means to travel beyond the confines of their own nation.[5]

The reason for quoting this report at some length is twofold: first, because it vividly encapsulates the range of anxieties voiced following Mexico's successful bid for the 1968 games. Several national Olympic Committees, particularly the British, expressed grave concerns over Mexico City's altitude and the ability of Mexicans to stage the Games.[6] Such fears intensified when after having been shown an open field where the rowing lanes were to be constructed, Thomas Keller, president of the International Rowing Federation, stormed back to Europe and with barely concealed rage predicted that the installation would never be built on time.[7] In private, the president of the IOC, Avery Brundage, sent reminders to Ramírez Vázquez regarding the need to keep construction projects on schedule. In public, however, Brundage never ceased to be supportive of the Organizing Committee's efforts, and he rebuffed all such criticisms by assuring that Mexico City "would stage the Olympic Games in a real Mexican way, according to Olympic regulations, and that there was nothing to worry about."[8] And in the event, Mexicans *did* do things their own way and everything *was* ready on time—just! The inventive architectural style of many installations won international praise, and as the Olympic Games began, even Thomas Keller was moved sufficiently to declare the rowing course the best in the world, as reported by James Samuel in a *Guardian* article on October 12, 1968.

Another reason for quoting the Mexican Olympic Committee report is to suggest that those worried about impending disaster included more than "an incredulous minority of Mexicans." We believe that members of the Organizing Committee shared the preoccupation of their social class; that despite Mexico's best efforts to project a positive image of itself on the world stage, ultimately this might be revealed to be yet another mask, laid bare not least by the behavior of its own people. In early 1968, an article written by Siefreid Kogelfranz in *Der Spiegel* caused an outcry in Mexico, as attested in reports in *El Nacional* and *Novedades* on March 3. The author referred to the mixed race of the Mexicans and questioned their ability to organize the Games, not to mention their ability to win any medals. While Mexicans dismissed Kogelfranz as one of a dwindling group who still embraced the racist sympathies of a Nazi past, his comments did strike a raw nerve. Only thirty years earlier, Mexico's own sports administrators had pointed enviously toward the widespread enthusiasm for sports in Western Europe (Germany included) and concluded that only by embracing sport would Mexicans develop the required characteristics to improve their racial stock and help the country advance.[9] The administrators were not, of course, referring to the entire population. For many years, Mexicans with sufficient time and money pursued interests that mirrored the pastimes of the "developed" world. Consequently, ballooning, golf, polo, horse racing, baseball, cycling, and rowing became popular sports for the wealthy (Beezley 1987, 15–52). The criticism was more focused upon the Mexican masses, who often spent their leisure time getting drunk and gambling on cockfights.[10]

In order to measure the degree to which these tensions still existed in the 1960s, we need to analyze the image of Mexico that the Organizing Committee sought to portray. Ramírez Vázquez claims that when he took over as president of the Organizing Committee the first question he asked himself was how to make the 1968 Olympics different, that is, truly Mexican.[11] Phrased differently, he was posing the same question that Octavio Paz had raised in *The Labyrinth of Solitude*: what did it mean to be a Mexican? In searching for an answer, we argue that Ramírez Vázquez offered an array of masks, some familiar, others less so. The 1968 Olympic Games would present Mexico as a modern, forward-looking nation; it would also portray a nation with proud ancient traditions, one that was both an aspirant to the First World, and a champion of the Third World, a standard bearer for Latin America, and a promoter of the Spanish language. How did these values and aspirations manifest themselves in the actions of the Organizing Committee? A promising line of inquiry would be to begin by speculating why Mexico City was chosen to host the Games over its competitors—Detroit, Lyon, and Buenos Aires.

Mexico City's selection to host the 19th Olympiad took place at a session of the IOC in Baden Baden held October 16–20, 1963. Not surprisingly, no incriminating evidence exists within the IOC archives to suggest why Mexico was favored over other cities. Nor is there any explanation of why its bid to host the 1956 Games had failed. But a report by Ing. Marte R. Gómez to the incumbent president of Mexico, Miguel Alemán, suggests that the 1956 bid had failed due to insufficient networking within the IOC and a polarized tussle between English-speaking and Spanish-speaking delegates in which Melbourne was eventually selected over Buenos Aires.[12] Any notion that it was Latin America's turn, however, is unlikely. In contrast to FIFA's management of the World Cup, maintaining a continental balance had never been a priority within the IOC. The Olympic Games had never been awarded to a Spanish-speaking host, let alone a Latin American city. It is all the more surprising, then, that Mexico City's bid for the 1968 games won so much support that a second round of voting was not necessary.[13] In the absence of hard evidence of why this occurred, perhaps we should begin by considering the local, regional, and global developments that formed a backdrop to the lobbying and bidding procedure.

An important factor that may have distinguished Mexico City's bid from all those previously emanating from developing countries was that its sponsors were able to make a convincing case that the country was sufficiently robust economically for the IOC to place its trust in them. Much of this confidence came from the fact that in preceding decades Mexico had indeed enjoyed a dynamic economy. Since the end of the Second World War, state investment and protective import tariffs had nurtured a homegrown manufacturing base. Unprecedented government investment had been channeled toward improving the country's infrastructure, with roads and hydroelectric stations bringing about real changes to provincial Mexico. The gross domestic product was growing at an annual rate of 6 to 7 percent, and the expansion of welfare programs contributed toward convincing ordinary Mexicans that they were indeed living through what politicians had called the "Miracle Years." In Mexico City itself, citizens could reflect upon the recent completion of the national university campus, new housing complexes, and the beginnings of a new underground railway network as signs of such investment.[14] In one important respect, then, Mexico's belief that it was an emerging nation was justified.

Yet when looking for reasons why Mexico City succeeded in 1963 where it had previously failed, one should also reflect upon the geopolitics taking place as competing cities lobbied for IOC votes. In recent years dramatic events had been taking place in Latin America that gripped the world's attention. Fidel Castro's revolution reached its successful climax on January 1, 1959. The disastrous Bay of Pigs invasion occurred in 1961, and less than a year later, time stood still as Kennedy and Khrushchev confronted each other over the missile crisis. Within such an environment, IOC members from the Soviet bloc were extremely unlikely to support any bid from a city in a NATO country: Detroit and Lyon had no chance of winning.[15] The stalemate between superpowers over Cuba heralded the beginning of a charm offensive by the Kennedy administration, as millions of dollars were poured into an Alliance for Progress program designed to boost Latin America's socio-economic infrastructure and thereby persuade would-be radicals from following Castro's move toward the Soviet Union.[16] During this period, the Mexican government trod a fine line between making supportive gestures toward Castro while never stretching the patience of its North American neighbor. For its part, the United States had learned to tolerate the more radical elements of Mexican foreign policy and had long seen Mexico as a cultural intermediary toward Latin America. During this delicate time in U.S. relations with Latin America, Mexico's support was highly valued. While not suggesting that the U.S. government could direct the IOC in the way that it tried to direct other international bodies, it should be noted that Avery Brundage, who had become accustomed to running the IOC as his own personal fiefdom, was a U.S. citizen. Again, we stress that no conclusive evidence points to why Mexico City won the bid. We merely observe that as Mexico's booming economy coincided with a most sensitive time in the cold war, a Latin American city for the first time ever was chosen to host the Olympic Games.[17]

The global and regional context within which the 1968 games took place inevitably impinged upon the way that the Organizing Committee assumed its responsibilities. Bearing in mind that the Mexico Olympic Games were taking place at the height of the Vietnam War, it is not surprising that the Organizing Committee chose to reiterate the IOC's apolitical ethos by declaring the Mexico Olympic Games the "Peaceful Games."[18] The games would take place in a harmonious environment in which, for two weeks at least, all political differences would be put to one side. The white dove was adopted by the Mexicans and appeared on all official publications emanating from the Organizing Committee.

Another early initiative by the Organizing Committee was to foster the games as a unique opportunity for Latin America. While Che Guevara's death in the Bolivian highlands in 1967 may have ended one vision for the continent, other ways forward still existed. The committee's own aspirations were made clear in June 1968, when it launched the first of a series of radio "chats."

> Mexico's commitment is, in reality, a commitment by all countries who speak Spanish, especially those in Latin America. That's why the committee wants as many Americans as possible to give a demonstration of what they can do through Mexico. Hence, the Olympic committee wants American radio stations to take a few minutes to inform their listeners of what's happening in Mexico and thus to show the organizing efficiency and capacity of Latin Americans.

Loyal listeners of these "chats" could be forgiven for breathing a sigh of relief when, months later, the announcer pronounced "upon transmitting our hundredth broadcast, we can say with satisfaction that Mexico has honored its commitment."[19] A dominant theme of the series was the fraternity among Latin American countries, a fraternity that the Mexican Ministry of Sport reinforced by offering training facilities and financial support to the less wealthy nations of Central America to help them prepare and compete in the Olympic Games. Furthermore, as a logical continuation of its promotion of the Spanish language, after the games a Mexican delegation tried (unsuccessfully) to have Spanish adopted as the third official language of the IOC. This initiative was given an extra edge due to the fact that Mexico did not have diplomatic relations with Franco's Spain. Since the Spanish Civil War, Mexico had played host to the Republican government in exile. Indeed, only due to the understanding and cooperation of the exile government was the Organizing Committee able to avoid an awkward issue concerning Spain's participation in the Games.[20] It seems clear, then, that at one level Mexico saw itself as the legitimate champion of both the Spanish language and the Latin American continent.

Yet at another level, Mexico's actions seem even more ambitious. While it is clear that few, if any, Organizing Committee members viewed Mexico as an underdeveloped nation, much of its official policy sought to portray the host nation as a standard bearer of the Third World.[21] The reasons for this may have been diverse, but in part it was a question of circumstances. Following a wave of decolonization, the Mexico City Olympic Games were the first to which many newly formed African nations were invited to compete. Mexicans were forced to go beyond their role as host when South Africa's invitation to the Games threatened to foster a widespread boycott by other African nations. Faced with such a situation, the Mexican president, Díaz Ordaz, added weight to the Organizing Committee's demand that the invitation to South Africa be withdrawn. Ramírez Vázquez, for example, recalls that at one meeting Díaz Ordaz stated that the dignity of the nation depended upon ensuring "that those South African bastards should not come to the Games."[22] This was a high-risk strategy, as almost all Western countries were adamant that the Olympic Charter demanded South Africa's right to participate. In the event, Mexico's unwavering stance and intense lobbying won through and, in turn, lent much credence to its image as a defender of the dignity of Third World countries.

Why did the Mexicans gamble so much in defense of the young African nations? One reason might well have been through a genuine sympathy with their argument. The Mexican government portrayed its own revolution (1910–1917) as the moment when the country banished all forms of colonial racism, hence it could not be seen to condone such behavior elsewhere. More pragmatically, if up to thirty-two African nations had boycotted their first Olympic Games, then it would have been a considerable blow to Mexico City's reputation as host.[23] Yet we believe that an equally strong factor stems from an attempt to overcome something that Octavio Paz highlighted in *The Labyrinth of Solitude*: a latent sense of inferiority that Mexicans had often shown in their relationships with "developed" countries. The need to prove itself on the international arena weighed heavily upon Mexico. It should be remembered that the Mexicans had already blamed the failure of their 1956 Games bid on an "English-speaking" voting bloc. In addition, as criticisms of Mexico City's preparations increased, the United States had suggested that Los Angeles would be ready to take over the hosting of the games if it got to be too much for the Mexicans.[24] Finally, only months before the games, the United States had joined forces with other English-speaking delegates to demand South Africa's inclusion.[25] As the nations of the IOC marshalled their forces on either side of the apartheid issue, the Organizing Committee was determined not to let the games be highjacked by international heavyweights.[26] As is often the case in such affairs, there is no hard evidence to confirm this as being behind official Mexican policy, but if we broaden our horizon a little to view the way in which the committee sought to use the Games as a whole, then a certain consistency of behavior becomes apparent.

According to Ramírez Vázquez, a crucial solution to his dilemma of making the 1968 Games different was to revive the original spirit of the ancient Olympics by placing cultural endeavor at the heart of the 19th Olympiad. His stated reasons for doing so are plausible: not everyone could win medals, athletes from poorer countries could not hope to compete realistically against those enjoying superior training facilities, and that what all countries could bring to Mexico, whether rich or poor, was a unique cultural heritage that defined their nation. By fostering a cultural Olympics within a non-competitive environment, Ramírez Vázquez maintained that all countries could leave Mexico feeling that national honor had been satisfied.[27]

While there is no reason to doubt such motives, it is worth remembering one of the criticisms recalled by the Mexican Olympic Committee after the games were over: that Mexican athletes would be ridiculed in front of the sporting world's crème de la crème. So worried were Mexican sports administrators that such a scenario would transpire that excuses were made for the poor showing expected of their athletes even before the Games began.[28] This may have been nothing other than a realistic appraisal. After all, Mexican athletes had hardly distinguished themselves at previous Olympics. Indeed, after its poor results at the London Olympics in 1948, one Mexican politician was moved to excuse the team's performance by pointing out "Mexicans are not athletes, they are poets."[29] His suggestion that Mexicans could hold their heads up in the field of culture is strengthened by the often-quoted observation, "Mexico has a lot of culture and no money, whereas the United States has lots of money but no culture." The sense that Mexicans might not win many medals but could do culture well was in itself a good enough reason for the Organizing Committee to make the 1968 Olympic Games different by staging a cultural Olympics. Combined with its desire to offer a cultural platform to Third World countries, the idea may have been too good to pass up.

The Mexicans certainly went to town on their cultural Olympics, launching a year-long series of events that attracted top performers and artists from all continents of the world.[30] So extensive was the program that some voices within the IOC movement began to doubt the wisdom of reintroducing this element to the Games. Overlooking the non-competitive dimension stressed by the Mexicans, Sandy Duncan, president of the British Olympic Association, feared that the program was getting out of hand and might turn into a mini-Olympics in which each country tried to outshine the rest.[31] Avery Brundage, initially a keen sponsor of the cultural events, did eventually admit that "Mexico is going a little too far, [and that] we had better notify both Sapporo and Munich to submit their programs before they get in too deep."[32]

For this chapter it is interesting to consider the ways in which Mexico sought to portray itself, both by its own contributions to the cultural Olympics and by the type of cultural projects that it included in the program. What we see is the same balancing act that had taxed the creative minds of those who alternatively offered pre-Columbian, Hispanic, and modernist representations of Mexico at world fairs in earlier decades. The range of events throughout the year celebrated the world's diverse traditions through folklore, music, and dance, yet it also encouraged contemporary arts, offering many venues at which high and popular culture could be enjoyed. Furthermore, through its sponsorship of exhibitions and conferences relating to space exploration, the Mexican organizers underlined that the country's future lay in embracing the most up-to-date technology.

A fundamental aspect of Mexico's own contribution to these cultural initiatives was the resurrected myth of a "Golden Age."[33] For a Mexican elite, long brought up on a diet of the classics, the rather tenuous link between the ancient Greeks and the Aztecs was too good an opportunity to miss. Poems, odes, and newspaper articles made knowing references to how the Hellenic spirits of the past would be rekindled among the temples of the Aztec gods.[34] The recent opening of Mexico City's National Museum of Anthropology and History was acknowledged in the first issue of Olympic commemorative stamps, which depicted pre-Columbian ceramic figures chosen by experts at the museum, each engaged in a sporting activity. The second series reflected designs that the Mexican muralist, Diego Rivera, had chosen to decorate the walls of the Olympic Stadium when it was built in the early 1950s. Although within a modern context, the way that the figures were formed and framed bore more than a passing resemblance to those of the classical Greek era.[35] The cultural program received a considerable boost when the Vatican sent a copy of the works of Pindaro as its contribution. For a Mexican-educated elite that prided itself on reading the works of the ancient Greek poet, the Vatican's unique gesture seemed to endorse Mexico's "Golden Age" credentials. Furthermore, the Organizing Committee's promotional literature placed considerable emphasis on informing foreigners of Mexico's pre-Columbian cultures.

Yet the great challenge for the committee, as it had been for designers of Mexican pavilions, was to celebrate Mexico's pre-Columbian civilizations without leaving the impression that all Mexico had to offer the world was its history. In the 1920s, the more convincing solutions had portrayed the past through a contemporary lens. And so, too, the Organizing Committee came up with a truly inspirational means of constructing a temporal bridge between past and present. Among the many pre-Columbian exhibits on display in the National Museum were stone and wooden seals used by the Huichol ethnic group to create designs characterized by concentric lines in black and white. Borrowing heavily from the Huichol past, the Organizing Committee fashioned what would become the official logo of the Olympic Games.[36] Moreover, the black-and-white patterns engaged directly with op art, a form of artistic expression that was pushing the boundaries throughout the Western world. The logo became a symbol of a nation that had found a harmonious fusion of past and present and that was confident about its future. The Mexico City of the late 1960s was a place where the ceremonies and dances of its Aztec ancestors could be reenacted amid the skyscrapers and futuristic architectural styles of the new sports installations.

As had been the case with Mexican pavilions forty years earlier, however, the images of Mexico that the Organizing Committee created were crystalline. Certainly, "popular" Mexico formed part of the cultural celebrations. Indeed, Mexican hospitality was underlined time and again, yet it was a distinct form of hospitality in which charming Indian women with broad smiles displayed teeth every bit as pristine and white as their freshly starched blouses. Nowhere in the Organizing Committee's promotional material does one find any hint of the emblem adopted by the organizers of the Mexican World Cup two years later. This portrayed a diminutive Mexican boy sporting a large sombrero and a cheesy grin. To have done so would have undermined the whole cultural ethos that the committee was trying to portray, and would have done little other than to bring to the fore the negative stereotypes of the Mexican so frequently held by foreigners: behind the cheesy grin lay an "apathetic, lazy, and backward" character. When asked why he believed the World Cup organizers had chosen to resurrect such an image, Ramírez Vázquez barely concealed his contempt, observing that the decision was made by "uneducated" men for an entirely different, much more limited audience.[37] While the audience may have been different, we believe that the sanitized, sophisticated image of Mexico avidly promoted by the Olympic Organizing Committee reflected a long-held concern among the Mexican elite. Behind the unifying façade of patriotism, it seems likely that the cosmopolitan members of the committee feared that their countrymen might let them down. In the World Fair exhibitions of the past, this had mattered little, as they took place overseas. This time, however, the world was coming to Mexico City. Could the mask be sustained for the duration of the Games?

In fairness, many of the measures taken by Mexico City's authorities were no different from those employed in any big city prior to an important international event. Streets were scrubbed, buildings were given a fresh coat of paint, and water fountains and wastepaper bins suddenly began to appear. Yet things in Mexico City went a little further. Reminiscent of centennial celebrations that took place in the same streets almost sixty years earlier, unsightly citizens were again swept aside. And in this respect, the student demonstrations that filled the streets during the summer of 1968 were every bit as embarrassing for the local and national authorities.[38] Like the vagrants, they too had to be removed, albeit in a much more brutal and tragic way. For those Mexicans who simply could not be taken out of sight, another approach was adopted. The Organizing Committee launched a huge media campaign designed to teach the people of Mexico City how "to establish a sense of national responsibility" and "to awaken the natural hospitality of Mexicans toward foreign athletes and visitors."[39]

Part of the campaign included a series of messages given in an official, paternalistic tone, informing Mexicans of the right and wrong ways to behave in front of foreigners. According to Ramírez Vázquez, he judged such a campaign counterproductive, and upon taking over the presidency of the committee he set about a more imaginative form of public education. The result was a series of humorous shorts, two-minute scenes that were broadcast on radio, television, and cinema. They featured Cantinflas, a favorite comic hero of Mexican cinema, in the guise of one of his most popular characters, an incompetent, pompous policeman who was the bane of his commanding officer's life.[40] In the clips, Cantinflas brings into the local police station a series of characters and situations that visitors might encounter during the Olympic Games: a taxi driver trying to overcharge a tourist; hooligans fighting at a football match in the Aztec stadium; a housemaid throwing rubbish onto the street; and a hippie making a nuisance of himself in a tourist area. In each case, the message was clear. Mexicans needed to modify their behavior to create a good impression, to present Mexico in the best possible light, and to lend dignity to the Mexican nation. Most revealing, however, are the aspects of Mexican life that the committee chose to highlight: dishonesty, untidiness, violence, drunkenness, predatory sexuality, and police corruption, all elements that the Organizing Committee either wanted to eradicate, or at least keep out of sight, until the Games were over.

Such initiatives were not without their critics. Some lamented that efforts to clean up Mexico City would only last for the duration of the Games.

Others, both at the time and afterward, claimed that the whole nature of the campaign was in danger of squeezing the essential elements of the Mexican character out of the Games. Newspaper articles criticized efforts to remake Mexico City in the cultural mode of a sophisticated West. One article criticized the city authorities for encouraging people to paint their houses. Only half in jest, the author alluded to the foreigner's view of the unkempt Mexican by asking, "Wouldn't it make more sense to wash the lion before cleaning his cage?" He went on to muse whether the policy would continue after the Games, or whether it was "only worth washing our faces for the benefit of foreigners."[41] What they were all pointing to, of course, was the fact that the city authorities and the Organizing Committee were being more than a little disingenuous. They were trying to mold their countrymen to suit their own aspirations rather than having the confidence to reveal Mexicans for what they were. The divisions within Mexican society that were clearly visible in the early twentieth century had not gone away. Indeed, in a strange way they reflected the diverse range of postures that Mexico sought to assume on the international stage. While many aspects of Mexico City's hosting of the Olympic Games did indeed suggest that it was a modern, capable nation, beyond the shining new sports installations lay humble dwellings reminiscent of the Third World that Mexico hoped to champion. Both worlds shared an uncomfortable coexistence in Mexico City, and while for the most part they barely met, during the Olympic Games they were forced to confront each other.

In the event, the true character of the Mexican people proved irrepressible and provided one of the highlights of the 1968 Games. Following the chaotic scenes that had taken place in Tokyo four years earlier, the IOC gave strict instructions regarding conduct at the 1968 closing ceremony. Instead of the entire complement of each team circling the Olympic stadium, one single representative holding his or her country's name on a banner was allowed to parade before the crowd. As part of the spectacle, the lighting for each section of the stadium slowly dimmed, until the Olympic flame remained the only source of light. As the flame itself was extinguished, the night sky was lit up by an amazing display of fireworks. Under the cover of darkness, a band of 1,000 mariachi musicians entered the arena, and as the firework display subsided, the lights went on and the band struck up a medley of popular Mexican tunes. Unable to contain his emotions, one African athlete broke ranks and ran toward the crowd, whirling his national costume in dramatic gestures. As others followed suit, the audience went wild, throwing their hats into the air, and they poured onto the track to help the world's athletes convert the solemn closing ceremony into a spontaneous Mexican fiesta.[42] Perhaps the Organizing Committee should have had more faith in its countrymen and women. On this occasion, at least, the raw emotions of the Mexican people proved not to be a weakness. On the contrary, it became a strength, as their genuine warmth created a most fitting climax to the 1968 Olympic Games.

NOTES

1. Keith Brewster interview with Pedro Ramírez Vázquez, Mexico City, April 26, 2001.

2. It is unlikely that the actual number of deaths will ever be known. After returning from Mexico, eyewitness sports journalist John Rodda stated, "An accurate figure of the deaths will never be known, but the 500 I reported the following day is not likely to be far off the mark." See Rodda (1968a, 1968b) and Pinchetti (1978). Student leader Marcelino Perelló claims to have overheard a police officer say that over 500 people were killed.

3. For a good overview of all of these issues, see Arbena (2002). On the ethnic issue, see Brewster (2004).

4. Archivo General de la Nación, Mexico City, Comité Organizador de los Juegos Olímpicos collection (hereafter AGN, COJO), Box 401, report dated April 28, 1969.

5. For vivid examples of such portrayals, see Dent (1999) and Pike (1997).

6. The first such concerns were raised immediately after the announcement that Mexico City had won the competition. See Archive of the IOC, Lausanne (hereafter IOC archive), CIO session in Baden Baden, October 16–20, 1963, pp. 5–6.

7. IOC archive, P.V. Sessions 1964–1966, CIO session in Madrid, October 6–9, 1965, p. 9. After the Organizing Committee gave its report, Brundage mentioned the objection lodged by the International Rowing Federation concerning rowing facilities; IOC archive, file 0100624, Correspondence COJO, 1963–1967. See letter dated December 7, 1966, from Keller to Brundage complaining about a lack of preparation for rowing lanes and suggesting a switch of countries for the trial regatta to be held in October 1967.

8. IOC archive, file 0100624, correspondence COJO, 1963–1967. See letter dated August 26, 1966, from Brundage to Clerk inquiring about the present state of constructions. For Brundage's reassurance, see minutes of IOC Executive Board, Mexico City, October 22, 1966.

9. Archivo General de la Nación, Mexico City (hereafter AGN), Lázaro Cárdenas, 532.2/1. Document dated September 1935. See details of the speech made by Senator David Ayala.

10. For an example of such sentiments, see AGN, Lázaro Cárdenas, 532.2/1. Document dated September 1935. For a more detailed discussion of the role that mass sport played in post-revolutionary Mexico, see Keith Brewster (2005).

11. Ramírez Vázquez took over the presidency from former Mexican president Adolfo López Mateos, who had resigned due to ill health. Interview with Ramírez Vázquez.

12. AGN, Miguel Alemán Valdés, 532/6 (no date).

13. IOC archive, CIO session in Baden Baden, October 16–20, 1963, pp. 5–6. The first round of voting was as follows: Mexico City, 30, Buenos Aires, 2, Detroit, 14, Lyon, 12.

14. Upon winning the competition in Baden Baden, Adolfo López Mateos said it was due to international recognition of Mexico's "economic and political stability." See *El Nacional*, October 19, 1963. For an overview of this economic growth, see Aguilar Camín and Meyer (1994), Carr (1992), and Handelman (1997).

15. We thank John MacAloon for highlighting this observation.

16. For an overview of U.S. foreign policy toward Latin America during the cold war period, see LaFeber (1994) and Schoultz (1998).

17. An insight of the United States' cultural efforts to gain favor with its Latin American neighbors can be gleaned from the various documents found within the official Web site of the United States Information Agency.

18. Mexican politicians proposed that 1968 be designated "The Year of the Peace Olympics." See AGN, COJO, caja 403, 154, tomo VI, December 29, 1967.

19. AGN, COJO, caja 403, Charlas Radiofónicas, nos. 1–104.

20. Interview with Ramírez Vázquez. See protracted correspondence between the Spanish delegation, the IOC, and Ramírez Vázquez in late 1967 over Spain's participation and possible reception by the Mexican people: AGN, COJO, caja 403, 152, tomo III, Control of Installations.

21. AGN, COJO, caja 401, December 18, 1967. In the margins of a report given to the Mexico City authorities by Dr. Joshua Saenz, the president of the Mexican Olympic Committee, Comité Olímpico Mexicano, informe a la asemblea, México DF by the president of the committee, an anonymous Mexican official put a line through text that described Mexico as an underdeveloped country and wrote "*en vías de desarrollo*" (developing).

22. Interview with Pedro Ramírez Vázquez.

23. *Excélsior*, February 27, 1968; *El Nacional*, February 29, 1968, editorial, covering the vote on February 26, 1968, by the African Supreme Sports Council to boycott the Olympic Games.

24. Interview with Ramírez Vázquez.

25. For details of the IOC correspondence and debate concerning the South Africa issue, see IOC archive, file no. 0101561, Comites nationaux olympiques (Afrique du Sud 1968). Also see various correspondence relating to South Africa in the IOC archive, Brundage Collection Reel 103, Box 179. There is no documentary evidence to suggest that the protest by Afro-American athletes within the Olympic stadium was connected to the stance of African nations. We thank C. L. Cole, Bob Edelman, and John MacAloon for their comments on this matter.

26. In this important matter, Latin American countries showed their fraternity by rallying to Mexico's position. Interview with Ramírez Vázquez.

27. Interview with Ramírez Vázquez. Ramírez Vázquez envisaged twenty cultural events to match the twenty sporting events that were already scheduled. Also see AGN, COJO, Box 300, 40, CO-Presidencia, copy of speech by Ramírez Vázquez to the Society of Architects of the Instituto Politécnico Nacional, dated November 15, 1967.

28. *El Universal*, on March 20, 1965, reports on the findings of trainer Bud Winter, who blamed an inadequate diet and a weak physical condition for the probability of Mexico's poor performance at the 1968 Olympic Games. AGN, COJO, caja 401, December 18, 1967. A report given by Dr. Joshua Saenz, the president of the Mexican Olympic Committee, underlines that Mexicans were "not a strong race." Mexicans had been unable to excel in sporting activities due to centuries of poor health, diet, and poverty. He stressed that the 1968 Olympic Games should be seen as a springboard for future development.

29. Even after Mexico's unprecedented medal haul in the 1968 Olympics, this attitude persisted. In an article (in *El Heraldo de México*, June 14, 1978) entitled "Why Mexicans Always Lose," the writer consoled his readers by suggesting that at least they could be proud that the Mexican was an "*artista de alma*" (artist by nature).

30. The full extent of the cultural program fills the pages of vol. 4 of the Official Report of the Mexican Organizing Committee.

31. IOC archive, file 0100677, Correspondence 1965–1971. See letters between Duncan and Johann Westerhoff, Secretary General of the IOC, dated July 15, 1968, and July 19, 1968.

32. IOC archive, file 0100624, Correspondence COJO, 1963–1967. See letter from Brundage to Lord David Killanin, dated July 17, 1967. This largely accounts for the scaling down of overseas contributions to the Munich Cultural Program and its concentration upon diverse aspects of German culture.

33. For a thoughtful essay on the links between a "Golden Age" and nationalism, see Smith (1997).

34. For examples in newspapers, see "Foro de Excélsior," *Excélsior*, December 22, 1966, and "Principio unificador," *Excélsior*, February 25, 1968. See also President Díaz Ordaz's inaugural speech to the Assembly of the IOC in *El Sol de México*, October 8, 1968, and a poem written as Pindaric odes that compares the Greek and Aztec cultures, Eusabio Castro, "Olímpica 68," in *Olympiad 68* (Chicago: Illinois State University Press, 1971).

35. See *Carta Olímpica 14: Timbres postales preolimpicos*, AGN, COJO, Mexico City.

36. Further details regarding the development of the Mexico 68 designs can be found in Ramírez Vázquez (1989, 143–58). See also Rivera Conde (1999, 13–38).

37. Interview with Ramírez Vázquez.

38. This should not be taken to infer that the Organizing Committee had any part in countering the student movement. Ramírez Vázquez convincingly argues that the committee did not share the government's view that the students were trying to disrupt

the Olympic Games. Indeed, as he points out, many of the temporary employees of the committee (*edecanes*) were students, and the Olympic Stadium located within the university campus was never targeted.

39. Cited in *Excélsior*, August 29, 1968.

40. Interview with Ramírez Vázquez. See also an interview with Cantinflas in *El Nacional*, February 10, 1965. Original footage of the Cantinflas clips can be viewed at the Filmoteca Nacional, Mexico City.

41. "La Brocha Olímpica," in *Excélsior*, January 29, 1968. "Vestir a la Ciudad," in *Novedades*, November 22, 1967, urges more effort to clean up the city; "Nuestro Rostro Limpio," in *El Nacional*, January 20, 1968, urges the citizens of Mexico City to do likewise. See also "Los Males de la Olimpiadad," *El Universal*, July 22, 1968, in which the article portrays Mexico City as an innocent country girl who tries to adopt the gestures and mannerisms of the big city.

42. Visual images of the closing ceremony appear in the Official Film of the 1968 Mexico City Games, but a more illuminating commentary and footage appear in "La Clausora de la Olimpiada XIX" Cine Mundial, to be found in the Filmoteca Nacional, Mexico City.

References

Aguilar Camín, Héctor, and Lorenzo Meyer. 1994. *In the shadows of the Mexican revolution*. Austin: University of Texas Press.

Arbena, Joseph L. 2002. Hosting the Summer Olympic Games: Mexico City, 1968. In *Sport in Latin America and the Caribbean*, ed. Joseph Arbena and David LaFrance. Willington, DE: Scholarly Resources.

Beezley, William H. 1987. *Judas and the Jockey Club and other episodes in Porfirian Mexico*. Lincoln: University of Nebraska Press.

Brewster, Keith. 2004. Redeming the "Indian": Sport and ethnicity in post-revolutionary Mexico. *Patterns of Prejudice* 38 (3): 213–31.

———. 2005. "Patriotic pastimes." The role of sport in post-revolutionary Mexico. *The International Journal of the History of Sport* 22 (2): 139–57.

Carr, Barry. 1992. *Marxism and Communism in twentieth century Mexico*. Lincoln: University of Nebraska Press.

Dent, D.W. 1999. *The legacy of the Monroe doctrine: A reference guide to U.S. involvement in Latin America and the Caribbean*. London: Greenword Press.

Handelman, Howard. 1997. *Mexican politics: The dynamics of change*. New York: St. Martin's Press.

LaFeber, W. 1994. *The American age*. New York: Norton.

Nairn, Tom. 1997. *Faces of nationalism: Janus revisited*. London: Verso.

Paz, Octavio. 1990 [1950]. *The labyrinth of solitude: Life and thought in Mexico*. London: Penguin.

Pike, F. B. 1997. *The United States and Latin America*. Austin: University of Texas Press.

Pinchetti, Francisco Ortiz. 1978. Políticamente, el movimiento triunfó. *Proceso*, October 2, p. 11.

Ramírez Vázquez, Pedro. 1989. *Ramírez Vázquez en la arquitectura*. Mexico: Editorial Diana.

————. 2001. 1910 Mexico City: Space and nation in the city of the centenario. In *Viva México! Viva la Independencia!: Celebrations of September 16*, ed. William H. Beezley and David E. Lorey. Wilmington: Scholarly Resources Books.

Rivera Conde, Sergio. 1999. El diseño en la XIX Olimpíada: Entrevista al Arq. Pedro Ramírez Vázquez. *Creación y cultura* 1 (1): 13–38.

Rodda, John. 1968a. After the Games are over. *The Guardian*, November 1, p. 10.

————. 1968b. Trapped at gunpoint in the middle of fighting. *The Guardian*, October 4, pp. 1–2.

Schoultz, L. 1998. *Beneath the United States: A history of U.S. policy toward Latin America*. Cambridge, MA: Harvard University Press.

Smith, Anthony. 1997. The "Golden Age" and national renewal. In *Myths and nationhood*, ed. Geoffrey Hosking and George Schopflin. London: Hurst and Co.

Tenorio-Trillo, Mauricio. 1996. *Mexico at the World Fairs*. Berkeley: University of California Press.

Chapter 7

Munich 1972

Re-presenting the Nation

Christopher Young

INTRODUCTION

"It was very quiet . . . looking down into that little walkway. In a sense you were looking down into the cockpit of world events. Of that year, of that decade, maybe of that quarter-century" (Reeve 2000, 57). The voice is that of Gerald Seymour, ITN reporter at the 1972 Olympic Games in Munich, and the scene being described is not that moment where a great athlete—an Olga Korbut or a Mark Spitz—stands on the cusp of greatness but the eerie silence that had broken into the sporting storm of the 20th Olympiad. In the early hours of September 5, heavily armed members of the Palestinian group, Black September, turned terrorism into a global televisual spectacle for the first time by entering the Olympic Village, where they murdered two Israeli athletes and took nine of their teammates hostage in 31 *Connollystraße*. For many, the day-long siege, and its disastrous dénouement at Fürstenfeldbruck military airport, where all of the hostages lost their lives during the Bavarian police's inept attempt to resolve the situation, has remained a Kennedy moment. For the state of Israel, it represented much more. Within days, PLO bases in Syria and Lebanon were razed to the ground in the largest operations of their kind since the Six-Day War (1967); within months, Golda Meir had given approval for Operation Wrath of God that, in a change to policy, would not only hunt down those directly involved in the specific attack but also launch a secret war against Palestinian leaders (Reeve 2000, 126–32). Over a third of a century later, as Uzi Mahnaimi noted in a *Sunday Times* article on August 24, 2003, participants in Ariel Sharon's security cabinet responded to a suicide bombing of a bus that killed twenty ultra-orthodox Jews in Tel Aviv by drawing parallels to the Munich massacre and the Israeli government's retaliation. For Israel, Munich is both still an open wound and a productive matrix of collective memory.

117

For Germany, the events of Munich reopened wounds that it was desperately trying to heal. Conrad Ahlers, Willy Brandt's press secretary, announcing—tragically incorrectly, as it was to turn out—that all of the hostages had been released, told the world: "For us Germans it was a tragic situation that all this happened to Jewish people." He was relieved that the danger had passed, "otherwise some of the old memories might have come back" (Reeve 2000, 107). In his memoirs, Brandt himself later underlined the sentiment: "My disappointment at the time was intense, first because the Olympics on which we had expended so much loving care would not go down in history as a happy occasion—indeed, I was afraid that our international reputation would be blighted for many years—and secondly because our counter-measures had proved so abortive" (Brandt 1978, 439–41). Both the order of Brandt's regrets (which prioritize the self over the other) and the list of key words—history, international reputation, loving care, and happiness—are telling. Munich was Germany's chance to showcase its rehabilitation as a peace-loving, democratic state where the past was a foreign country. For such a purpose, the Olympic Games, where the host nation can allow its own world vision to rub up against the set elements of Olympic ritual, is the perfect vehicle and medium.

Going by current estimates, one person out of two of the world's population watches the Olympic Games; in its wonderfully stereotypical fifth bulletin to foreign journalists, *2638 Fakten*, the organizers of the Munich Games calculated that it would have taken thirty-four years of filling the 80,000-seat Olympic Stadium every day to have reached the equivalent of the world TV audience for the opening ceremony alone. With this much immediately transmittable symbolic capital at stake, it is hardly surprising that state and regional governments are keen to get their hands on the Olympic Games. Over the last ten years, the Turkish government has spent in the region of 100 million pounds on three unsuccessful bids for Istanbul; in the late winter of 1965, it took Willi Daume (president of the West German NOC) just one month to secure guarantees of equal funding from the city of Munich, the regional government of Bavaria, and the federal government. Any remaining doubt about the symbolic power of the Olympics would have been erased by the devastatingly eloquent observation of Issa, the leader of the Palestinian group, Black September, in Munich. Replying to the offer of Hans-Dietrich Genscher and several others, including Willy Brandt's son, to stand in for the hostages, Issa apologized, saying "the Germans had produced an excellent Olympic Games, but it offered the Palestinians a showcase where they could bring their grievance to the millions watching around the world" (Reeve 2000, 51). Much has been written about the Israeli and Palestinian side of this story. This chapter looks at the German perspective.

THE OLYMPICS IN GERMAN POLITICS, 1945–1972

It is ironic that the best seat in the house for the terrorist attack on September 5 was in the block opposite 31 *Connollystraße* that housed the team of the GDR (German Democratic Republic). This tragic spatial configuration, which had athletes from the "other Germany" watch as Jewish blood was spilled on German soil again, could well stand as a metaphor for the major tensions in relations between politics and sport during the cold war standoff between the GDR and the FRG (Federal Republic of Germany). Sporting institutions—and above all those that interacted with the IOC—were caught up in highly politicized discourses (often against their will) about *Vergangenheitsbewältigung* ("coming to terms with the past") and recognition of the GDR.

Borrowing terms from Foucault's theory of discourse (particularly 1972), who draws our attention away from the rhetorical mechanisms of the spoken word to the various pressures and forces that make the linguistic articulation possible, we could say that the notion of the Federal Republic as the sole representative of Germany in the postwar years could be described as the formation of an object; the non-recognition of the GDR in Western discourse is the non-formation of an object; sport is a surface of emergence, or thwarted emergence; and the West German government, other Western governments (primarily the allies and NATO), and various sporting bodies, both international (primarily the IOC, IAAF [International Amateur Athletic Federation], and FIFA) and national (e.g., NOC), act as the authorities of delimitation. The basic unit of Foucault's analysis is the "statement"—a type of *basic meaning* that can have various non-identical individual enunciations. *The* statement that sustained postwar German political discourse and which postwar German political discourse tried to make a part of sporting discourse is the *Alleinvertretung* ("sole representation"). It soon became apparent that this was not going to be an easily transferable statement. Adenauer described FIFA's decision to give official recognition to the GDR as a "deep blow" (Blasius 2001, 110).[1] But even internally, sport had its own dynamic—a prime example of this is the way in which Manfred Ewald, sport supremo of the GDR, was able to directly defy Honecker by not bringing his athletes home from Munich as a result of the attack on the Israeli team (Krebs 1999, 281). The combination of external global institutions and the internal dynamic of sport was to mean a gradual slippage between the discourses of sport and politics in Germany.[2]

This slippage was no more apparent than in the later years of Adenauer's government. After years of shifting and mounting pressure between the IOC, the Federal Republic, the GDR, and the USSR—manifest on the world stage (from 1956) by a joint Olympic team with a neutralized flag but separate national anthems—the cracks were beginning to show. While the Western world gradually moved on—the flag of the GDR was flown at the World Ice Hockey Championships in the United States in 1963—Adenauer's stance hardened. The proto-*Realpolitik* of Willi Daume and the then mayor of Berlin, Willy Brandt—to bid for a Berlin Olympics after the erection of the Berlin Wall—fell on deaf ears in governmental circles. Daume's proposal for two separate teams under one flag for the 1964 Tokyo Olympics was rejected by the ministry of the interior and the IOC alike, both holding firm to their own projected realities of one Germany. At the same time, West German clubs were forbidden from arranging matches with East German counterparts at the grassroots sporting level.

But change was not far around the corner. When the IAAF, under Cambridge alumnus Marquis of Exeter, gave full recognition to the Athletics Association of the GDR in 1964, the game was up. After the capitulation of the most Olympic of Olympic sports, the IOC could do little else than recognize the GDR in 1965—as "Ostdeutschland," a geographical area, participating along with the West German "Deutschland" as two separate teams under one Olympic German flag (equating almost exactly to Daume's rejected suggestion for 1964). Despite some discussion of a separate NATO Olympics as a consequence, the Olympic 1968 Games went ahead as planned.

The German government's loss was German sport's gain, and things began to happen all at once for Daume. Cashing in on the sensitive way he had been seen to handle the recognition battle, and—as he was later wont to recount—doing a deal with the Russians (who eventually got the 1980 Olympic Games), Daume bid for and won the 1972 Olympic Games for Munich in April 1966. Not long afterward, the change of government from the conservative Christlich Demokratische Union (CDU) to the *Große Koalition* ("grand coalition" of CDU and the social democratic Sozialdemokratische Partei Deutschlands [SPD]) brought a fresh wind to the relation between sport and politics. But there was one final snag that even caught the new foreign minister, Willy Brandt, unaware. How could the FRG host an Olympic Games but not hoist its own flag? The foreign office feared that having to fly the German Olympic flag rather than that of the Federal Republic proper would be viewed as a "sort of national sacrifice," with "extensive and long-lasting psychological consequences" (Blasius 2001, 297).[3] The GDR was also aware of the symbolic capital to be made by appearing in Munich as a completely separate NOC with its own flag, and after the success of 1968 it began pushing for full recognition. By 1968, the Munich organizers were asked to give assurances that they would abide by IOC regulations, *whatever these might be*, in 1972. The West Germans hesitated. At the 1968 session, the GDR was fully recognized by the IOC as Deutschland D. R. Having already invested DM 900 million, and understanding the huge loss of face that giving up the Olympic Games would have entailed, the German government considered all possibilities, including declaring the city of Munich to have Vatican City status for the duration of the Olympic Games, thus effectively banishing the GDR flag to foreign soil (Blasius 2001, 305). In the end, the West Germans capitulated, and the way was paved for the flags of both Germanies to be paraded and celebrated for the first time at the Olympic Games.

But with the new SPD government under Kanzler Brandt (from September 1969), this was far from an own goal for the home team. With two *Realpolitiker* at the helm, sport and politics found themselves in the closest harmony since the earliest days of the republic. Moreover, there might well have been one very direct way in which Brandt allowed the discourse of sport to stabilize political discourse. It had often been the case that sport ran ahead of politics in ways in which politics found uncomfortable. It could be postulated, however, that Brandt instrumentalized the Olympics in the Olympic year itself. Various movements within his coalition with the FDP (Freie Demokratische Partei) left him without an absolute majority in April 1972, and there was heavy opposition from the CDU toward plans for the *Ostverträge* (Treaties with the Eastern Bloc whereby both Germanies, without official recognition of each other, would not treat each other as foreign territory). Brandt agreed to call for a vote of confidence, but not until after the summer recess (on September 20—ten days after the scheduled end of the Olympic Games). It was widely rumored at the time that there had been a pact made to postpone the inevitable election so as not to disrupt the Olympic Games (Mandell 1991, 4). This might well have been the case, but Brandt was surely not unaware of the power of sport to influence popular perception. Surely the election—which was essentially a referendum on the *Ostverträge*—would go better after the GDR had been recognized on German soil in the hermetically sealed but hugely symbolic arena of the Olympic Games. Indeed, running under the banner of "Deutsche, wir können stolz sein auf unser Land!" ("Germans, we can be proud of our country"), Brandt led the SPD to its best election result ever, just two months after the close of the Olympic Games.

While the awarding of the Olympic Games to Munich brought about some form of resolution to the notion of *Alleinvertretung*, it did, however, re-open the issue of *Vergangenheitsbewältigung*. This re-emerged from two directions: directly from the GDR with typical cold-war brio (an aspect that for economy of space this chapter will bracket out; see Krebs 1999, 275) and in a much more indirect and tortured way from within the Federal Republic itself. The focus of this chapter now shifts from Olympics in German politics to politics in the German Olympics.

POLITICS IN THE GERMAN OLYMPICS

When Lord Killanin rose to the climax of his closing and farewell speech at the Moscow Games, he pulled no punches. With the double blow of Montreal's financial disaster and Moscow's boycott, Killanin, who had taken over from Brundage in 1972, had found the presidency of the IOC no sinecure:

"I implore the sportsmen of the world to unite in peace before the holocaust descends. . . . The Olympic Games are for the benefit of our children" (Lord Killanin 1983, 219). Eight years earlier, however, with the Games held almost in the physical shadow of Dachau and, from the halfway stage on, with the stain of Jewish blood on the freshly laid floors of the Olympic Village just a five-minute leisurely stroll from the main site, it was very much a case of "don't mention the war." There is no better place to outline the ways in which the Organizing Committee dealt with the German historical legacy than in the opening statement of its Official Report—1.1 *Die Anregung* (Official Report, 23). Three interesting strands comprise the argument: Germany's projected role as savior of the Olympic movement; claims of continuity with the past; and, then, in relation to the past, silences and ruptures.[4]

Regeneration: The idea for the Olympic Games was not "spontaneous" but rather a "sacrifice and duty" on the part of Germany and "an attempt to make a small contribution to the survival of the Olympic ideal" (Official Report, 23),[5]—a gesture toward debates about rising nationalism and professionalization in Olympic sport. The notion of "regeneration" is highly significant, for if Coubertin's driving vision was that of the renovator of ancient ideals, then in modern Olympic history these renovated ideals more often than not acted as a regeneration for the host city or, indeed, the nation. In most recent times, the city of Barcelona had a full Olympic makeover, and this was certainly the case in Munich, too, which received its underground as an Olympic spin-off, as recently recalled positively by the head of Berlin's now shelved bid for the 2012 and 2016 Olympics. But more importantly perhaps in the present context is the way in which the Olympic Games gradually brought the defeated nations of the war back into the international family. The first three Games after the war went to victors, neutrals, and semi-neutrals, London (1948), Helsinki (1952), and Melbourne (1956), then to the losers, Rome (1960) and Tokyo (1964)—Olympic Games reputed with giving Japan a new image of efficiency with which we stereotype it today, rather in the same way that the Barcelona Games killed off the mañana image of Spain)—and then, after the Third World interlude of Mexico City (1968), Munich. Far from regenerating the Games, the Games were intended to regenerate Germany: it was, to quote Killanin again, "an event of immense world significance. It was intended to show the world that Germany had risen from the ashes of war, and that its youth could take part in wholesome sporting competitions" (Lord Killanin 1983, 63).

Continuity: More interesting than Germany's transferral of regeneration is the reasons it claims that Germany is *the* country to act as regenerating agent, for this is based on two key continuities. First, it is stated that although a Frenchman might have reinvented the Olympic Games, the Germans in the form of nineteenth-century archaeologists (Curtius and Schliemann) had actually *been there* first (Official Report, 23). Second, Germany had an organizational pedigree when it came to the Olympic Games themselves: the "good intention" of the 1916 games "entrusted" to Berlin in Sweden "had been ruined" by World War II (Official Report, 23), but then there were the successfully executed games of 1936.[6] This organizational history assured the bidding team for 1972 that it could rely on the "the latent willingness, consent, and support of broad sections of the population" (Official Report, 23).[7] On the one level, these are extraordinary words. On the other hand, how do you create a sporting *Stunde Null* ("zero hour") within the framework of an event that lives off an unbroken tradition reaching back at least to the nineteenth century and, in terms of its self-image, back to antiquity? And it is, after all, this continuity that makes the Olympics such a powerful engine of regeneration. So, by definition, the *Stunde Null* effect cannot escape the strictures of continuity. For the Germans, it was a difficult balancing act. In 1962, for instance, Daume delivered a damning verdict on the 1936 Olympic Games to Foreign Minister Schröder in an attempt to get him to support the idea of a Berlin Olympics in 1968 to foil a potential bid by the Soviets: "Hitler's greatest hour and the greatest hour of the Third Reich, according to international opinion, was in 1936 during and after the Olympic Games in Berlin. Moscow would pursue the same goals with even more cunning propaganda and greater means."[8] Yet here is Daume (who carefully proofread every word of the report) using the 1936 Olympic Games to create a sense of German Olympic credentials. These credentials were well anchored in Olympic collective memory, as IOC President Brundage's letter to Daume in November 1965 clearly shows: "The 1936 Games in Berlin were outstanding and are still remembered by all of us as establishing new standards in Olympic organization and performance."[9]

In fact, the continuities were more than localized linguistic occurrences in the official report. There is room here to give just two examples. First, the arts. Coubertin had a vision of an all-encompassing festival to celebrate human achievement in which the arts would play much more than just a supporting role to sport. There can be no doubt that the Munich Olympics put on a splendid festival of the arts. There were top class theatrical and musical performances (e.g., the Berliner Ensemble, the Royal Shakespeare Company), fabulous exhibitions (e.g., *Weltkulturen und Moderne Kunst*), and a limited edition of posters based on twenty-eight specially commissioned paintings from Olympic-standard stars of the modern art world (e.g., Kokoschka, Hockney). Munich claims that it is returning the Olympic Games to the principles of Coubertin. Keith and Claire Brewster's work in this volume on Mexico City 1968 (which hosted a huge arts festival) would indicate that this is—at best— a much-overstated claim. In fact, the Germans' willful neglect of Mexican achievements amounts to an act of Western self-absorbsion and says a great deal about Germany's self-image as a *Kulturnation*. More interesting still, however, is that Diem's 1936 Olympic Games set standards in the provision for the arts unparalleled until well into the postwar era. Munich's return to Coubertinian principles cannot therefore stand in isolation from Berlin. Second, civic boosterism—a different sort of example altogether, but one that shows the range of areas in which continuities exist. For the 1936 Olympic Games the Berlin organizers put on an exhibition entitled *Die deutschen Leibesübungen des Mittelalters in Buch und Bild* ("German Physical Exercises in the Middle Ages in Book and Picture").[10] In fact, it ranged from the courtly period (with some of the finest medieval manuscripts, e.g., Manesse Codex, Veldeke, *Tristan*), over the early modern period (fencing manuals), and into the nineteenth century ("Turnvater Jahn"). In the earliest period, there are many examples of the *buhurt* (a particular type of medieval joust). Exactly the same sorts of examples are dredged up by Munich's second brochure to journalists in a section entitled *Spiel und Spaß in München* ("Fun and Games in Munich"): "But the Munich citizen's joie de vivre is not simply measured in terms of beer. In previous times there were also colorful games in the form of chivalric tournaments and pitched battles, known as *buhurt*."[11] On a pictorial level, Munich indulges in the same historical rhetoric, printing almost a replica of the 1936 exhibition catalogue.

Discontinuity: As a cursory knowledge of postwar German history and society would lead us to expect, where there is continuity, there is also rupture and silence. These are equally clearly visible and audible on the first page of the Official Report. The mention of Coubertin's reinvention of the Olympic Games in 1896 (Official Report, 23) is too brief to include the fact that it was boycotted—like all prewar Olympic Games (except London)—by all but a handful of rogue *Turner* for no other good reason than the fact that it was the brainchild of a Frenchman. The cancelled Olympics of 1916 are mentioned, but the 1940 Winter Olympics in Garmisch, for which Hitler authorized the beginning of construction work and which were cancelled as late as April 1940, are omitted. The archaeological pedigree of the Germans is underlined by further work on Olympia in the postwar years, but this completely ignores the fact that it was a Nazi initiative in 1936 under Walter Wrede to continue the work begun in the nineteenth century at Olympia, with 300,000 Reichsmarks over six years appropriated from Hitler's personal disposition fund (Marchand 1996). But the most interesting silence in the Official Report is the way that the 1936 Olympic Games themselves are dealt with: there is great emphasis on how they are bid for (in 1930), how they are awarded (in 1931), and how they are planned in detail (in 1932)—all before the Nazi's ascension to power in 1933. This emphasis is not by chance, as the very precise wording shows: "The document of Carl Diem, later General Secretary of the Organizing Committee, which he put together in October 1932, included all plans as they were later executed on the *Reichssportfeld* in Berlin" (Blasius 2001, 291).[12] As Christiane Eisenberg (1999, 409–29) has recently—controversially, but I think convincingly—shown, the organization of the Berlin Games was marked by an institutional and ideological combination of collaboration and resistance in which sport and politics exploited each other to varying degrees of mutual benefit. In the case of the Munich organizers, however—despite (mainly unacknowledged) continuities—the Berlin Games were like the whole of the German past and national history: in the words of Peter Pulzer (1995, 6–7) "a black hole [. . .], a liability." The uneasy relation to the past comes up in many other areas of the Games, such as the holding of a ceremony at Dachau on the eve of the Games, which goes completely unmentioned in the Official Report. This is a clear example of what W. G. Sebald has referred to as the West German's propensity to "recognize, yet look away" (Sebald 2003, 12). This uneasy encounter with the past was torn between the equally important needs for continuity and rupture.

I now leave the first page of the Official Report to exemplify how this "difficult past" and politics in general impinge on just one other area of the Games: their aesthetic presentation.

In his excellent book on Munich architecture after the war, *Munich and Memory*, Gavriel D. Rosenfeld notes that throughout the Federal Republic, modernism had become identified as the architecture of democracy (e.g., Sep Ruf's 1964 private residence for the German chancellor): "Constructed of light materials such as glass and steel, open and transparent in appearance, modern architecture stood in clear contrast to the heavy, monumentalized neoclassical architecture favored by the Nazi (and Stalinist) dictatorship" (Rosenfeld 2000, 153). Rosenfeld cites Munich's Olympic Stadium as "the most dramatic demonstration of the widespread acceptance of modernism's political and historical symbolism." Certainly most voices within the public debate in 2000–2001 in reaction to Franz Beckenbauer's bid to have the stadium modernized beyond recognition or ripped down to accommodate his beloved Bayern Munich in a more football-friendly arena would bear out Rosenfeld's claim. Almost thirty years on, Munich's stadium was to be saved not only on aesthetic grounds, but due to its essential role in portraying a transparent, democratic, and, above all, new Germany (see Young 2003). One needs only to think of the technologically groundbreaking and stunningly beautiful *Zeltdach* (tent roof) that cost over a quarter of the final bill for the whole Olympic site to grasp the essence of the enterprise.

But the roof, although defining, in no way dominated the site. It might have been transparent, but it was not simply a democratic overlay. The Olympic venues were situated at the *Oberwiesenfeld*, which lay to the north of the city in a largely unattractive industrial area. The field itself had a significant history. Until World War I it was the parade ground of the Munich Garrison; after World War II it became a dumping site for the rubble removed from the city center. The architects, Gunther Behnish and partners (a sort of 1960s'–1970s'

German Norman Foster), had a clear vision of what was to be done. They were to mold the rubble into a rolling landscape, dam up several canals to make a lake, and at all cost avoid the axial monumentalism of the Berliner *Reichssportfeld*. Munich was to gain not just new sports facilities but the legacy of a park where its citizens could walk in peaceful surroundings. One gets a clear picture of their task and aims when one considers that Behnish and the vast team of specifically chosen up-and-coming young architects played around for months with sand-pits to make their initial model. The specific objective was to design the build-ings in perfect proportion with the *Menschen* (human beings) who would use them and walk around them (Official Report, 29). To this end, as Günther Grzimek, the landscape architect, describes it, the buildings were "pressed into the ground" (Grzimek 1992, 33), many of them sunk up to halfway into the ground (a problem, incidentally, that undid the Bayern plan to sink the pitch by several meters, which would have plunged the stadium into a deep-lying water basin). The main stadium itself was roofed on one side only, letting the other almost spill out into the rest of the site, in particular, allowing it to open out onto an Olympic mound, where a great deal of the rubble had been pushed together. The Olympic mound, which redefined the perspective of the Olympic spectacle by allowing the public to look down into the stadium and the spectators inside of the stadium to look beyond the stands outward, was covered, like most of the rest of the site in pasture taken from the nearby Bavarian Alps.

But as I have pointed out, the site, with its alpine grass and Plexiglas roof, is more than a cover-up of the past. And here I disagree with Rosenfeld's con-clusion that the success of Munich's modernist Olympic memory was bought ironically at the cost of a "declining consciousness of the Nazi past" (Rosenfeld 2000, 156). It is helpful to consider the relationship between landscape and memory following the dynamic cultural political model of Simon Schama (1996), for in Munich the relationship between nature and architectural design is deliberately a highly reflective one. The Official Report talks repeatedly about the constructedness of the park's nature: it is "new nature," "created na-ture," and, most tellingly, "the nature of nature-alienated cities" (Official Re-port, 29).[13] In this nature, created out of the remains of devastation, buildings become "part of the landscape" (Official Report, 29).[14] The *Zeltdach* was com-plemented by trees; sky, roof, and lake were to merge into one. But there is more. If you stand at the top of the stadium and look across to the rest of the park, there is a wonderful optical illusion: the gently rising and falling curves of the *Zeltdach* in other parts of the site look as though they could be the Alps (which in fact can be seen from the top of the *Olympiaturm*). This can be gleaned from pictures of the site, although the effect is not mentioned in any of the main accounts of Behnisch's achievement. The observant spectator at the stadium, however, will notice that the effect is not only a real one, as it were, not just a photographic one, but also that from the bridge over the outer ring at dusk there is an equally striking alienation effect between the *Zeltdach* and the Olympic Tower, whose sheer size casts the roof from which one has walked minutes earlier into such perspective that it appears momentarily to the observer as though it has to be the Alps. In his essay "Toward a Poetics of Culture," Stephen Greenblatt describes a similar moment of optical reflexivity as he looked at the plaque pointing the way to the Nevada Falls in Yosemite Park, an event that called "attention to the interpenetration of nature and artifice that makes the distinction possible" (Greenblatt 1989, 9). No doubt about it, Munich's architecture and landscaping is a sophisticatedly constructed site of reflection and self-reflection.

The reflection that is part of its very fabric did not, however, prevent the site from making statements. It was to be a *Welt ohne Verbotsschilder* (world without signs of prohibition)—an aspect rather comically articulated in the official journalists' pack: *Bitte den Rasen betreten! Bitte die Blumen pflücken!* (Please go on the grass! Please pick the flowers!) And it was to create a sense of time and space. Grzimek (1992, 33) describes the *Zeltdach* as being similar to a circus and Peter Blundell Jones (2000, 65) as that of nomadic tribes (in this case, sporting nomads). The architecture creates, therefore, the perfect setting for what anthropologist Victor Turner describes as the temporal essence of all rituals: the fact that they are "time out." It was to create "time for pausing" so that the "Olympic fluidity could be experienced" (Official Report, 30).[15] Spatially, Munich was to be a "space of understanding, of truly supra-regional communication" that would be possible "without great words" (Official Report, 30). Whoever came to marvel at the electronic communication systems, of which the Germans were so proud, would find in greater measure "human communication."[16] All of this is most neatly captured in the development of the pictograms that have since become a lingua franca of the sporting world. The park was constructed with amazing attention to this detail: paths were given the optimum width to encourage "forums of unforced human movement" (Official Report, 30), set at the right incline to make their users relax, and plotted to take them exactly along the lines that they would have walked naturally.[17]

The architectural construct was supported by the aesthetic vision of graphic designer Otl Aicher, who took control of every visual aspect of the color scheme for the whole event, from the seats in the stadium (which he also designed) to the design and layout of every document, file, poster, and even the flags that adorned the site, the city, and its transport hubs. Aicher's guiding principle was "equality/uniformity through relationship" (this and following quotations from the Official Report, 269), which he understood in a metaphorical as well as pragmatic sense. The key was to devise a "uniform and harmonious visual presentation" that would bring out the "meaning of the festival" and strive for *Leichtigkeit* (lightness) and avoid *Konformität* (conformity).[18] To achieve this, a wide range of experts was consulted: artists, sociologists, and (child) psychologists. The results were used for the pictogram system already mentioned, the color scheme, and the very font for every document. The main color was light blue, which was supported by green, white, and silver. Daume was wont to describe the color scheme as a Bavarian summer's morning. His designers were even more detailed at translating their scheme into the Munich landscape: for instance, the grassy banks of the lakes were planted exclusively with a silver leaf-bearing tree. Aicher was also famous for stating: "*Mit Farben kann man Politik machen*" ("You can do politics with colors"). It is why the Rainbow Games had a rainbow of violet, orange, yellow, green, and light blue, but not the color red, for Aicher and Daume, *the* color of dictatorship and to- talitarianism (Mandell 1991, 3). The font chosen after painstaking considera- tion by Aicher had one main purpose: it had to avoid "aggressive sizes" (Official Report, 269).

But not everything was new. The reverse side of the Olympic medals that was left free for each host nation to design, for instance, was made the re- sponsibility of one of the last surviving members of the *Bauhaus*, Gerhard Marcks. His design of Castor and Pollux not only fits clearly with the mini- malist elegance of the overall visual concept but invokes clear memories of the *Bauhaus* style. The design, therefore, is not without a certain historical resonance—Nazi persecution—and it surely cannot be accidental that the two figures holding onto each other give a clear impression of emaciation. Günther Grzimek's concluding remarks on the Olympic site set this tension into the broader scheme of things: "In its conception as the people's park, the Olympic Park was an answer to our time. We didn't want to remain silent about who we were, where and how we lived" (Grzimek 1992, 37).[19] But no- tice: an *answer to* not a *reflection of*. In projecting a new Germany, Munich was not at all a package of neat solutions but in some way an answer to a set of German questions.

This sense of tension is most apparent in the arrangements for the Olympic spectacle.[20] The opening ceremony was a reflection of all of the ele- ments I have just been mentioning: *Leichtigkeit, Heiterkeit*, and so on. The music was performed by the Westdeutscher Rundfunk's Entertainment Or- chestra under the sky-blue suited Kurt Edelhagen, who conducted his band at a rhythm set at 114 beats per minute—the scientifically proven optimal relaxed pace for a stroll. It was the first time that athletes entering an Olympic stadium had not been accompanied by a military band—a fact noted with some relief by Sebastian Haffner in the *Frankfurter Allgemeine Zeitung*, August 28, 1972: "Marching steps took a break—a remarkable event, especially in Germany."[21] The potential list of examples is endless. Yet outside the stadium, perambulat- ing along the pathways nestling gently into the rolling hills and leading down to the lake, there was street theatre. These free, spontaneous, and accessible *Spielstraßen* were supposed to not only set a contrapuntal note to the highly tuned performances of the sporting arena but through their sense of carnival (deep-sea diving in a paddling pool, the blind discus thrower) pose critical questions about the relation between sport and politics. Some of the major, planned sketches had very dark overtones: *Müllwagen der Geschichte* (the dustbin of history) ended with the world being destroyed at the 2000 Olympics by extremists. But as fate would have it, Bakhtinian devices were the last thing that Munich needed to conjure up a sense of doom. After the terrorist attack, the closing ceremony, which was supposed to seal a fortnight of *Heiterkeit*, had to be toned down beyond recognition. Security was heightened, and the machine guns that the Germans had hoped to avoid for the sake of their image were very much in evidence. During the ceremony, Joachim Fuchsberger, the stadium announcer, noticed that the VIP boxes were being vacated at an alarming rate. A colleague appeared at his box and pressed a scribbled message against the glass: "Two unidentified flying objects on course for the Olympic stadium; possible bombing; say what you think best."[22] Fearing a stampede, Fuchsberger kept his council, and the two off-course private planes found their bearings again. The date, coincidentally, was September 11.

This chilling anecdote could hardly provide a better example of the tragic uncertainty and dismay that reigned at the end of the Munich Olympic Games. For if the *Süddeutsche Zeitung* on September 7, 1972, is anything to go by, the terrible events of the Munich massacre utterly obliterated the Games organizers' attempt to rejoice in a new future and once again plunged the present deep into the past: "There may not exist a great city whose people are less imperialistic, less aggressive, more peaceable, more full of simple human qualities than those of the Bavarian metropolis. However, various slogans have stuck to the name 'Munich'. Capital of the [Nazi] 'movement'. Originator of politically ideological lawlessness. Site of the capitulation of the law before naked power. 'Brown' Munich. Bulwark of vengeance. However contourless and emotional these notions seem to us, they now appear to be confirmed."[23] Munich, 1972, it seems, offers a tragic illustration of what Sebald has recently re-emphasized: "Coming to terms with the past may be a contradiction in terms, because the past never gives up" (Phillips 2003, 17).

NOTES

1. Original: "tiefer Einbruch."

2. For an in-depth overview of this aspect of the period, see Blasius (2001).

3. Original: "eine Art nationale Selbstaufgabe"; "weitreichende und fortwirkende psychologische Konsequenzen."

4. These latter two categories are picked up by Kuhn, Lakämper, and Wimmert (2000, 27) of the *Deutsche Sporthochschule*, Cologne, in their document written to train student helpers for work with the public at the *Deutsches Sport-und Olympiamuseum* in Cologne: "Die Spiele von München 1972 waren aber nicht nur Kontrapunkt zu 1936,

sie waren gleichzeitig Fortsetzung, Weiterentwicklung." Like the notion of regeneration, however, I shall be subjecting continuities to a more critical analysis than the German sport museum.

5. Original: "spontan"; "opfervolle Aufgabe"; "den Versuch zu machen, einen kleinen Beitrag zum Überleben des Olympischen Gedankens."

6. Original: "gute Absicht"; "anvertraut"; "zunichte."

7. Original: "latente Bereitschaft [...] die Billigung und Unterstützung breiter Bevölkerungsschichten."

8. Original: "Hitlers größte Stunde und die größte Zeit des dritten Reiches, was internationalen Konsens angeht, waren 1936 während und nach den Olympischen Spielen in Berlin. Moskau würde das ganze Unternehmen mit noch geschickterer Propaganda und auch mit dem Einsatz noch größerer Mittel anlagen."

9. Stadtarchiv München, Olympiade 71 (cited in Schlüssel 2001, 524).

10. Die deutschen Leibesübungen des Mittelalters im Buch und Bild. Ausstellung des Reichs- und Preußischen Ministeriums für Wissenschaft, Erziehung und Volksbildung in der Preußischen Staatsbibliothek in Berlin (15. Juli bis 22. August 1936).

11. Original: "Aber nicht am Biergenuß ist die Lebensfreude der Münchener zu messen. Da gab es schon früh das farbenfrohe Schauspiel der Ritterturniere in der Form des Massenkampfes, der 'Buhurt' genannt wurde."

12. Original: "Die Denkschrift des späteren Generalsekretärs des Organisationskomitees, Dr. Carl Diem, die er im Oktober 1932 vorlegte und die die Billigung des NOK fand, enthielt alle Pläne so, wie sie auf dem Reichssportfeld später verwirklicht worden sind."

13. Original: "neue Natur"; "Natur geschaffen"; "die Natur der naturentfremdeten Großstädte."

14. Original: "Teil der Landschaft."

15. Original: "Zeit zum Verweilen"; "olympisches Fluidium gespürt werden könnte."

16. Original: "Raum des Verstehens, der wirklich überregionalen Kommunikation"; "ohne große Worte"; "menschliche Kommunikation."

17. Original: "Foren der ungezwungenen menschlichen Bewegung."

18. Original: "Gleichheit durch Verwandtschaft"; "uniformes, harmonisches Erscheinungsbild"; "Bedeutung des Festes."

19. Original: "Der Olympiapark ist in seiner Auffassung als Volkspark wie in seinen Einzelheiten eine Antwort auf unsere Zeit gewesen. Wir wollten nicht verschweigen, wer wir waren, wo und wie wir lebten."

20. An excellent discussion of the music at the opening ceremony is given by Schlüssel (2001, 519–714).

21. Cited in Schlüssel (2001, 701). Original: "Der Marschtritt hatte Pause—gerade in Deutschland ein bemerkenswerter Vorgang."

22. Cited at http://www.olympia72.de/110972a.htm. Original: "Zwei nicht iden-
tifizierte Flugobjekte im Anflug auf das Olympiastadium; möglicherweise Bombenab-
wurf; sag, was du für richtig hältst" (accessed June 1, 2003).

23. Cited in Reeve (2000, 229).

REFERENCES

Blasius, Tobias. 2001. *Olympische Bewegung, Kalter Krieg und Deutschlandpolitik 1949–1972.* Frankfurt am Main: Peter Lang.

Blundell Jones, Peter. 2000. *Günther Behnisch.* Basle: Birkhäuser.

Brandt, Willy. 1978. *People and politics: The years 1960–1975.* New York: Little, Brown and Company.

Eisenberg, Christiane. 1999. *"English sports" und deutsche Bürger: Eine Gesellschafts-geschichte 1800–1939.* Paderborn: Ferdinand Schöningh.

Foucault, Michel. 1972. *The archaeology of knowledge.* Translated from the French by A. M. Sheridan Smith. London: Tavistock.

Greenblatt, Stephen. 1989. Toward a poetics of culture. In *The new historicism,* ed. H. Aram Veeser. New York: Routledge.

Grzimek, G. 1992. Gedanken zur Gestaltung der Olympialandschaft. In *Behnisch und Partner: Bauten 1952–1992,* ed. J.-K. Schmidt and U. Zeller. Stuttgart: Verlag Gerd Hatje.

Krebs, Hans-Dieter. 1999. Die "doppelten Deutschen" (1965 bis 1988). In *Deutschland in der Olympischen Bewegung: Eine Zwischenbilanz,* ed. Manfred Lämmer. Frankfurt am Main: NOK für Deutschland.

Kuhn, Heike, Olaf Lakämper, and Jörg Wimmert. 2000. *Handreichung für die Erstel-lung und Durchführung museumpädagogischer Angebote am Deutschen Sport-und Olympiamuseum Köln.* Unpublished document, Institut für Sportgeschichte, Deutsche Sporthochschule Köln.

Lord Killanin. 1983. *My Olympic years.* New York: William Morrow and Company.

Mandell, Richard D. 1991. *Olympics of 1972: A Munich diary.* Chapel Hill: University of North Carolina Press.

Marchand, Suzanne L. 1996. *Down from Olympus: Archaeology and philhellenism in Ger-many 1750–1970.* Princeton: Princeton University Press.

[Official Report]. Organisationskomitee für die Spiele der XX. Olympiade München 1972. [1974] *Der Offizielle Bericht. Die Spiele, I.* Munich: proSport München.

Phillips, Adam. 2003. The truth, the whole truth. Review of *On the natural history of destruction, with essays on Alfred Andersch, Jean Amery, and Peter Weiss,* ed. W. G. Sebald. *The Observer* (Books) February 23, 17.

Pulzer, Peter. 1995. *German politics 1945–1995*. Oxford: Oxford University Press.

Reeve, Simon. 2000. *One day in September*. London: Faber and Faber.

Rosenfeld, G. D. 2000. *Munich and memory: Architecture, monuments, and the legacy of the Third Reich*. Berkeley and Los Angeles: University of California Press.

Schama, Simon. 1996. *Landscape and memory*. London: Fontana Press.

Schlüssel, Elizabeth Audrey Leckie. 2001. Zur Rolle der Musik bei den Eröffnungs- und Schlußfeiern der Olympischen Spiele von 1896 bis 1972. Ph.D. dissertation Deutsche Sporthochschule Köln.

Sebald, W. G. 2003. *On the natural history of destruction, with essays on Alfred Andersch, Jean Amery, and Peter Weiss*. Translated from the German by Anthea Bell. London: Hamish Hamilton.

Young, Christopher. 2003. Kaiser Franz and the communist bowl: Cultural memory and Munich's Olympic Stadium. *American Behavioral Scientist* 46 (11): 1476–90.

Chapter 8

Argentina 1978

Military Nationalism, Football Essentialism, and Moral Ambivalence

Eduardo P. Archetti

INTRODUCTION

In the novel by Antonio dal Masetto, *Hay unos tipos abajo* (1998), Pablo, during the weekend of the final of the World Cup played by Argentina against Holland, sees a suspicious car with two people inside parked at the corner of his house, located in a central neighborhood of Buenos Aires. He is not engaged in politics, but as a journalist he knows that he could be defined as an enemy of the military Junta. He and his fiancée undergo two extremely paranoid days. Dal Masetto recreates an odd atmosphere in which Pablo's fear of being kidnapped by a police or military squad is contrasted to the excitement and enthusiasm of the Argentines anticipating their World Cup triumph. We are in the middle of a sporting competition that covers over political repression, torture, and death. What goes through Pablo's head as a frightening possibiltiy takes on tragic dimensions in the novel by Martín Kohan, *Dos veces junio* (2002). The narrator is a soldier serving as a driver to a military doctor during the period of the World Cup. While the masses follow the matches by radio or television, the soldier waits outside River Plate stadium for the doctor, who is urgently needed: a tortured political prisoner is dying, and the experience and competence of Dr. Mesiano is required. Dr. Mesiano is more interested in football and the fate of Argentina's team in a crucial match than in saving a life— after all, terrorists do not deserve to be treated as human beings. The dying person could have been Pablo. In *La crítica de las armas* (2003) José Pablo Feinman has dramatically portrayed the contradictions of Argentine society that claimed order and peace while kidnapping and killing reigned. The main character, Epstein, a philosopher who has written revolutionary texts in the past, is obsessed by the idea of being kidnapped, and night after night he waits for the noise of the lift stopping on the floor of his flat, announcing the arrival of the military squad. Feinman writes:

> If he did not die, if he was not assassinated, Pablo Epstein knew that he would live in a country of cowards and accomplices. But he knew something more, even worse: he, necessarily, would participate in one of these two conditions, or in both, because he knew that he would behave as a coward, and he was unable to imagine how, in the terrible coming country, he could not be an accomplice. (2003, 21)

Argentine fiction has forcefully elaborated the moral dilemmas of the 1970s and reflected on the dark side of the World Cup. These recent novels show that the military period is still an open wound that produces both emotional consternation and controversial meanings. Nobody will deny that a mere thousand meters from the River Plate stadium, where the Argentine team played the first round and the final, was the ESMA (Navy Mechanical School). This was the largest torture and detention center of the military dictatorship. The horror was such that the prisoners could hear the celebration and joy coming from the stadium mingled with the screaming of the tortured inmates. Was it legitimate to be obsessed with the World Cup, pretending to ignore what was going on? Was it acceptable to support the national team under those circumstances? Was it justifiable to desire victory, knowing that this victory was the main explicit political aim of the military in power? Was it defensible to go onto the streets, singing and waving the national flag after Argentina's victory?

Twenty-five years after the World Cup, the journalist, de Vedia, summarizes the contradictory situation of Argentina in 1978:

> The core of the Argentine tragedy was the existence of a country divided in the middle, a nation cut by a dichotomy in which football and death competed in the most absurd contests. . . . In 1978 there was pain and death but also football and contentment. Life always flows in this way, with light and shadow . . . countries write their histories, with the soul full of joyfulness, and at the same time, full of pain. . . . We will play football without the shadow of death invading the stadiums, and we will cry for the lost lives. (*La Nación Deportiva*, June 25, 2003, p. 2)

In this chapter I shall attempt to reach a better understanding of the complex relationship between the Argentine passion and love of football and the nationalist ideology of the military junta. In the final section I shall elaborate on the moral ambivalence over the victory of the national team, a victory that has stimulated continuous discussions on what was right and wrong in Argentina.

Military Nationalism and the World Cup

The beginning of 1976 was extremely chaotic due to the extreme, gross political violence used by the paramilitary and military forces to combat opposing left-wing guerrilla groups, to the institutional crisis that began after the death of President Peron, and to the economic decline and crisis that, among other things, provoked an annual rate of inflation of 566.3 percent. In March of that year the inflation reached a historical peak: 56 percent. This was accompanied by a political assassination every five hours and a bomb explosion every three hours. From December 1975, the killings were aggravated by the uncontrolled activity of the paramilitary groups supported by the state and the rightist wing of the Peronist party in power. On March 24, the military overthrew President Isabel Martínez de Perón and installed a regime euphemistically called *Proceso de Reorganización Nacional* ("Process of National Reorganization"). Its proclaimed objectives were the reestablishment of the lost social order, the reorganization of the institutions, and the creation of better conditions for the return to an authentic democracy (Novaro and Palermo 2003, 20). In their own words, they intended to stay in power until the true values of Christian morality, the national tradition, and the dignity of being Argentine had been reinstated. The most important means were the eradication of the subversive leftist groups and the promotion of harmony between the state, the capital, and the workers. The insertion of Argentina in the western bloc of Christian nations fighting communism and opposing the socialist countries was defined as crucial (*La Nación*, March 25, 1976). The diagnosis of an intense moral, political, and social crisis was not far from reality, but of course the military forces were also an important part of the syndrome. They decided to act with the idea that they represented the only guarantee of order and that, in the process of governing, the required social consensus would be obtained. General Videla, who had been appointed president by the junta, declared that once its values and goals were accepted by civil society and political groups, a gradual transference of power could be made (Novaro and Palermo 2003, 27). The military forces, though, decided to hold power for a long period of time, and this time perspective was different from the other military regimes that had been in power in the recent past. The use of repression, torture, kidnapping, and assassination became normal. The results were dramatic: 30,000 people were murdered between 1976 and the end of the dictatorship in 1983. A country accustomed to military intervention and violence had never experienced cruelty and madness on this scale.

This was the context in which the World Cup was organized and carried out in an exemplary way. One could ask in retrospect: how could FIFA allow the World Cup to be played under such circumstances? How was it possible for fifteen other countries, many of them old democracies governed by progressive governments, to participate? The answer is simple: the dominant ideology prescribes that football and sport belong to civil society, thus independent of partisan state policies. It is assumed that football is not politics and never will be. The ideologist Polakovic clearly expressed this conceptual framework:

> The World Cup is not politics, it is the manifestation of the national . . . of the community of belonging . . . each person is part of a nation, independently of the State . . . nationality accompanies the individual and marks his personality . . . and from the point of view of sport, the national team is like the folkloric ballets that represent the best of a nation . . . thus the national ties are the most powerful . . . the nation gives protection and pride . . . and the World Cup engenders deep national emotions . . . and football is a factor of national reunion . . . the Argentine football present in the River Plate stadium activated the ethnic forces and helped in the reinforcement of the Argentine soul . . . we knew of the national value of tango, and now we discover the national value of football. (*La Nación- Suplemento Cultura y Nación*, June 22, 1978, p. 6)

Moreover, FIFA, as a transnational organization, depends on the independent national football associations and sponsorship of multinational firms, both interested in the global impact of championships and the consolidation of sport's worldwide profile. Neither FIFA nor Coca-Cola engage in politics or take moral standpoints, putting the qualities of hosting countries at the core of their concerns. The junta knew very well that FIFA was not prepared to cancel the World Cup on ethical grounds. The military rightly understood that the periodical evaluations carried out by the FIFA were based on an assessment of the organizational capacity of the national committee (Ente Autártico del Mundial—EAM) that was in charge of rebuilding stadiums, transforming airports, and providing a new television and communication structure. The junta inherited a World Cup finals given to Argentina in 1968, a competition for which it had not asked. One can imagine how influential generals might have considered it a gift to a society that loved football so much. But it was a poisoned chalice: if the country was not pacified, their time was running out. The total annihilation of guerrilla groups was crucial. A World Cup with bombs, protests, and demonstrations was unthinkable. A few weeks after the military coup, the EAM was taken over, and the World Cup was defined as a national priority.

Alfredo Cantilo, the president of the Argentine Football Association, recognized that the preparations initiated in 1968 were not sufficient. The military in 1976 was confronted with a chaotic situation. The main obstacle was the lack of time. However, the presence of the military in the EAM finally made possible all of the delayed building work. The military, Cantilo says proudly, demonstrated to the world the possibilities of a new nation and confirmed the importance of planning and discipline (*La Nación*, June 1, 1978, p. 8). General Antonio Merlo, who was in charge of the EAM, had declared some months before the opening ceremony that "in spite of the World Cup being a modest event compared with the Olympics, the main objective is to show the world our organizational talent. Two years ago nobody believed in us, and now the world is convinced that the Argentines are capable of doing important things. For us the moment of truth has come" (*Somos*, April 28, 1978, p. 14). There were expectations when it came to the sporting competition itself. At his last meeting with the national team, General Videla proclaimed that the footballers were obliged

> to show that they were the best of the nation and the best Argentina could present to the universe . . . and they were obliged to demonstrate the quality of the Argentine man. This man that at the individual level or working in a team is able to carry out great enterprises when guided by common goals . . . I claim from you the victory, the winners of the World Cup, winners because you will show courage in the games . . . and will be the right expression of the human quality of the Argentines. (*Suplemento Clarín Mundial*, May 27, 1978, pp. 6–7)

The World Cup turned out to be a success in a "pacified" society. The wave of popular nationalism was extreme. The demonstrations of joy in the stadiums and the streets after the Argentine victories that culminated in the triumph against Holland in the final were interpreted by the junta as the success of a national project. General Videla said that the cry of "Argentina, Argentina" and the millions of flags all around the country were signs of a recovered nation celebrating its dignity. General Saint Jean, governor of the province of Buenos Aires, proclaimed that Argentine history divided into a time before and a time after the World Cup. The World Cup was seen as the beginning of a new epoch in which the unity of the people was finally formed and sealed. The junta declared with pride that the competition showed that the matches were played not by the eleven players on the field but by 25 million Argentines. Argentina won peacefully against subversion. A new country was born (see *Página 12*, June 26, 1988, pp. 10–11). The media, without exception, showed no critical distance in the explosion of joy, optimism, and chauvinism (see Ulanovsky 1997; Gilbert and Vitagliano 1998; Blaustein and Zubieta 1998). Even a critical intellectual of the stature of Ernesto Sabato observed that "the World Cup was a proof of maturity, nobleness, a popular mobilization marked by generosity and altruism" (*La Razón*, June 13, 1978, p. 4). Defined as *La fiesta de todos* (the feast for all), the title of the official World Cup film, the junta enjoyed its best days that June. Without any doubt or hesitation, the regime believed that it had achieved some of the most important symbolic and real goals through football: the image of a victorious nation projected to the entire world (Novaro and Palermo 2003, 166). In the next section we shall see how this was also made possible by the values and ideologies of Argentine football that created a particularly favorable environment.

FOOTBALL ESSENTIALISM

Football in Argentina is an old national passion, an obsession, a locus of pride and disenchantment, of joy and sadness, an important arena for obtaining victory and global recognition (see Archetti 1999, 2001; Alabarces 2002). A country that had exported thousands of players to the world, and especially to Europe, and had gained many international titles with its clubs and national teams had never been crowned "World Champions." Their last involvement in the World Cup of 1974 had not been successful, with the 0–4 defeat in the second round against Holland proving rather traumatic. The defeat was put down to the erratic systems of play chosen by the coaches. The leading sports weekly magazine reported that Argentina played without conviction and, even worse, without a philosophy that reflected a vision or an expressed historical continuity (*El Gráfico*, July 9, 1974, p. 1). In the same issue, Perfumo and Babington, two of the most talented players who played in the World Cup of 1974 in Germany, confessed that they did not know how to play because they were more preoccupied with how their opponents played than with their own tactics. Babington said that it was necessary "to have clear ideas about our style, we need a plan reflecting our idiosyncrasy, our ability and technique, combined with more dynamics and rhythm" (*El Gráfico*, June 9, 1974, p. 3). In the long article there was a consensus between players and journalists on the right strategy: an imperious need to return to the sources of Argentine style based on dribbling and virtuosity. It was emphasized that Argentina, a world power in exporting players, should now concentrate on its own possibilities, creating a process that would culminate in winning the title in 1978.

In October 1974, César Luis Menotti was appointed national coach. He had been a talented inside left: languid, tall, elegant, and very technical, a scorer with great vision. He started his career with Rosario Central, a traditional team from the city of Rosario, with great success. Later he moved to Buenos Aires and played on two important teams: the Racing Club in 1964 and the Boca Juniors in 1965. His time at Boca was very problematic. His style, based on a slow tempo and elegant touches, did not fit very well with the kick-and-run tactics that has always characterized the Boca Juniors. Like many Argentine players, he too had an international career. In 1967, as a true pioneer, he joined the Generals of New York and in 1969, he joined the famous Santos of Brazil, the mythical team of Pelé (Gasparini and Ponsico 1983).

Menotti coached Huracán in 1973, when the club won its first national title playing what Argentine football lovers perceived as the typical national style. He understood that a clear philosophy was needed. Menotti was educated, having spent two years as a university student. He was politically engaged, a member of the Communist Party, and, above all, very articulate. He was able to create a discourse about the relationship between the historical roots of football and national identity. Moreover, to accept the post of national coach was in accordance with the political strategy of the Communist Party, which was more opposed to the guerrilla groups than to the junta. After so many failures, the public expected a kind of messiah, and he was prepared to perform this role. In a long interview in *El Gráfico*, Menotti summarized his football philosophy in a few principles:

1. Talent and technical ability should predominate over physicality and power.
2. A dialectical articulation between bodily and mental speed was needed: he did not want players running without thinking or thinking without running.
3. A flexible system of zonal and man-to-man marking was the best defensive strategy.
4. Attacking with two wings and one center-forward was the best response to the system 4–4–2 imposed by the Brazilians and followed by so many teams.
5. Continuity, as exemplified by the Dutch in the 1970s, was crucial: possession should be regained as soon as possible after the ball is lost.
6. A sense of belonging to a football tradition with great heroes was important for the players. (August 1, 1975, p. 2)

He decided to select the best established players and also to give opportunities to a lot of talents playing in the provincial leagues. His project was defined as a "national enterprise" and he deliberately constructed a national squad, including players from the interior. He also began systematic work with the youth national team that culminated in victory in the prestigious Toulon Cup in France in 1975. In this tournament Tarantini, Gallego, Passarella, and Valencia, who were to join the national team in 1978, were outstanding figures. He insisted that football was only a sport, and that his work was carried out in order to defend the prestige of Argentine football traditions. He said that "playing we do not defend our borders, the Motherland, the flag. With the national team nothing essentially patriotic dies or is saved" (*El Gráfico*, April 19, 1977, p. 65). The systematic preparation of the national team lasted almost four years. Menotti was even successful in persuading the Argentine Football Association in October 1976 to ban the selling of Argentine players to foreign clubs. Menotti experimented with many players, and he was confident of reaching 1978 with the majority of them playing in Argentina. This was achieved, and the only one selected from outside the country for 1978 was

Kempes, who at that moment was playing for Valencia in Spain. In four years he was able to form a dedicated group of young players with the mission of becoming world champions.

For Argentine football supporters and the media, winning the World Cup was seen, paradoxically, given the political context, as an act of redemption and justice. In *El Gráfico*, Onesime wrote that on the day of the finals "justice was achieved with great transparency . . . Argentina was World Champion for the first time" (June 27, 1978, p. 23). In a special issue of the magazine, the importance of a dream transformed into reality was emphasized; the national side played in the style people liked (*la nuestra*) against Holland, which represented modern and functional European football. Once more, the technique and ability of the Creole players (*jugadores criollos*) were hailed as being superior to the robotic Dutch way of playing (*El Gráfico*, June 30, 1978, p. 58). The attempt by Menotti to create a national discourse based on tradition, cultural continuity, and a return to the sources was undoubtedly successful. Menotti repeated time and time again throughout 1978 and 1979 that the best way of understanding the triumph was to see it as a tribute to "our old and loved football" (*El Gráfico*, June 26, 1979, p. 63). He constantly denied that he created a Menotti style. He was just recapturing the memory of the people and their love for "the inner nature of the Argentine football player: his creativity" (*Viva*, May 19, 1988, p. 54). He recreates a history of purity through an explicit ancestral cult, that of the great Argentine players who pursued success with fantasy, imagination, and a sense of duty.

Menotti, in spite of his exaggerated modesty, was declared the "master of the victory," because he initiated and brought to conclusion a long process based on continuity and a profound respect for the qualities of his selected players. The daily *Clarin*, in an editorial note the day after the final, wrote that the plan of Menotti's

> was seen as unachievable madness. To believe that it was possible to build a competitive side taking as the premise the qualities of the Argentine player. To play well and to win . . . during this process of searching for a distinct style was a hard struggle. . . . For four years the team played well and not so well. Won and lost. But the religion of ability and touch was accepted by all the players. . . . Now the victory covers all the moments of darkness. Argentine football is the best in the World . . . but the achievement of Menotti is great. His style won. His convictions won. It is possible to be World Champions with technical and attacking players. Argentine football will always be remembered for this triumph. (June 26, 1978, p. 15)

Years later, it was clear that Menotti, a progressive figure, desperately tried to rationalize the success, searching in the history of football and not in current political history for categories and concepts to interpret the joyful events. He developed a clear ideological standpoint: politics is based on hypocrisy and tricks; his "philosophy of football" tried to demonstrate the importance of playing with generosity, creativity, and honesty, and without tricks. Football, then, in a difficult period of Argentine history, could be perceived as a performative field crossed by "permanent" values of decency. Menotti observed the following eight years later:

> Many people would say that I have coached teams during times of dictatorship, in an epoch when Argentina had governments with which I had nothing in common and, moreover, which contradicted my way of life. And I ask myself, should I have done that, should I have coached teams that played badly, that based everything on tricks that betrayed the feeling of the people? No, of course not. . . . We were conscious, and we knew all the time that we were playing for the people. A people, that in this moment in Argentina, needed a new point of departure to do something different together. . . . We tried to play in the best way possible, because we understood that we were obliged to give back to the people the spectacle of football. To give it back through victory, if this was possible, but, after all, through the pleasure of playing honest football. Each of us had an order when we went on the field on the day of the final: to look at the people in the stand. We are not going to look up to the authorities in the VIP box, I said to the players, we are going to look into the stands, to all the people, where each of our fathers perhaps is sitting, because there we will find the metal workers, the butchers, the bakers, and the taxi drivers. (Menotti 1986, 27)

For the junta it was clear: the victory articulated the excellence of the nation and the importance of staying together, like the national team, against all kinds of enemy. Football was defined as a privileged arena as far as patriotism was concerned. Videla proclaimed four days after the final that the "triumph was obtained with capacity, courage, and discipline" and not, as Menotti stated, with "technical ability." Furthermore, it was even more important to observe the joy and enthusiasm of the people, and this "could be seen as a profound wish for national unity felt by all Argentines." The World Cup expressed the "purist sentiments because they are the best proof of our identity and our will to win. The entire nation has triumphed" (*Clarin*, June 29, 1978, p. 15). Menotti used the category "people" instead of "nation." Nation relates to traditional Argentine nationalism, while people relates to a left-populist discourse. In a note published on the day of the final in *Clarin*, Menotti wrote that he dreamed of a victory that belonged to one alone: the Argentine people (not the nation) (June 25, 1978, p. 6).

However, despite this difference, the patriotic tales of the junta joined the essentialist narrative of Menotti in a symphony of victory.

It was accepted that the Argentines, governed by the rules of fear and repression, also participated in the feast. Claudio Tamburrini, an imprisoned political activist, student of philosophy, and professional football player who escaped from a house of detention in March 1978 (see Tamburrini 2002), wrote the following twenty years later:

> What is the fascination of sport that makes it possible for torturers and tortured to embrace each other after the goals scored by the national team? During the 1978 World Cup, the Argentines—including myself—replaced the critical political judgement of the situation of the country with sporting euphoria. Sports, in particular, football, produce passions. Passions don't always help when decisions are made. To support the national side of a country that is subjected to a dictatorship is an example of a costly irrationality, but perhaps salutary for a people. Given the imperfectability of life and history, it is perhaps rational to celebrate football triumphs alongside a society's concrete political context. Argentines should commemorate the title again . . . Luque, Fillol, Kempes, and Bertoni, together with the other heroes of 1978, should return to the River Plate stadium. Now they will be the undisputable champions. This time, Videla is in prison. (*Perfil*, June 12, 1998, p. 14)

Tamburrini indicates the paradoxes, contradictions, and moral ambivalences that the World Cup brought about in Argentina. In the next section I shall show that football in Argentina is a crucial field for gaining a better understanding of some of the dilemmas experienced by the main actors engaged in the drama of 1978.

EPILOGUE: TWENTY-FIVE YEARS ON AND MORAL AMBIVALENCE

On June 19, 2003, I was present at a commemorative act organized by the University of Belgrano in Buenos Aires, at which the key invited participants were two of the best Argentine players from the 1978 final: Bertoni and Larrosa. The idea was to discuss with the students the importance of the country's first World Cup victory. There was not a large audience, which initially surprised both of the players, who had expected a packed and admiring crowd. Their reactions as the event proceeded, however, were different. Bertoni said that he was not surprised, because what characterized Argentina was "a lack of memory, or, better, the fact that we have a short memory." Larrosa agreed with him but speculated that the students were reticent perhaps because they "had a great deal of memory." I asked him to develop this statement. Larrosa explained that the victory was obtained in a difficult political context, that there were allegations that the military junta paid some of the Peruvian players in the quarter final match that Argentina won 6–0, and that Maradona, the superb player who dominated world football in the 1980s, was not chosen by Menotti at the last minute. In other words, the victory was a locus of polemics and moral ambivalence. Later in the debate, both players were asked to comment on their reactions to the indiscriminate and unjust repression launched by the junta. They emphatically denied any knowledge of it, maintaining that football was not politics, and that they played and represented the people and not the military—an argument reminiscent of Menotti.

Democracy returned to Argentina in 1983. All of the members of the junta and many prominent military figures were arrested and brought to justice. The atrocities were open to public scrutiny. It was obvious that Menotti and the players could no longer remain silent. The majority chose Menotti's explanation: they represented the people, and they played for the people. Moreover, they also said that, like the majority of Argentines, they did not know the scale and brutality of the military and paramilitary forces. In 2000, Ricardo Villa, another important player from the 1978 squad, who later had success in England playing for Tottenham Hotspur, agreed to discuss the World Cup with Tati Almeida, a mother from the Plaza de Mayo, who had lost her son Alejandro on July 17, 1975. Villa said that he agreed to the meeting because he did not feel that he was an accomplice of the military. He was a footballer who unfortunately lived in a terrible epoch of Argentine history. "Now," he says, "I feel that I would have liked to fight for a better country." Even he admits that if he had known what was going on, he would have declined to join the Argentina team, like the captain, Carrascosa, who refused to play in the World Cup finals but never presented clear arguments why he made that decision. Almeida admitted that she wanted Argentina to win. She also wished that her son, Alejandro, had been alive to be together with so many young people in the public feast that followed the final. Villa concluded the dialogue, saying,

> we are talking about a horrific period. Today I realize that we were used to [giving] joy to the people. But I don't like the fact that we, the players, are represented as sons of the military Junta, because I assure you that I did not know what was going on then. As the years went by, I became aware that I had been deceived, but this had not been difficult: I was a player who just wanted to be a world champion. (*Clarin Deportivo*, June 26, 2000, pp. 12-13)

With the arrival of democracy in the 1980s, Villa decided to become active in local politics. He joined the social-democratic Radical Party. In 1990, he was elected and presided for many years in the municipal council of his town, Roque Pérez.

Villa's later political commitment is exceptional, but he is not the only player to exercise self-criticism. Oscar Ortiz, one of the most regular players during the championship and a dedicated socialist, declared, "I would have swapped the title we won to stop what happened during the military dictatorship. But it must be clear that it was not our fault, we were not the cause of the tyranny," adding that even civil society and the political leaders had been more responsible by passively accepting the coup d'état. He feels that too much blame has been put on the players because, as many argue, the match against Peru was fixed by the junta, and the team played to "wash the face of the military." But this is wrong: Ortiz insists, "We were not the champions of the dictatorship, we just happened to be champions during it, and we played good football" (*Veintitrés*, June 26, 2003, pp. 78–79). Menotti supported Ortiz's reasoning when he asked rhetorically, "Why is there so much criticism of the team and not of the entrepreneurs, the media, or the politicians" (*La Nación Deportiva*, June 25, 2003, p. 3). In the interview, he insisted that on the day of the final he ordered all of the players to ignore the junta. He emphasized that they belonged to a football tradition with a certain style, and that their main purpose should be to defend Argentine football history (*La Nación Deportiva*, June 25, 2003, p. 3). He pleaded for a better understanding of what happened in 1978: "Without minimizing the dictatorship, it is important to keep the World Cup in its real context" (*Página* 12, June 15, 2003, p. 20).

The players and Menotti are not exceptional in their arguments. This appeal to Argentine ignorance has been described as dialectical, "the show of horror and the myth of innocence" (see González Bombal 1988; Novaro and Palermo 2003). From the second half of 1982 onward, the revelation of the scope of torture and murder was such that after a few months of incredulity there followed a general indignation and repulsion about what the military had done since 1976. The complex mechanism of denial built up by the repressors, the lack of witnesses, and indeed the extreme nature of the cruelty conditioned the skepticism of public opinion. This was slowly undone by hard evidence, and a feeling of guilt came over the nation. How had it been possible to ignore what was being done by the military and other repressive forces? The fear and terror were, together with the supporting role of the media, important factors in creating passivity and a lack of interest. Villa, Ortiz, and the rest of the players were part of a people that preferred to adhere to the logic of innocence. It is clear now that the military years provoked in Argentina an extreme situation of social alienation (see Vezzetti 2002).

I have shown in this chapter that the genuine passion for football in Argentina was articulated in a double discourse: the narrative of tradition and style of play and the ideology of a nation fighting a just war against communism and subversion. Julio Marini writes that the main dilemma twenty-five years on is how to understand a popular love for a sport in the midst of a "cruel time." He describes the engagement of the supporters inside and outside the stadium, of those without knowledge of what was going on and of the others who ignored it. He even points out the most blatant of the paradoxes: the prisoners listened to the radio and showed sincere joy on the day of the final (*Clarín Deportivo*, June 25, 2003, p. 7). The story of Captain "Tiger" Acosta, one of the most violent torturers of the navy, has entered Argentine mythology. He is said to have entered a room after the final because the prisoners were shouting, "We won, we won," and then participated himself in this authentic and spontaneous display of euphoria. As an example of his cruelty, it is said that he took a group of prisoners out in a car so that they could see with their own eyes that the people did not care about them or human rights. They just cared about the World Cup. One of the victims told journalist Fernández Moore that she asked Acosta to open the roof of the car to have a better view of the masses in the streets. And when he had done this, she thought about screaming that she was one of "the disappeared," held in a secret place. But she realized that this was pointless, because the people would just think that she was a crazy woman in the middle of the national carnival (Fernández Moore, 2003, 11).

Writer Alfredo Leuco provocatively acknowledged that in full knowledge of the junta's atrocities—he had friends who had disappeared—he participated in the celebrations in the streets. He writes:

> The dictatorship tarnished the history of Argentina with blood. But neither the ball was stained, nor the supporters. . . . Football is not the opium of the masses. . . . I would even argue the contrary. Football mobilizes a collective creativity, harvests multitudes that unify interests and goals, democratizes class relations. . . . It is the expression of what we are and what we have. . . . Twenty years have passed since one of the most cruel paradoxes was lived out in this country. The happiness of being world champions combined with the painful tears of thousands of Argentines who died in the prisons. The passion and the horror together. . . . Football and death playing the same match on a field called Argentina. (*Página* 12, June 25, 2003, p. 21)

It is clear that the 1978 victory will always be perceived as being morally difficult, generating the ambiguities and ambivalences that I have been able to present. Larrosa was one of the organizers of the commemorative event twenty-five years after the success. The day chosen was July 9, 2003, the day of the national independence, the location River Plate stadium. At the University of Belgrano he emphasized the generous attitude of the committee: "The celebration was not only for the triumph of 1978 but also a tribute to Argentine football." In this way, it had operated within the ideological framework developed many years before by Menotti. The testimonial match, he said, would be played by old and young players who had represented Argentina in different World Cups and international competitions. He told us that the Argentine Football Association had even commissioned the delivery of medals to such charismatic players as Batistuta and Simeone. Maradona had also been invited, and he had promised to come from Cuba. Sixty thousand were expected, but only 9,000 found their way to the stands. It was a sad day for the heroes of 1978. The people they represented did not bother. Maradona did not leave La Havana, and even Kempes, the greatest player of the tournament, did not come. Everyone just ignored them. They were part of history; they were, in many ways, the players of a match between football and death. They symbolized a traumatic epoch that will never be forgotten and in the middle of which they are like a dark diamond, the names and bodies of the first great victory of Argentine football.

REFERENCES

Alabarces, Pablo. 2002. *Fútbol y patria: El fútbol y las narrativas de la nación en Argentina*. Buenos Aires: Prometeo.

Archetti, Eduardo P. 1999. *Masculinities: Football, polo, and the tango in Argentina*. Oxford: Berg.

———. 2001. *El potrero, la pista y el ring: Las patrias del deporte argentino*. Buenos Aires: Fondo de Cultura Económica.

Blaustein, Eduardo, and Martín Zubieta. 1998. *Decíamos ayer: La prensa argentina bajo el proceso*. Buenos Aires: Colihue.

dal Masetto, Antonio. 1998. *Hay unos tipos abajo*. Buenos Aires: Planeta.

Feinman, José Pablo. 2003. *La crítica de las armas*. Buenos Aires: Norma.

Fernández Moore, Ezequiel. 2003. *The many faces of Argentina 78*, unpublished manuscript.

Gasparini, Roberto, and José Luis Ponsico. 1983. *El director técnico del proceso*. Buenos Aires: El Cid.

Gilbert, Abel, and Miguel Vitagliano. 1998. *El terror y la Gloria: La vida, el fútbol y la política en la Argentina del Mundial 78*. Buenos Aires: Norma.

González Bombal, Inés. 1988. *Los vecinazos: Las protestas barriales en el Gran Buenos*

Aires. Buenos Aires: Ediciones del IDES.

Kohan, Martín. 2002. *Dos veces junio*. Buenos Aires: Editorial Sudamericana.

Menotti, César Luis. 1986. *El fútbol sin trampas*. Barcelona: Muchnik editores.

Novaro, Marcos, and Vicente Palermo. 2003. *La dictadura militar (1976–1983): Del golpe de estado a la restauración democrática*. Buenos Aires: Paidós.

Tamburrini, Claudio M. 2002. *Pase libre: La fuga de la Mansión Seré*. Buenos Aires: Ediciones Continente.

Ulanovsky, Carlos. 1997. *Paren las rotativas*. Buenos Aires: CEAL.

Vezzetti, Hugo. 2002. *Pasado y presente: Guerra, dictadura y sociedad en la Argentina*. Buenos Aires: Siglo veintiuno editores.

Chapter 9

Moscow 1980

Stalinism or Good, Clean Fun?

Robert Edelman

INTRODUCTION

In this chapter I ask a fundamental question about the 1980 Moscow Olympics. Were the Olympic Games a grand remnant of Stalinist sporting practices that emerged in the 1930s, or were they, rather, what I have chosen here to call "good, clean fun," that is, a spectacular global sporting entertainment, devoid of the didactic purposes usually associated with Soviet sport (Riordan 1979, 1). In seeking an answer, I examine three historical aspects surrounding the 1980 Olympic Games: (1) the events surrounding the U.S.-led boycott of the Moscow Olympic Games; (2) the historic relationship between the International Olympic Committee and the Soviet Communist Party; and (3) the sporting rituals seen during the 1980 Olympic Games, set in the larger context of the history of Soviet sporting rituals.

THE BOYCOTT OF MOSCOW

I begin with the awarding of the Olympics to Moscow in 1974. That step came after what was deemed, perhaps not fully correctly, to have been the successful holding of the 1973 university games in the "capital of world socialism." For the Soviets, this victory was, first of all, a sign of international acceptance. The first Olympics to take place in a socialist country meant that the USSR, while communist, could now be seen as a "normal" nation. The importance of this victory was rooted in the historic Russian sense of backwardness and outsiderness that predated the revolution by a good 500 years. Now, with this stamp of international approval, the Soviets could claim to be just as good as the rest of the world (Shteinbakh 1980, 33–39).

One of the historic purposes of Soviet sport had been to demonstrate the superiority of communism as a social and economic system to both international and domestic audiences, but that theme was largely absent from Soviet discourses during the run-up to the Olympic Games (Riordan 1979, 12). Instead, winning the right to hold the games was described as a vindication of the Soviet Union's "peaceful foreign policy" (Dobrov 1974, 9–12). The USSR was not to be seen as a better place than any other but rather as, again, a "normal and civilized" nation. Foreign guests were supposed to come to Moscow to see a well-developed traditional and elite culture and a comfortable standard of living—in other words, a place that was really not so different than the rest of the world and, most importantly, a country that did not threaten the rest of the world (Salutskii 1981, 7–13).

In 1980, the Soviets thoroughly embraced the ideology of Olympism and claimed that the decision to hold the event in Moscow was a reward for their many services to the movement (Salutskii 1981, 18). Acceptance within the Olympic movement had been gained after more than twenty years of struggle. During those years, Soviet sports officials had always been very conscious of their place as outsiders in world sport. They had complained endlessly about biased judging, about rigged draws that always put them in tougher brackets, about harassment by local hosts, and a mass of other things, including, of all things, bad food. Yet within two decades, their athletes had come to dominate the games, and Soviet officials were eventually accorded positions (and the accompanying perks) in the highest councils of the Olympic movement and in most international sports federations as well.

This did not mean so much as social acceptance by the elite gentlemen of the IOC. Rather, it was a recognition, even a grudging recognition, of the achievements of Soviet athletes and coaches. Like their sportsmen and women, Soviet sport bureaucrats came to be accorded the right of international travel, the greatest privilege that could be granted to any citizen of the USSR. They got to go to the same watering holes as Olympic committee members, to drink the same champagne and eat the same hors d'oeuvres at the same parties. As the games approached, life did not look altogether bad for the Brezhnev cronies, most notably Marat Gramov, head of the State Sport Committee (Goskomsport), who were to organize and present the Moscow Games. They had achieved acceptance from global sport's most elite bodies, and they came to enjoy the good life that came with membership in that elite.

The invasion of Afghanistan in December 1979 pulled the rug out from under this world of comfort. To this day, we do not know if the question of the Olympics ever entered into the decision to invade. More generally, however, we do know that the central aim of postwar Soviet foreign policy had been to surround itself with friendly buffer states in order to forestall yet another of the many invasions experienced by Russia and later the USSR over the course of a thousand years. While Afghanistan had never formally been a Soviet satellite, relations were always cordial, starting from the 1920s. Afghanistan was deemed a backward nation but not, by itself, a military threat. This stasis changed in April 1978, when leftist army officers, many of them educated in the USSR, seized power. While the Soviets did not engineer the coup, they did come eventually to support it. The new government began a process of modernization, which in turn provoked a violent traditionalist response that the West today confronts in all of its horrible magnitude. In defense of their clients, the Soviets installed some 7,000 troops in September 1979. However, internal bickering among the new regime led to the violent installation of an even more militant faction of officers, convincing party leader Leonid Brezhnev of the need to install a more moderate Marxist government. Soviet troops moved into Afghanistan on December 24 and soon found themselves in a quagmire that came to corrode the authority of the regime and played a crucial if not decisive role in the collapse of the Soviet Union. Fifteen thousand Soviet soldiers would die, and Afghanistan would be devastated, paving the way for the Taliban (Suny 1998, 444–45).

While there had been calls for a boycott from the time Moscow was awarded the Olympic Games, those suggestions gained no traction until President Jimmy Carter took up the matter. Carter had come to be perceived in the United States as a weak and an indecisive figure. Now, with the era of detente over after the invasion, Carter decided on a grain embargo and a boycott of the Games as ways of laying down the gauntlet to the Russians (Hazan 1982, 123–74). This last step raises another unanswered question—this time about the U.S. administration's actions. Did the Americans seriously believe that the Soviets' devotion to sport was so great that a boycott would get them to withdraw from Afghanistan? (Barton 1983, 105). Researching the debate as it played out between January and April 1980 did not, it must be said, prove to be an edifying experience. Each side indulged in immense hypocrisies and acts of convenient historical amnesia. The Americans acted as though big powers were not supposed to do such things as invade small countries, neighboring and otherwise. Such a thing was unthinkable. Yet despite the long American presence in Vietnam and various adventures in South and Central America, the Soviets had not, for their part, usually boycotted international events in the United States. In fact, in only one instance did U.S. actions even provoke a Soviet boycott of an international event in the United States. That moment came in 1966, at the beginning of the Vietnam War, when the Soviets decided not to take part in the annual US-USSR dual track and field meet (Turrini 2001, 439). More typically, the Soviets did not object when Denver was awarded the Winter Games for 1976 at a time when the United States was still in Vietnam.

For their part, the Soviets had the stunning chutzpah to protest that sport should be kept separate from politics, this from a nation that had virtually invented the concept of openly politicized sport (Hazan 1982, 149; Salutskii 1981, 175). In fact, in their counteroffensive against the boycott, Soviet spokesmen, acting like the new teacher's pet, went so far as to claim that the United States had no understanding of the history and character of Olympism (Gutin 1990, 45–48). Of course, in the preceding three decades, the Soviets had engaged in a series of smaller boycotts, visa denials, and other attempts to use international competitions in various parts of the world to make political points. Some of these actions, such as the campaign against apartheid, were authentically admirable. Perhaps the best known such moment came with the Soviets' refusal to play Chile in a World Cup elimination match just after the overthrow of the leftist Salvador Allende government in 1973, an event we now know to have been fomented by the U.S. government. The national stadium in Santiago had been used to imprison thousands, perhaps hundreds were executed there, and the Soviets refused to play in such a tainted site. FIFA refused, in turn, to move the game, and the Soviets were disqualified (Sugden and Tomlinson 1998, chapter 7). One could even argue that there was a trace of principle in this step, given the enormous importance that the Soviet citizenry, at least its male part, attached to the World Cup. In fact, it attached much more importance to the World Cup than it did to the Olympics.

In any case, the Soviets stayed in Afghanistan, and the games went on. Only eighty-one nations came to Moscow, while some thrity-six did not. In some cases, such as Great Britain, teams were sent as representatives of National Olympic Committees. Others who did show up protested by not attending the Opening Ceremonies. This step turned out to be a significant gesture. Their absence from the parade of nations made a strong impression. Pictures of the delegations lined up in the infield after the parade showed vast, embarrassing swathes of green (Novikov 1980, unpaginated).

To the people who were there, the Moscow Olympiad felt like a "sporting holiday" (Geskin, interview). Watching the event on Soviet television from Helsinki, which I was able to do in 1980, I cannot say that I was unimpressed. The Finns also thought that the Games were a big deal. Yet there can be no doubt that the spectacle was diminished by the absence of so many strong athletes. While it may well have been that Pietro Minnea would still have won the 200m, can anyone in their heart say that Alan Wells would have taken the 100m? Soviet sports officials knew full well that in certain sports their Games were damaged goods. The Soviet haul of eighty gold medals, which was some thirty more than their peak at Munich, did not have the same meaning.

We now also know from Soviet archives that as soon as the Moscow Games ended, these sport bureaucrats wished to take revenge four years later. Within the Kremlin's corridors of power, they organized a lobby in favor of a boycott of the

Los Angeles Games. The internal arguments raged for three years. Finally, the political winds of the moment (1984) were such that the pro-boycott camp was able to prevail when the neo-Brezhnevite, Konstantin Chernenko, who was briefly in power between the death of Iuri Andropov and his own demise, supported the boycotters' cause. Even today, the U.S. boycott still rankles among ordinary Russian citizens along a wide spectrum of political opinions.

For their part, Soviet athletes are still bitter about the 1984 boycott, and U.S. athletes remain equally angry about 1980. Both groups felt cheated about lost opportunities. Over the years as I have come to know more athletes, I have become more sympathetic to those feelings of betrayal by political leaders who were using athletes for their own purposes. On the other hand, I do think athletes take it for granted when the galaxy of political forces and events conspires to give their efforts visibility and importance. None of the members of the United States' ice hockey team that beat the Soviets in 1980 at Lake Placid refused to go to the White House, because to do so was an "interference of politics in sport." On the other side, I do not know of any Soviet medal winner from the 1968 Olympic Games refusing to attend the official Kremlin Olympic reception in protest of the invasion of Czechoslovakia.

Can it then be said that the boycott was a success? Partially. It did put a dent in performances and diminished the size of the spectacle. Needless to say, it did not get the Soviets to leave Afghanistan. Were the Games a success? Again, partially. The events were well organized, something the Soviets did not always succeed in pulling off. Moscow was spruced up enough to appear to be a showcase city—the mother of all Potemkin villages. Large crowds attended. Sports, like field hockey, that had attracted few fans before the Games sold out their arenas. The Games played to 96 percent of capacity (Novikov 1980, unpaginated). Yet surely the worldwide TV audience, especially in the United States where the Games were not shown, was a good bit smaller than had been hoped for. Three hundred thousand foreign visitors had been anticipated, but only half that number showed up.

STRANGE BEDFELLOWS—THE IOC AND SOVIET SPORTOCRATS

The 1980 Olympic Games brought together two of the major international causes of the twentieth century—Olympism and communism. On the surface, this closeness seems puzzling. How could two such politically different kinds of movements eventually come to work so closely together? Given the thorough embrace of Olympism required in bidding for and organizing the Olympic Games, it is important to remember that when the Bolsheviks came to power in 1917, the

Olympic movement was anathema to them, and they were anathema to the Olympic movement. The Games excluded workers and minimized the participation of women. The new state wanted no part of them. Tsarist officers who had been on the IOC before 1917 were not kicked off the committee after the revolution. They wanted no part of this strange and threatening regime. Yet it appears that the high councils of Olympism were not unanimous in rejecting the Bolsheviks. According to one recent post-Soviet Russian source, de Coubertin wished to invite the Soviets to Paris in 1924, but their participation was rejected by the pro-czarist Russians still on the Olympic committee (Vartanian 1997, 62).

Yet for all of the tensions, there was something about the Olympic-style, multisport festival that appealed to segments of opinion in the commissariat of enlightenment (i.e., the ministry of culture) and to other groups of sports officials as well. In the wake of the revolution, the Bolsheviks had not yet decided which course to take in organizing sport. This uncertainty extended to a vast range of other forms of human activity, especially in the cultural realm. Different camps proposed all manners of different solutions (Stites 1989, 79–100; Gorsuch 2000, 116), yet there was no question in any of the minds of the participants in these debates that sport, regardless of its organizational form, was a marker of modernity, and that the party's overwhelming and fundamental task was to modernize this backward country in which it had managed to make a socialist revolution. As we all know, the Olympics also embraced the modern world, although with a version of modernity highly different from that of the Bolsheviks. Both movements celebrated human progress, much of it measured in statistics, whether running times or production quotas. Finally, both movements, especially in their early years, were internationalist and cautious about embracing strong expressions of nationalist sentiment (Hoberman 1995).

For the Soviets, the multisport festival had political advantages over a single sport competition. Multisport events more easily allowed the organizers to ascribe a series of slogans and messages to these grand assemblages of youth. In single-sport championships, tactics, strategy, and personnel dominated the discourse around the event and even got in the way of the organizers' goals, which in the Olympics and for communists were always didactic. Following Richard Gruneau's characterization of the Olympics, it is, I think, fair to say that both movements were concerned, first and foremost, with social improvement (Gruneau 1993). As we all know, both Olympic and communist sport were always about more than play, more than mere entertainment. Both were about getting better, maybe even about changing human nature, and that common vision was buttressed by a shared belief that getting better was even possible.

While the party had held a variety of sports festivals and parades as early as 1919, the first serious attempt at a Soviet version of an Olympiad came in 1928 (Van Geldern 1993, 3). This event was the first Spartakiad, named after the rebel slave of ancient Rome. In addition to some 7,000 male and female athletes from all over the USSR, more than 600 foreign guests competed. The games were organized by the Communist Red Sport International to compete with the bourgeois Olympics in Amsterdam. It was also to offer a contrast to the larger and more successful efforts of the Social Democratic Lucerne Sports International, particularly the Frankfurt Worker Olympiad of 1925. Unlike the "bourgeois" Olympics, the Spartakiad was to be a mass rather than an elite activity. In addition to Olympic-style events, there were non-competitive hikes, reenactments of great events in revolutionary history, and a bit of the carnivalesque. Female performers, while not a majority, were highly visible. Interestingly, less than half of the participants were members of what was called the "working class." Scarcely any peasants took part. Rather, the majority of athletes was drawn from an extremely amorphous social category called "employees" or "white-collar workers" (Edelman 1993, 37–41).

This event took place in the pivotal year 1928. Stalin was in the final process of consolidating his power in the party. The nation had gone through a war scare in 1927. Military concerns were now more important, and the organizing model of the Spartakiad fit the regime's changing needs. The program was even modified to include such events as the grenade toss and underwater swimming in full battle dress (no reported deaths during the competition). This first event was judged a success, and the Spartakiad became the prime organizational model for most subsequent Soviet sport competitions. During the 1930s , along with All-Union Spartakiads, there were army Spartakiads, police Spartakiads, trade union Spartakiads, collective farm Spartkiads, and even Spartkiads for medical workers. In other words, the "system" that emerged so surprisingly in 1952 had first been put into place much earlier. It developed through the 1930s as an elitist and a statist version of competitive but noncommercial sport.

In particular, Soviet sport came to share Olympism's highly hierarchical approach to society, power, and privilege. As Soviet society became increasingly hierarchicized from the mid-1930s on, sports would play a crucial role in the complex process that has been called by specialists the "Great Retreat." This concept, first put forward by the émigré sociologist Nicholas Timasheff in 1946, described a move toward more traditional and less revolutionary practices (Timasheff 1946, 7). Consistent with this trend, the Red Sport International passed a resolution in 1937. This document, recently found in the Comintern archive by Barbara Keys, cited the "progressiveness" of Olympic principles and urged communists in capitalist countries to strengthen National Olympic Committees by joining them (Keys 2001, 206).

But there was one part of the first Spartakiad that fit poorly into this statist model, and that was football. Dinamo Stadium, the first sizable Soviet facility holding 55,000, had been built for the Spartakiad. It was not a historical accident but rather a sign of coming times, that the sport club of the secret police, Dinamo, was the institution given the task and the funds for building such a structure. Yet during the Spartakiad it was filled only for major soccer matches. No other sport came close to attracting even a quarter of the attendance that soccer did, but soccer, as we shall see, fit badly into the Soviet version of Olympism that the state had come to favor.

Again, when the Soviets came to take part in the Olympic Games, this did not require a radical revision of their sporting practices. By the time of the Moscow Games, the IOC and the Communist Party of the Soviet Union (CPSU) were locked in a warm embrace. They had come to share not only a belief in modernity and social improvement but also a convenient amorality about their working partners and political bedfellows. By the end of the Moscow Games, so intimate was the Soviet-IOC relationship that the Moscow Organizing Committee published an instant memoir that included a fawning interview with the soon-to-be-former Spanish ambassador to Moscow and the new incoming head of the IOC, no less than Juan Antonio Samaranch (Salutskii 1981, 7). While Samaranch was praised for his deep love of art and culture and the beauty of his wife, the piece never mentioned the words Franco, Fascism, or dictatorship a single time. Veteran Russian sportswriter Vladimir Geskin, who today writes for the daily *Sportexpress* and covered the Olympic Games for *Sovetskii Sport*, attributes much of the closeness between the IOC and the Soviet side to Samaranch. Getting himself posted to Moscow as Spain's ambassador to the USSR did much to rid Samaranch of the odor of Franco, and he was able to use his cordial relations with the Soviets to woo backers from the Third World in his campaign for the IOC presidency (Geskin interview).

SOVIET SPORT: THE RITUAL AND THE UNRULY

Finally, I have tried to understand the nature of the Soviet Olympic enterprise by interrogating the choices of ritual made by the Moscow organizers. I embarked on this task despite my limited knowledge of how ritual works (Brownell 1995, 11). Along those lines, I have spent more time then I care to admit examining Soviet television footage of the Opening Ceremony. Early on in the official part of the ceremony, a group of marchers dressed as ancient Greeks, some astride a chariot, entered the stadium. A giant card section presented a picture of the Parthenon. The announcer offered a thoroughly positive reading of classical history, listing all of the great thinkers of ancient Greece. This approach to antiquity is especially curious when one considers that every world history textbook then used in the Soviet Union would also have noted that the society was based on slavery and involved the massive oppression of women, facts conveniently forgotten for the occasion. Then, as the parade of nations finished, large, embarrassing patches of green appeared on the infield, giving visual demonstration to the absence of so many countries. The official part of the event ended with greetings from two cosmonauts from their craft floating in space.

The "cultural" segment consisted entirely of the dances of the many Soviet peoples. The national dance troupes of each of the fifteen republics presented their national dance. In all, more than 3,000 dancers took part, ranging from the dashing, thoroughly macho Georgians to the demure, choreographically challenged Estonians. In trotting out this warhorse of Soviet parades and festivals, Soviet organizers were emphasizing the internationalism of the games and emphasizing the Soviet Union's own internationalism as a multinational state. Given the fact that we now know centrifugal nationalisms played a crucial role in the collapse of the USSR, what can one make of this part of the ceremony? There is a bit of the Disneyesque "It's a Small World, After All" in watching so many brightly costumed smiling dancers, each group showing its national specificities. Still, one must ask, is this a globalized festival of shared, equally valued customs or rather a multicultural minstrel show that masked the imperial character of the Soviet Union? Perhaps, the tip-off came with the cultural part's last number. The dancers from all of the republics joined with their Russian comrades for one final rousing version of the Russian folk song "Kalinka"—many nations, but one giant Kalinka (Gosteleradio 1980). Finally, the "sporting" part of the program presented the mass gymnastics, body sculptures, and heroic posing seen in virtually every Soviet sporting festival.

Crucially, there was nothing original about the choices made for the opening ceremony. They were based on a tradition of sports festivals and ceremonies that dated back to the Civil War period. Spartakiads always had opening ceremonies that became increasingly pompous and shallow with each year after the somewhat carnivalesque event of 1928. Yet the real template, or better the apotheosis, of the Soviet sports festival and with it the best expression of Stalinist body culture, was the annual Physical Culture Day Parade that took place each summer on Red Square. This tradition was reinvented in 1931 and petered out around the time of Stalin's death. These events featured body sculptures, precise marching, mass gymnastics, rapturous adulation of the party leadership atop Lenin's tomb, the participation of groups from the national republics, and a collection of exceptionally wacky floats with sporting themes, something interestingly but not surprisingly eschewed by the 1980 organizers who seemed allergic to the possibility of humor.

The 1980 opening drew from this catalogue of devices and routines first established during the 1930s. Virtually the only part of the ceremony that could be described as "original" was the greeting from the cosmonauts. Everything else had been done (to death) before. When I began studying the Physical Culture Day Parades in the early nineties, I , like everyone else, saw them as monolithic, even totalitarian or Orwellian. Yet recent work, much of it archival, by the young American scholar, Karen Petrone (2000), has revealed that the parades were something quite different. First, they were far from orderly. In the newsreels and documentaries, we see only those moments when people did manage to march in line. In fact, the parades appear to have been fairly chaotic affairs. Second, but more importantly, Petrone has revealed that the parade itself was, to use a familiar but useful term, "contested terrain." Rival groups within the political structure were constantly struggling over proper slogans, pride of place in the parade, and the right to present their segments as they wished. These were struggles over ways of presenting and displaying the human body, and those competing body cultures revealed different approaches to what I would call "being Soviet." Finally, it must be noted that the Physical Culture Day Parades were very much a part of the process of the hierarchization characterized by the Great Retreat, mentioned earlier. The November 7 and May Day parades were mass events, open to anyone who wanted to amble through Red Square after the formal part of the ceremonies. On the other hand, not everyone could take part in Physical Culture Day. One had to be fit, attractive, and nominated by one's sports group. Only the talented and beautiful could apply (Petrone 2000, 23–45).

Perhaps the most flamboyant and famous contestation to the imposed and intended orderliness of the parades came in 1936 with the participation of the Spartak sport society's hugely popular Moscow soccer team. Spartak athletes sewed a giant green carpet the size of a soccer field. They then proceeded to roll out this early Soviet version of Astroturf over Red Square's cobblestones and played a match. This move proved a huge success and was a part of all future parades. What Spartak was trying to do was create an oasis of spontaneity in an otherwise highly planned event. It was trying to show the limited, elite audience of party leaders and other honored guests crammed into the small reviewing stands in Red Square another body culture and that was, of course, the body culture of football (Starostin 1989, 29–32).

Football, over the course of Soviet history, was always something other, something different, something that fit poorly into the Stalinist template that emerged in the late 1920s. We have seen the rituals that were designed to make the practices of Soviet sport seem sacred. Yet as Susan Brownell (1995) has argued, not all rituals are sacred. There are profane rituals as well, and football, in the USSR as elsewhere in the world, succeeded in producing a variety of thoroughly profane rituals over the course of its history. This was a thoroughly male world, often violent, highly corrupt, spontaneous, and unpredictable—a place for drinking and humor. It fit badly into the model of sport on display in the 1980 Opening Ceremony. Yet football was by far the most popular sport in the USSR.

While it would be stretching things too far to call soccer subversive, it did allow certain safe forms of resistance for disadvantaged social groups and nationalities.

As proof of soccer's problematic position in the Soviet context, I offer a 1959 article from the national sports daily, *Sovetskii Sport*, written by a female physician and unearthed and described by Julie Gilmour. The piece suggested that there was a need to distinguish real athleticism from the male soccer culture of nicotine, alcohol, rough play, and raw strength. The author called instead for a higher, more cultured Soviet masculinity to counter the crudeness on display at soccer matches. She also observed that the ancient Greek sports ideals could still be found among weight lifters, gymnasts, and discus throwers, but not among soccer players (Gilmour 2002, 218–19). This piece, it must be noted, appeared in a newspaper that gave more attention to football than to any other game.

CONCLUSION

The 1980 Olympics were a grand Stalinist gesture in a society that had changed significantly, if not totally, from the worst days of Stalinism. The Moscow Games were supposed to be the great shining moment for the Soviet Olympic sports system. That system was a product of the Stalinist period, and it operated according to Stalinist principles, even after the end of the USSR's existence. Even today, the Russian Olympic Committee offers a refuge for hundreds, perhaps thousands, of officials and coaches from the previous regime.

The year 1980 was also a time in Soviet history when the economy had begun to slow down dramatically. To twist Stalin's famous phrase of 1935 when he said "Life has gotten better Comrades," life in 1980 was not getting better at all. Yet the state and party were in complete denial of these facts. In that moment, when happy media descriptions of life clashed so harshly with the grim realities of daily existence, the Olympic Games allowed the Brezhnevite sclerocracy to make claims that it ruled over the happiest place in earth. For sixteen days, millions of Soviet citizens, but certainly not all of them, actually believed this claim. Open political dissidents (those not forced out of the city for the duration) had to cover their heads and remain silent. Others among the dissatisfied would have to wait for another day to raise their complaints, but let us not forget that that day did finally come.

REFERENCES

Barton, Lawrence. 1983. The American Olympic boycott of 1980: The amalgam of diplomacy and propaganda in influencing public opinion. Ph.D. dissertation, Tufts University.

Brownell Susan. 1995. *Training the body for China: Sport in the People's Republic.* Chicago: University of Chicago Press.

Dobrov, Aleksandr. 1974. *Moscow is ready to host the 1980 Olympics.* Moscow: Novosti.

Edelman, Robert. 1993. *Serious fun: A history of spectator sports in the USSR.* Oxford: Oxford University Press.

Geskin, Vladimir. 2003. Interview with author. Moscow, September 7.

Gilmour, Julie. 2002. "If you want to be like me, train": The contradictions of Soviet masculinity. In *Russian masculinities in history and culture,* ed. Barbara Clements, Rebecca Friedman, and Dan Healy. New York.

Gorsuch, Anne. 2000. *Youth in revolutionary Russia.* Bloomington: Indiana University Press.

Gosteleradio (Soviet State Television). 1980. Footage from the sports library of the Amateur Athletic Foundation of Los Angeles.

Gruneau, Richard. 1993. The critique of sport in modernity: Theorizing power, culture, and the politics of the body. In *The sports process: A comparative and developmental approach,* ed. Eric Dunning, Joseph Maguire, and Robert Pearson. Urbana: Human Kinetics.

Gutin, A. T. 1990. Olimpizm kak element gumannisticheskoi kul'tury. In *Novoe myshlenie i olimpiskoe dvizhenie,* ed. S. Guskov. Moscow: Izdatel'stvo Instituta Fitzkul'tury.

Hazan, Baruch. 1982. *Olympic sport and propaganda games.* New Brunswick: Transaction Press.

Hoberman, John. 1995. Toward a theory of Olympic internationalism. *Journal of Sport History* 22 (1): 1–37.

Keys, Barbara. 2001. The dictatorship of sport: Nationalism, internationalism, and mass culture in the 1930s. Ph.D. dissertation, Harvard University.

Novikov, I. T., ed. 1980. *Games of the XXII Olympiad, Moscow, 1980: Official report of the Organizing Committee of the Games of the XXII Olympiad.* Moscow: Organizing Committee of the XXII Olympiad.

Petrone, Karen. 2000. *Life has become more joyous, comrades: Celebrations in the time of Stalin.* Bloomington: Indiana University Press.

Riordan, James. 1979. *Sport in the USSR and the 1980 Olympic Games.* London: Collet's.

Salutskii, Anatoly. 1981. *Moskva: Olimpiskoe Leto.* Moscow: Novosti.

Shteinbakh, Valeri. 1980. *The Soviet contribution to the Olympics.* Moscow: Novosti.

Starostin, Nikolai. 1989. *Futbol skvoz' gody.* Moscow: Sovetskaia Rossiia.

Stites, Richard. 1989. *Revolutionary dreams: Utopian vision and experimental life in the Russian revolution.* Oxford: Oxford University Press.

Sugden, John, and Alan Tomlinson. 1998. *FIFA and the contest for world football—who rules the peoples' game?* Cambridge: Polity Press.

Suny, Ronald. 1998. *The Soviet experiment: Russia, the USSR, and the successor states.* Oxford: Oxford University Press.

Timasheff, Nicholas. 1946. *The great retreat.* New York: Fordham University Press.

Turrini, Joseph. 2001. "It was communism versus the free world": The USA-USSR dual track meet series and the development of track and field in the United States, 1958–1985. *Journal of Sport History* 28 (3): 427–69.

Van Geldern, James. 1993. *Bolshevik festivals.* Berkeley: University of California Press.

Vartanian, Aksel. 1997. *Sto Let Rossiskomu futbolu.* Moscow: Gregory Page.

Chapter 10

Los Angeles 1984 and 1932

Commercializing the American Dream

Alan Tomlinson

INTRODUCTION

In 1984, the Los Angeles Olympics rewrote the formula for staging the global sports spectacle. On the eve of the Olympic Games Gruneau could "argue that the Los Angeles Games are in no way a significant departure from practices established in earlier Olympics," and that they "are best understood as a more fully developed expression of the incorporation of sporting practices into the ever-expanding marketplace of international capitalism" (Gruneau 1984, 2). Two decades on, though, it had become clearer that the Los Angeles (LA) Games occupies a pivotal place in the history of the modern sports event, transforming the worldwide perception of their political and economic potential and, consequently, their international profile. After the 1980 Moscow Games, evaluated by Robert Edelman in chapter 9 of this book, the Olympics was in severe crisis, and it took the radical, ruthless, and ambitious vision of the new IOC president, Juan Antonio Samaranch, combined with LA's model for the staging of the Games, to restore credibility to the Olympics as a desirable modern cultural product to which cities and nations would continue to be drawn. Within a little over a decade of the LA Olympics, the United States would host both the men's football (soccer) World Cup finals (1994) and the Summer Olympics (Atlanta, 1996). Just ten years after the LA Olympics, Los Angeles staged the final of the most commercially successful World Cup ever, in the very same venue as the 1984 Olympic football final. For 1984, the organizers used the same stadium as had been used for the 1932 Olympics, claiming both financial prudence and a historical pedigree. Comparing and contrasting the conditions of the staging of the 1932 and 1984 events provides a basis for the analysis of fundamental shifts in the cultural and political meanings and significance of the international sports event.

THE HAMBURGER OLYMPICS: LOS ANGELES 1984

Peter Ueberroth took on the presidency of the Los Angeles Olympics Organizing Committee (LAOOC) in 1979. The IOC had been in a quandary in 1978, with Los Angeles the only candidate for the 1984 Olympic Games. Iran's capital, Teheran, had tabled a bid, but then withdrew. This seems remarkable to write, in a year in which the IOC's president, Dr Jacques Rogge, commented that all the bidding cities for the 2012 Olympic Games might well make the final ballot—including Havana, Istanbul, Leipzig, London, Madrid, Moscow, New York, Paris, and Rio de Janeiro. But the terrorist massacre of the Israeli team at Munich in 1972 and the spiralling costs of staging the Montreal Games in 1976 had left the Olympics looking like a terminally tarnished product. The IOC had no choice but to accept any conditions laid down by LA, and when Los Angeles' population voted against the use of any taxpayers' funds going toward the cost of the event, the bidding committee president, John Argue, "had to go back to the IOC and restructure L.A.'s bid and negotiate a rule that allowed a private group to stage the Games" (Ueberroth 1985, 27). In his ebullient, self-congratulatory account of the Olympic Games, Ueberroth lists the five main objections made by those predicting that the Games would be a disastrous failure: U.S. people would be inhospitable to visitors; Americans, being too selfish, would not volunteer; terrorists would flock to the site; smog, traffic, and crime would plague the city and the event; and a private organizing committee would never muster the necessary finances. Smugly, Ueberroth countered with the benefit of hindsight, "I knew we could succeed," and relates how he accepted the challenge on the basis of what he called "three simple assumptions":

1. The United States of America is the greatest country in the world, and every one of us knows how lucky we are to live here.
2. If enough Americans believe in an idea or project, anything is possible.
3. Patriotism is alive and well and all the people needed was a rallying point to give them reason to stand up and cheer for their country, their communities, themselves, and share their great spirit with the peoples of the world. (Ueberroth 1985, foreword, 10)

For Ueberroth, the Olympics "was the perfect vehicle to join the public and private sectors in a partnership . . . for private enterprise to enhance itself and show what is good about mankind" (1985, foreword, 9). On this basis, the LAOOC signed up thirty-five sponsors, "large, often multinational corporations which contributed a minimum of $4 million in cash and/or in-kind products or services" (Perelman 1985, 95). For this, sponsors got the right to use all of the LAOOC symbols for advertising and promotions. This included the "Star in Motion" symbol, the mascot (Sam, the Olympic Eagle), and the sports pictograms, LA's version of that Esperanto of the body innovated twelve years earlier for the Munich Olympics (see Christopher Young's analysis in chapter 7 of this book). This financial strategy was presented as both an innovative self-financing model and a form of selective control of commercial trends: "the LAOOC was determined to limit the commercialization of the Games by reducing the number of firms with licenses for various items from the Organizing Committee" (Perelman 1985, 94). The projected target of funding to be raised from the corporate sector was set at $116 million. This was exceeded. And what the controls or constraints on commercial exploitation really meant was a concentration of revenue generation and an exclusivity of brand association: "In comparison with past Games, the LAOOC succeeded well in limiting the commercial spread of the Games' symbols" (Perelman 1985, 94). Montreal had had 42 official sponsors, 124 suppliers, and 140 licensees; Moscow 35 sponsors, 290 suppliers, and an incredible 7,272 licensees. Los Angeles boasted a streamlining that held the number of official sponsors at 35, reduced the number of suppliers to 64, and slashed the number of licensees to 65. The 35 official sponsors comprised a litany of the United States' corporate elite and a celebration of consumer capitalism: ABC radio and television, American Express, Anheuser-Busch (Budweiser), ARA Services, Arrowhead Puritas Waters, American Telephone and Telegraph (ATT), Atari, Atlantic Richfield, General Motors, Canon, Coca-Cola, Converse, First Interstate Bank, Fuji Photo Films, International Business Machines, Levi Strauss, McDonald's, M&M Mars, Motorola, Pacific Bell, Sanyo Electric, Southern Pacific, Southland Corporation, *Sports Illustrated*, Times Mirror, Trans America, United Airlines, Warner Communications, Westinghouse Electric, and Xerox. Dentsu, Inc., had a "special designation" status as the official marketing agent for Japan (Perelman 1985, 95–97).

The sixty-four companies accepted into the "supplier program" included long-term Olympic and World Cup partner Adidas, providing handballs and soccer balls, and suppliers covering services ranging from poultry to metal detectors (there was of course a massive security alert for these Olympic Games), floor coverings to Muzak, pianos (which certainly made their mark in the opening ceremony) to floral services, and hair care to waste management. While the official sponsors could share between them blocks of tickets totaling 585,700 and had their pick of LA's top hotel suites and rooms, the suppliers had to make do with only 14,300 tickets. The suppliers "provided a combination of cash, products and/or services needed by the organizers to stage the Games. Total contributions . . . reached into the hundreds of thousands of dollars, and suppliers could use only the 'Star in Motion' symbol in advertising and promotional activities" (Perelman 1985, 98). Licensees comprised the third category of corporate support for the economics of the Olympic Games. Companies were "authorized specifically to manufacture and sell a variety of souvenir products featuring all LAOCC symbols" (Perelman 1985, 102). The companies paid the Organizing Committee a standard royalty rate of 10 percent, linked to a guaranteed minimum royalty, a proportion of which was paid at the time of the signing of the deal. Of the sixty-five companies to be so authorized, eight were sublicensees of Adidas (France), selling bags, towels, caps, balls, and swimwear, peddling the Adidas triple strip everywhere any Olympic punter might look and showing the degree to which the influential sports entrepreneur, Horst Dassler, was already influencing the commercial profile of the world sports event (Tomlinson 2005a), in tandem with Samaranch's IOC and the world football governing body, FIFA. This all added up to LA's strategy to control the commercialization of the Olympic product.

Los Angeles reported a $222 million profit. The program of revenue generation and a "careful control of costs by the organizers" (Perelman 1985, 115) were stated as the key factors. Audited in March 1985, the LAOOC's operations were as follows:

Revenues	
Broadcast rights sales	$286,794,000
Ticket sales	$139,929,000
Sponsorship and licensing	$126,733,000
Interest income	$ 76,319,000
Coin program	$ 35,985,000
Other (primarily non-monetary contributions, revenue from accommodations, and ticket handling charges)	<u>$102,884,000</u>
Total revenues:	$768,644,000
Expenses	
Operating expenses	$398,394,000
Payments related to the use of venues and facilities	$ 97,389,000
International Olympic Committee	<u>$ 50,145,000</u>
Total expenses:	<u>$545,928,000</u>
Excess of revenues over expenses:	$222,716,000

(Perelman 1985, 118–19)

The U.S. Olympic Committee received 40 percent of this surplus, the national governing bodies of U.S. Olympic sports 20 percent, and 40 percent went to the Los Angeles Olympic Committee Amateur Athletics Foundation, "for the promotion and development of sport" (Perelman 1985, 119). Looking back at these figures, and recalling early estimates of required manpower requirements, Ueberroth spoke with revealing candor of the finances: "One of the miracles of the Games was the financing, that we were even within several hundred million of what we thought we were going to be, from 1979 to 1985, is a miracle. Now, I don't know how you do that with all the unknowns. I think we were very lucky. It wasn't any great skill that I have" (Reich, 1984–1985). It was also a very opportune moment as sport's place in the media marketplace was strengthening. Paul Ziffren, chairman of the LAOOC from March 1979 onward, confirmed this, talking to *LA Times* journalist Ken Reich in March 1985. In negotiations for television rights, he and his colleagues were looking to seal a deal at $150 to $200 million: "None of us hoped for more than 200 . . . I was at David's, and when ABC made its $225 million offer, everyone's eyes were open. Everyone was amazed. That included Ueberroth and Wolper" (Reich 1984–1985). "David" was David Wolper, veteran of the television and film industries. He had predicted $185 million for the rights and recalls how "ABC came in and made one bid, one individual bid of $225 million, take it or leave it, 48 hours, yea or nay in 48 hours. That's exactly what happened. Yea or nay in 48 hours, there wasn't one other fucking word said" (Reich 1984–1985). Except, pretty soon, "yes." This was a deal that the organizers could hardly turn down.

None of the organizers' financial calculations recognized formally the volunteer labor on which the success of the event depended. Ziffren had, though, built this into the planning right from the start, telling Reich that his "insistence on the use of volunteers" was one of the areas of which he was most proud: "And I certainly feel that not only did it save millions and millions of dollars, but it contributed greatly to turning around the apathy in the community and creating the enthusiasm that finally exploded with the Games" (Reich 1984–1985).

AT&T sponsored the torch relay, amidst much controversy over the ownership and symbolism of the flame and the torch. And the opening and closing ceremonies celebrated California's rescue act in inimitable Hollywood showbiz style. The Olympic Games were produced with only 5 percent of the budget used for Moscow. Twenty-six sites were renovated. Only two new venues were constructed, the swimming pool (located at the University of Southern California and funded by a $3 million allocation from the McDonalds Olympic Trust) and the velodrome (at California State University, the $2,911,585 costs underwritten by sponsor Southland Corporation) (Perelman 1985, 73, 76). Use of so many existing facilities lent the event what one design specialist has called "an essentially ephemeral physical quality" (Friedman 1985, 2). Much thought was given to the design and the look of the Olympic Games, led by a principle of "festive federalism":

> The overall Look, designed as an "invasion of butterflies" or "urban confetti," succeeded in turning the streets, sites, and other public areas into a constellation of ephemeral colors that brought residents a heightened sense of excitement, emotion, and history. (Perelman 1985, 107–108)

Ephemeral enough for many not to notice. In fact, the Los Angeles Games lacked a popular festive dimension, as ethnographic observations by John MacAloon (see chapter 2 in this book) bear out. With heightened terrorist alerts and massive security around sites and the three university-based athletes' villages (one 125 miles north of the LA city center, in Santa Barbara), the 1984 Olympic Games were a quintessential television event.

LA's achievement was based upon the combination of the optimistic and opportunistic ambitions of a regional elite, the mobilization of private capital in the corporate support strategy, the free labor of 30,000 volunteers (when only 3,000 were initially anticipated), and national political backing from the Reagan administration. This constituted a reframing of the Olympic project and became the first case of a significantly profit-making modern Olympics, according at least to the forms of accounting reported after the event. The opening and closing ceremonies celebrated the globally resonant image of U.S. culture: grand pianos, Western genre, jazz, dance, slavery, and the conquering of outer space (Tomlinson 1989). Analysts of economic impact could claim that total revenues from overall economic impact would benefit the region to the tune of another $202 million (ERA 1984, 14), but the real legacy of the LA Games was a model for the revitalization of the Olympics as a commercial product and a prime commodity for the global media.

The Dustbowl Games: Los Angeles 1932

"I'm a Dustbowl Refugee," sang Woody Guthrie in the Great Depression years following the 1929 crash. California beckoned for many, land of milk, honey, and false promises immortalized in John Steinbeck's *The Grapes of Wrath*, the Westward trek of the Joad family from Oklahoma, testimony to the contradictions and tragedies at the heart of the American Dream of mobility and prosperity:

> And while the Californians wanted many things, accumulation, social success, amusement, luxury, and a curious banking security, the new barbarians wanted only two things—land and food; and to them the two were one. And a homeless hungry man . . . in the south he saw the golden oranges hanging on the trees, the little golden oranges on the dark green trees; and guards with shotguns patrolling the lines so a man might not pick an orange for a thin child, oranges to be dumped if the price was low. (Steinbeck 1990, 273–74)

It was an extraordinary period in which sport offered a public spectacle that combined the themes of escapism, hope, individual accomplishment, and collective pride. From dance marathons to horse racing, popular culture and sport provided potential escape routes, or temporary diversions, sometimes tragic, as epitomized in the fate of West Texan would-be Hollywood starlet Gloria, seduced by the movie magazines into the showbiz fantasy, but aware that it is "Always tomorrow . . . The big break is always tomorrow" (McCoy 1965, 120). Gloria's will-to-death in McCoy's 1935 novel, showed in the dance-marathon phenomenon a seamy and ruthlessly exploitative side to the dream of success. Laura Hillenbrand, in her epic account of the achievements of the horse Seabiscuit also captures this context well, identifying

> a burgeoning industry of escapism. America was desperate to lose it-self in anything that offered affirmation. The nation's corner theaters hosted 85 million people a week for 25-cent viewings of an endless array of cheery musicals and screwball comedies. On the radio, the idealized world of *One Man's Family* and the just and reassuring tales of *The Lone Ranger* were runaway hits. Downtrodden Americans gravitated strongly toward the Horatio Alger protagonist, the lowly-bred Everyman who rises from anonymity and hopelessness. They looked for him in spectator sports, which were enjoying explosive growth. (Hillenbrand 2001, 141–42)

It is important to recognize the broader cultural context in which any Olympic Games takes place, and Guiney (1982, chapter 3) lists several other 1932 cultural moments: the debut of four-year-old Shirley Temple, Cary Grant's first film, Greta Garbo in *Mata Hari*, Bogart's return to the stage, the death of sixteen-year-old Rin Tin Tin, and, more weightily, or at least solemnly, the strides made by Nazism and other political movements in Europe, the consolidation of the Great Depression in the United States, and the Lindbergh death. Again, we see the popular cultural sphere providing solace, consolation, and diversion for many from the political and economic realities of the day.

Documentation on the 1932 Olympic Games, though, is sparse, and predictably the genre of souvenir literature memorializes a sanitized California, a cocooned and privileged world of sport—the *Official Pictorial Souvenir* (attributed to the Xth Olympiad Los Angeles, 1932, Olympic Games) comprises pictures of arrivals and training, and of rosewood trees, motion pictures, beaches, and riding tracks. But beneath this glossy representation, the cultural entrepreneurs behind the 1932 Olympic Games were acutely aware of the wider context of their plans, and of the social tensions that the Games might potentially exacerbate. To the organizers, a spirit of Olympism "illuminated" the "dark abyss of Depression, people from all over the world have gone home with new hope, and 'a finer understanding of and a more intimate friendship for their fel-low man, regardless of race or creed'" (Xth Olympiad Committee of the Games of Los Angeles. U.S.A. 1932 Ltd., 1933, 30; for the rest of this section, this source is referred to as the OR, the Official Report, and it is this source to which references refer when pagination only is cited). The event generated "memories of a splendid spectacle, splendidly staged, splendidly acted" (p. 29). The authors of the OR mixed a Christian conscience with a reformulation of the ideals of Olympism:

> Forty nations actually sent their representatives to sustain the flame of the Olympic Torch and to carve again in imperishable form the inspiring Olympic doctrine of good sportsmanship and peace and better understanding among the peoples of the earth.
>
> To us the matter is one of reverential sentiment. We make this statement without fear of those who may scoff at such an idea in this materialistic age. Sentiment, moulded from the finest of human emotions, rests at the very foundation of the Olympic movement. Sentiment achieved the glorious success of the Games of the Xth Olympiad. Sentiment sustained the whole Olympic family in carrying on, in a period of worldwide economic depression and political strife, and even at the cost of extreme self-sacrifice, in the determination to make the Games of the Xth Olympiad an outstanding success. (p. 29)

Here we see the zealous religiosity that has fueled successive Olympiads, offered as an antidote to the material dilemmas and problems of the contemporary world. Such a missionary motif is expressed even more emphatically in the opening commentary to a collection of the official programs of the Olympic Games (Times Mirror 1932). The program for Saturday, July 30, Olympic Park, costing ten cents, profiled a flaxen-haired youth (fairly androgynous), holding a green flower draped around his shoulders, clad in white, the torso layered so that the rib cage and the chest protruded, the latter breastlike. The commentary in the program focused not on the idealized body as so represented but an idealism of the (religious) spirit. Dr. Robert Gordon Sproul, president of the University of California, entitled his contribution "The Same Great Pattern." He summarized the Greek Olympiads as a "social and intellectual symposium, held under a sacred truce, during which the states, ceasing from war, cultivated friendship (p. 18). In their Games, as in all their life, the Greeks aimed at balance and harmony, the beauty of the spirit reflected in the beauty of the flesh, recognizing, as Plato put it, that 'the same great pattern enters into both'" (pp. 18, 19). Sproul went on to draw comparisons between the "lofty and reverent spirit that characterized the athletic festivals of ancient Hellas" and the aspirations for the 1932 event that could, "like their ancient pattern, help the life of men to higher physical, spiritual, and moral values" (p. 19):

With one heart and one voice, we who are here assembled, spectators and competitors alike, dedicate these Games to the high purposes in which the original Olympiad was conceived and to which it ideally ministered—to clean sport and fair play, to the development of sound minds in sound bodies, to the loyalties of the team underwriting the loyalties of life, to respect for opponents, win or lose, and to the brotherhood of mankind. We ask for the Xth Olympiad, conceived in this sprit, the blessing of the Most High, that in His awful hand it may prove a potent instrument for the peace of the world, for the goodwill of peoples, for the upbuilding of His kingdom upon the earth. (p. 19)

Such rhetoric could justify the staging of the event in the midst of the Great Depression. The organizers, though, had more mundane things on their minds. In a number of ways, their decisions helped shape the modern conception of the Olympic event in terms of timing, schedule, and promotion. The official line was that no stain of the commercial was permitted to taint the ideal:

The record of our city's conception of its responsibility, and of its preparations from beginning to end, discloses one fundamental and guiding principle, which was to adhere strictly to the Olympic ideals and to make such contributions in the organization of the Games as would strengthen and perpetuate those ideals. Not a single note of commercialism was allowed to permeate the consummation of the task. (p. 30)

For all but swimming and rowing, facilities and stadiums were already in place. In altering existing stadiums, future use was also considered. The principle here was the simple one of drawing on the past and creating a legacy for the future. A tribune had to be constructed for VIPs and could seat 809. Two thousand seats were eliminated and replaced with 706 special places for press correspondents (p. 67).

The organization underpinning the Olympic Games was developed out of established community and development projects. The Organizing Committee assumed responsibility from 1928, but there was already a foundation on which to build. In 1919, the California Fiestas Association had been established to revive old Spanish fiestas. It had planned the Los Angeles Memorial Coliseum stadium. In 1920, the association dissolved, and its members formed the Community Development Association (CDA), a non-profit organization that in partnership with the city and county of Los Angeles financed and erected the Coliseum. In 1919, a member of the Fiestas Association had suggested holding the Olympic Games, and its president went to Antwerp in 1920 to present the city's case to the IOC. He—William May Garland—was then asked to join the committee. In Rome in 1923, the IOC supported in principle a United States Games, designating Los Angeles the most suitable city location. The CDA in 1927 had got together with the state to secure a financial base for the planning, leading to the California Olympiad Bond Act of that year—this led to a million-dollar issue and the formation of a five-person California Olympiad Commission to administer the bond. Economic plans were therefore established before the Great Crash, so securing the economic security of the event. The Games could therefore claim not to be diverting resources in a time of need but to be contributing to higher spiritual ideals and social goals at little cost. The Games reported a $1 million profit.

"Between 1900 and 1928," Wallechinsky notes, "no Summer Olympics was shorter than 79 days" (2000, xxiv). Los Angeles 1932, modernized this sprawled-out event. The Official Report summarizes the scale of the streamlined, rationalized event in a section on tickets and attendance:

> The schedule, covering a sixteen-day period, consisted of competitions in sixteen sports and demonstrations, and comprised a total of approximately one hundred and thirty-five individual programs, to be held in nine different stadiums, auditoriums, and water courses. It was the responsibility of the Executive Committee to present this complex schedule to the public simply and intelligibly, and at the same time in sufficient detail to enable purchasers to make an intelligent selection of events they desired to attend. (p. 95)

Sensitive to the effects of the Great Depression, the organizers also agreed that prices should be set as low as possible. Los Angeles was also the first Olympic Games to be marketed in any serious way and covered by various new communications technologies. To communicate publicity, "the first organized department should be the Press Department, to serve as a bureau of information to Olympic Groups as well as a news disseminating agency for the World Press" (p. 45). It became the first systematic news service for a preparatory Olympiad period.

Realizing very early the paramount importance of athlete comfort, the committee came up with the idea of the Olympic Village. This innovation is made much of in the OR. At the beginning of the report, de Coubertin's 1892 announcement is cited: "Let us export our oarsmen, our runners, our fencers into other lands. That is the true Free Trade of the future," and this sentiment was taken to heart by the 1932 organizers: "For the first time in history men from all lands, speaking many tongues, were to live together in one communal establishment" (OR, 255). For two dollars a day athletes were housed, fed, transported, and entertained. Not all athletes were accepted into the village, the hundred or so women athletes being based in the Wilshire district of the city, visited by and socializing with film stars and celebrities. The men's teams are pictured training together, wrestling playfully, and eating together. The OR makes much of this "harmonious commingling" (p. 233) and reports that many athletes "left with regret": "Swayed no doubt in some instances by racial and national prejudices . . . they found themselves members of a community without prohibition or class distinctions. . . . In all likelihood the Olympic Village presented the purest cross-section of the world ever assembled, and each delegation in turn was a cross-section of a nation. The athletes came from all social strata. Twenty-three scions of nobility conformed to the same rules as their fellows, lived the same life, and liked it. For many of their athletes it was their first encounter with genuine democracy. All were quick to grasp the prevailing spirit, and all gave it their whole-hearted cooperation" (p. 287). For the Californian organizers at the heart of the depression, the Olympic Games were a reassuring cultural and political experiment. As the 3,500 volunteers, bedecked in white, took part in the musical program, the organizers could look on with satisfaction at a show that created some diversion from the everyday realities of the Great Depression, and that raised the international profile of their city.

CONCLUSION

What binds the Brazilian men's World Cup victory over Italy in the Rosebowl in 1994, Team USA's triumph over China in the women's World Cup Final at the same stadium in 1999, Carl Lewis's strutting presence in his home-club state in the Coliseum/Olympic Stadium in 1984, and the first gold-medal achievement by a black athlete at the Olympics when Eddie Tolan claimed the 100-yard title in the same stadium at which Lewis peaked half a century later? On one level, the answer is simple: cultural entrepreneurs in the United States, driven by a combination of personal ambition and patriotism, believing that the United States is the perfect location for the staging of a large-scale event at which the world's elite performers are on display. There is a pride in putting on the best show in town. There is added pride in commercializing it and making a profit. The successful Olympic Games of 1984 laid the foundations for the World Cup 1994 to be staged in the United States, again with little in the way of new infrastructure, and at a vast profit (Tomlinson 2005b, chapter 4). The 1984 event had some glorious sporting moments, as all Olympics have had, but it is the commercial success that marks them as a pivotal case in the contemporary history of international sport.

There are different ways of writing the history of the Olympic Games, and the levels of human endeavor and achievement should not be left out of analyses and accounts. All Olympics generate their own fund of stories. Guiney, in the foreword to his 1982 book on the Games of a half century earlier, went for the label *The Friendly Olympics*. He remembers the homecoming of a local hero, a gold-medal winning shot-putter to his village in Ireland. Guiney recalls that a brass band was playing, enlivening

> the greying image of a parade in the little town of Kanturk, [County Cork], where I was born. . . . I can vaguely picture the parade—and the gathering in the Market Square. . . . A giant of a man, Dr. Pat O'-Callaghan, was back in triumph from the other side of the world, back from the strange, wonderful, exotic city of Los Angeles on the remote West Coast of America—and home again, all the way across the Atlantic, to Kanturk, which in those days—and I looked it up when I set out to write this book—had a population of 1,518 people. And with him he had brought the supreme prize of international sport—an Olympic Gold medal. . . . Little wonder that Kanturk went on a glorious celebration for that homecoming—and of course the day. (Guiney 1982, unpaginated)

This folksy reminiscence sets the tone for an account of the Olympic Games revolving around the personally heroic, the quirkier the better. English runner Robert Tisdall's story is one of these, training while living in a railway carriage in Sussex, as preparation for 400-meter hurdle gold glory. The tone saddens to relate the tragedy of Japanese horseman Baron Takeichi Nishi, winner of an equestrian gold on Uranus, who died at Iwo Jima twelve and a half years later. Guiney gives a central position in his book to Mildred "Babe" Didrikson, who set world and Olympic records in the first heat of the 80 meter-hurdles and in the final. Next morning in the newspapers, Damon Runyon wrote: "'Miss Babe (Whatta-gal) Didrikson leaps the hurdles like a gay gazelle and runs on the flat like a sacred coyote. The California breeze sifts through her bobbed black hair. She runs in a neat costume of white, consisting of a skimpy shirt and little panties which reveal many of her muscles'"(cited on p. 51 of Guiney 1982). She then leant her name to a car promotion and was suspended by the AAU and banned for life from track and field, before moving into vaudeville and golf, and marrying a 285-pound wrestler, George Zaharias. Reinstated in golf, she kept winning, receiving the Athlete of the Year award five times before turning professional and sweeping the world. She died in 1956 of cancer, age forty-six. The significance of such individual stories should never be underestimated (nor should the voyeuristic mode in which such achievements and stories are sometimes described). They are the personalized narratives that make the Olympic story so enduring. But however central such stories are to the collective Olympic memory, they can hardly account for the historically established hold that the Olympics has established on the popular global consciousness in the modern era.

Whatever the commonalities in the rhetoric of sport used to justify Olympic and comparable events, and the claims for cultural continuity binding the Olympics of 1932 and 1984, there are critical differences in the social meanings and cultural values of the events. Ronald Reagan represented a right-wing, Republican U.S. government, using the Olympics as a propaganda tool in the cold war; Herbert Hoover and his administration operated from a different political base, committed to a New Deal solution to the deepening inequalities of the capitalist order. Reagan could hardly resist the media opportunity in staging the Olympic Games, seeing in them an embodiment of the qualities of the free world and unbridled capitalism. Hoover did not make it to the 1932 ceremonies, delegating this to his vice president. Beyond some superficial comparisons and cultural continuities in hyperbole and rhetoric, there are revealing differences in the nature of the two events, best understood in terms of the relationship of public service to private capital. In 1932, the private sector committed itself to a notion of service by those who had benefited from capitalism, a notion fueled too by a religious zeal. The 1984 Olympic Games reveal service as capitalism, a condition in which public interest is equated with capitalism rather than capitalism putting aside its gains in favor of the public interest. Both events would generate dramatic narratives of individual accomplishment, tales to warm the heart of any Olympic idealist or apologist. But upon closer scrutiny, the half century between the two events demonstrates the triumph of an unbridled market model in the staging of the major sports event. Los Angeles 1984, gave permission to nations and cities worldwide to manipulate the Olympic ideal in any way suited to their developmental agenda and ideological priorities. With Samaranch at the helm, the Olympic sponsorship program in place, and the cold war soon to be won by the champions of global capitalism, the 1984 Olympic Games ensured that the Olympic future was secure in the embrace of commercialism and its effects, and the commodification of the Olympic ideal.

NOTE

I am grateful to the staff at the IOC Museum/Study Center, Lausanne, for its exceptional hospitality, induction, and guidance to historical sources; to Dr. Wayne Wilson at the Los Angeles Library of the Amateur Athletic Foundation, a positive outcome of the profits of 1984 that is a dream resource and source for scholars of sport; to all participants at the Pembroke College symposium where a first draft of some of the material in this chapter was presented; and to Professor Toby Miller for his typically astute theoretical comments on the comparison between the 1932 and 1984 events, which have been absorbed into the concluding comments to this chapter.

REFERENCES

Economic Research Associates (ERA). 1984. *Community economic impact of the 1984 Olympic Games*. Los Angeles: Economic Research Associates.

Friedman, Mildred. 1985. LA 84: Games of the XXIII Olympiad. *Design Quarterly* 127: editorial, p. 2.

Gruneau, Rick. 1984. Commercialism and the Modern Olympics. In *Five-ring circus—Money, power, and politics at the Olympic Games*, ed. Alan Tomlinson and Garry Whannel. London: Pluto Press.

Guiney, David. 1982. *The friendly Olympics*. Dublin: PR Books Ireland/Brendan Press.

Hillenbrand, Laura. 2001. *Seabiscuit—The true story of three men and a racehorse*. London: Fourth Estate.

McCoy, Horace. 1965. *They shoot horses, don't they?* Harmondsworth: Penguin.

Perelman, Richard B., ed. 1985. *Olympic retrospective—The Games of Los Angeles*. Los Angeles: Los Angeles Olympic Organizing Committee.

Reich, Kenneth. 1984–1985. *The Reich manuscripts*. Los Angeles: Amateur Athletics Foundation of Los Angeles.

———. 1986. *Making it happen—Peter Ueberroth and the 1984 Olympics*. Santa Barbara, CA: Capra Press.

Steinbeck, John. 1990. *The grapes of wrath*. London: Mandarin.

Times Mirror. 1932. *Complete collection of the 39 official programs: Games of the Xth Olympiad* Los Angeles U.S.A. 1932. Los Angeles: Times Mirror.

Tomlinson, Alan, 1989. Representation, ideology, and sport: The opening and closing ceremonies of the Los Angeles Olympic Games. In *The Olympic movement and the mass media — Past, present, and future issues*, ed. Roger Jackson and Thomas McPhail. Calgary: Hurford Enterprises.

———. 2005a. The making of the global sports economy: ISL, Adidas, and the rise of the corporate player in world sport. In *Sport and corporate nationalisms*, ed. David Andrews, C. L. Cole, and Michael Silk. Oxford: Berg.

———. 2005b. *Sport and leisure cultures*. Minneapolis: University of Minnesota Press.

Ueberroth, Peter, with Richard Levin and Amy Quinn. 1985. *Made in America—His own story*. New York: William Morrow and Company.

Wallechinsky, David. 2000. *The complete book of the Olympics—2000 edition*. London: Aurum Press.

Xth Olympiade Committee of the Games of Los Angeles. U.S.A. 1932 Ltd., 1933. *The Games of the Xth Olympiade **Los Angeles 1932** Official Report*. Los Angeles.

Chapter 11

Barcelona 1992

Evaluating the Olympic Legacy

Christopher Kennett and Miquel de Moragas

Introduction

Roche (2000) described the Olympics Games as a "show" that is constantly on the road, traveling from city to city every four years. In 1992 the show stopped in Barcelona for sixteen days of sporting competition that left an indelible mark on the city, its residents, all those involved in organizing the Games, the spectators who experienced the event live, and the millions that watched it on television. The legacy of those days lives on in Barcelona in many tangible and intangible ways; it is still an "Olympic city" (Moragas et al. 2003, 279–88).

The Barcelona Olympic Games were widely heralded as a success in the mass media, and the keys to that success have been researched and documented perhaps more than any other Games in Olympic history (see Moragas and Botella 1995, 2002). The organizational model adopted in Barcelona has affected IOC policy (Felli 2002, 65–76) and was highly influential in the staging of the Sydney 2000 Olympic Games (Cashman and Hughes 1999) and other mega-sports events.

This chapter analyzes the political leverage of the Barcelona Olympic Games by interested political actors in the bidding, organizing, and staging of the games, leading to a discussion of the legacies of the Games and enabling an evaluation of whether the explicit and implicit objectives have been achieved to date.

Globalization and City Marketing

All Olympic Games occur within a specific set of historical circumstances at the local and global levels. For the Barcelona Games, these historical circumstances were dominated by the beginnings of accelerated globalizing processes, changing international relations after the breakup of the Soviet Union and the establishment of Catalonia as an autonomous region within the newly democratic Spanish state.

Giddens (1998) described the consequences of globalization for the nation-state, subject to three main sets of movements hollowing it out. First, nation-states experience a loss of power to intergovernmental organizations (e.g., the European Union). Second, and simultaneously, a reinforcement of local and regional governance may occur, involving a decentralization of nation-state power. Third, central governments may be bypassed through agreements between regions and cities from different countries. While Giddens emphasized that an important role for the nation-state still existed, it is clear that this role had changed in the context of these movements.

A further consequence of accelerated globalizing processes, in particular an increased flow of global capital, has been competition between cities to attract investment. In order to increase competitive advantage, many cities have entered into what has been identified as "city marketing," which van den Berg and others defined as

> the set of activities intended to optimize the tuning of supply of urban functions to the demand for them from inhabitants, companies, tourists, and other visitors. (2000, 6)

City marketing involves investment in the "product," which is the city itself and the infrastructure required to support foreign investment, in particular, service-sector activities such as information technology (IT), finance, or tourism. Combined with this product development, cities also undertake promotional activities to communicate their product to target groups. Van den Berg and others (2000) highlighted the role that sport, including hosting sport events, has played in the marketing of European cities, including Helsinki, Manchester, Rotterdam, Turin, and Barcelona. Evidence from these cities revealed how mega-sports events can be a catalyst for urban change and the promotion of cities on a global scale.

However, the following sections will show that urban change as part of a city marketing process represented only one set of objectives behind the Barcelona Olympic Games. It will be necessary to extend this analysis to tangible and intangible considerations at the local level to consider regional and national interests, as well as the role of the IOC as an international nongovernmental organization. Only by understanding the objectives behind the organization of Barcelona 1992, will it be possible to evaluate the legacies of the Olympic Games.

The Bid

The city of Barcelona had already played host to two major events, the World Fair in 1888 and the International Exhibition in 1929, which served as vehicles for modernization and urban change in a very similar way to the Olympic Games in 1992. Barcelona had also unsuccessfully attempted to host the Games in 1924, 1936, 1940, and 1972—thus the Olympic dream was an enduring one through the twentieth century.

The 1992 bid was formulated in a period of transition to democracy that was particularly important for Catalonia and its capital city. The establishment of Catalan autonomy was a priority in cultural and economic terms, but also politically. The Catalan language and many cultural traditions had been banned under the Franco regime; it was now time to reestablish Catalan national identity. The Generalitat (Catalan Autonomous Government) was reinstalled in 1979 with primary responsibility for implementing this process.

A commonly stated factor in the successful organization of the Barcelona Olympics has been the political consensus that was achieved between political parties and the local, regional, and national tiers of government (Joan Botella 1995, 139–48, 2002, 105–18; Truño 1995, 43–56, 2002, 77–103). However, the real key to success came in securing this consensus at the beginning and maintaining it to the end of the bid process among the political parties in the new Spanish democracy.

Indeed, Juan Antonio Samaranch, then preparing his candidacy for the IOC presidency, was a catalyst behind the process, encouraging Barcelona's Mayor Narcís Serra (Catalan Socialist Party) to bid for the Olympic Games, and then he intervened to establish and maintain the political census.

The bid jigsaw came together to produce a political elite consisting of key individuals in 1982 when Felipe Gonzalez, a supporter of the Barcelona bid, won the general election representing the Spanish Socialist Workers' Party (PSOE). Barcelona's Serra was appointed minister of defense (eventually becoming deputy prime minister), a key role in the new cabinet. Pasqual Maragall took his place as mayor; he also represented the Catalan Socialist Party, was a supporter of the bid, and eventually became head of COOB '92 (Comitè Organitzador Olímpic Barcelona, the Games' Organizing Committee). With Jordi Pujol, another bid supporter installed in the Generalitat, the political links between national, regional, and local levels were strong and provided a united front to the public, the IOC, and ultimately the rest of the world.

Private-sector support was secured in the form of the Association of Businesses Barcelona '92 that brought together high-profile businessmen from Catalan society. After the bid was won, this strong, public-private partnership was deepened in the establishment of HOLSA '92 (Barcelona Holding Olímpic, S.A.), which was responsible for the construction of the main Olympic facilities, the Olympic Village, and 78km of new roads (Brunet 2002, 245–74).

The bid documents presented an extremely detailed and convincing plan for the staging of the Olympic Games, involving a mix of self-belief in the need to transform the city, extensive research and planning, and negotiation and improvisation, reflecting the traditional Catalan characteristics of *seny* and *rauxa* (common sense and drive).

However, Miquel Botella (1995, 18–42) identified that these documents were far from complete and did not include the press village, hotel plan, telecommunications tower, park and ride, nor the Olympic Port—one of the major urban changes that Barcelona was to undergo. In addition, many of the financial estimations eventually proved unrealistic.

Indeed, it was initially estimated that staging the Olympic Games themselves would incur the highest cost at $667 million or 84 percent of the total budget, while $125.8 million (16%) was to be spent on the four main Olympic areas (Montjuïc, Diagonal, Vall d'Hebron, and Marina Park). These figures did not include any investments such as the improvement of communication infrastructure not directly related to staging the Games. Total spending on the four sites actually totaled $3.6 billion, twenty-nine times more than the estimate (Brunet 1995). In fact, the financial records show that the budget reached $9.4 billion with the main volume of costs being created by construction projects (85.5%–55% of which were not directly related to the Olympic Games), as opposed to organizing the Games themselves (14.5%) (Brunet 1995).

POLITICAL ACTORS AND THEIR OBJECTIVES

While political consensus was achieved, the political actors involved in the management of COOB '92 pursued different objectives as part of their involvement in the Barcelona Games, which are summarized in Table 11.1.

TABLE 11.1
Main Aims of the Political Actors Involved in Barcelona '92

Political Actor	Main aim for Barcelona '92
Barcelona City Hall	Urban change and modernization
Generalitat	"Catalanization" of the Games
Central Spanish Government	The "1992 project"
Spanish Olympic Committee	Spanish sporting success
EU	European representation
IOC	Risk management

Source: Adapted and expanded from Joan Botella, 1995, 143.

TABLE 11.2
Public Sources of Revenue for the Barcelona Games

Public revenue	$US (2000)	% Total Funding
Generalitat	1.47bn	12.7%
Central State	1.197bn	10.4%
HOLSA Public Revenue	1.160bn	10.1%
Other	369m	3.2%
Barcelona City Hall	235m	2.0%
Transfer Payments	133m	1.2%
EU	84m	0.2%
Total	4.6bn	40.3%

Source: Brunet 2002, 247.

Josep Miquel Abad, councillor delegate of COOB '92, explicitly stated after the games that they formed a pretext for Barcelona's larger, longer-term plans and functioned as a vehicle through which to achieve them. He explained:

> All those involved . . . in the decision-making process knew that the Games were clearly a sporting event. I confess without shame, however, that this did not concern us, since what mattered . . . was to determine the dominating idea that would allow us to do in five or six years what had not been done in fifty, with the risk of taking another fifty if the opportunity was not taken. (Abad 1995, 12)

The promotion of the city's image was a priority. Moragas and others (1995, 76–106) described the desired image as modern, yet historic, designed to encourage projects that stimulated local economic activity and development. Attempts were made to position Barcelona as the economic hub of Southern Europe, a vibrant, cosmopolitan city with a rich cultural heritage.

It is important to understand that the political consensus that was achieved and maintained through the bidding and organizational phases of the Barcelona Games was all the more exceptional due to the intense rivalry between the Socialist Party that controlled the Barcelona City Council and the Provincial Council, on the one hand, and the Convergence and Union Party that controlled the Generalitat, on the other hand.

The overriding objective for the Generalitat was the "Catalanization" of the Barcelona Games (Joan Botella 1995, 139–48). Botella described the role of the Generalitat as participatory, seeking representation and exposure at an international level for Catalan national identity. The Generalitat, however, contributed directly more than any of the other tiers of public administration to the funding of the Olympic project, although this must be considered in the context of the complexities of the Spanish fiscal system (see Table 11.2). Fear that Spanish identity would overshadow Catalonia served as motivation to ensure that Catalonia was represented first and foremost but also that it was shown to be distinct from Spain (Moragas et al. 1995, 76–106).

Catalan nationalists formed the *Acció Olímpica* pressure group, which included members of the Convergence and Union Party that used the English slogan "Freedom for Catalonia" to demonstrate its claims for independence to a global audience but was not against the staging of the Games themselves (Crexell 1994). Hargreaves (2000) described the process of tense negotiations that took place between the political parties and the IOC over the representation of Catalan national identity, which eventually resulted in agreement and avoidance of nationalist disruption of the Games.

Much more subtle leverage by the Generalitat came in the use of symbols of Catalan identity, particularly in the torch relay, the international press, the presence of Catalan flags at the Olympic venues, the use of Catalan as one of the official languages of the Games, and, perhaps most importantly, the use of the ceremonies as a cultural display.

The Catalanization of the Olympic Games created particular tension with the central government. The socialist government, led by Felipe Gonzalez, had a bigger project of which the Barcelona Games played a key part. The "1992 project" included the Expo in Seville, and Madrid as the European "city of culture". The central Spanish government was interested in leveraging the Games in the promotion of Spain's image, and activities undertaken focused on projecting Spain as a "passionate and democratic" country distant from Franco's dictatorship (Moragas et al. 1995, 76–106). This was increasingly important after Spain's entry into the European Community in 1986. The aim was to reposition Spain internationally and to overcome some of the tourist stereotypes of siestas, bullfights, and *mañana*. Spain was to be redefined as a land of passion, closely linked to the sun, but also as a country of possibilities and opportunities, highlighted in the slogan "everything under the sun." This combination of passion, sun, and dynamism was captured in the Games' logo.

The Spanish government also made direct contributions to the funding of the Games (see Table 11.2), as well as passing a fiscal law that encouraged private investment in the infrastructural developments and sponsorship of the games. The Spanish Olympic Committee, the other main organization directly involved in the Games at the national level, was primarily concerned with the preparation of the Spanish athletes and organizing press accreditations. The success of the Spanish athletes, winning twenty-two medals (including thirteen gold) and coming in sixth in the medal tables, has been identified as one of the keys to the wider success of the Games, inspiring public and media support. The European Union also contributed a limited amount to the funding of the Games, ensuring its representation in the ceremonies and the identification of the Games as European, as well as Barcelonese, Catalan, and Spanish.

The IOC has an inherent interest in the successful organization of the Olympic Games and exercised a high degree of influence in the staging of the Barcelona event. In addition to the huge public investment in the Games and the cost of urban changes, more media and commercial interest was shown in the Games than ever, the TV rights being sold for $636 million and the TOP II (the Olympic program of sponsor—phase two) program contributing $175 million. This meant that the stakes were high, with the total cost of staging the Barcelona Games estimated to be $9.4 billion, making it three times more expensive than the Montreal '76 Games (see Table 11.3).

The Olympic Games were also of great personal significance to IOC President Juan Antonio Samaranch, who went on to state in his memoirs that if the bid had failed, he believed it would have forced his resignation. He seemed to view the bid as a direct reflection of his ability and credibility as IOC president and that the failure of his members to vote for Barcelona would have been effectively a vote against him and his presidency (Samaranch 2002). He kept close control over the bidding and organization processes, maintaining an objective position publicly but privately meeting frequently with political leaders (Moragas and Botella 2002). Samaranch undoubtedly played a pivotal role in securing the Olympic Games for Barcelona, as well as in maintaining the political consensus around the Olympic project. In addition, the Games signified a change in image for Samaranch in Barcelona and Catalonia: he received repeated praise from the democratic political leaders, culminating in a public homage paid to him in the celebration of the tenth anniversary of the Games in 2002.

TABLE 11.3
The Scale of the Games: Barcelona '92 Key Facts and Figures

People

Olympic Family: 39,461 people, including:
- 169 National Olympic Committees
- 9,368 athletes (16,000, including officials and delegation staff)
- 284 competitions
- 4,880 journalists
- 7,951 TV and radio staff

Operations Staff: 89,723

Finance

$6.9bn Total private investment (59.7% of total)
$4.6bn Total public investment (40.3% of total)
$9.4bn Total estimated cost of staging Barcelona '92 Games
Source: COOB '92 1992; Brunet 1995, 203–37, 2002, 245–74.

THE LEGACIES OF THE OLYMPIC GAMES, 1992–2004

When considering the multiple political interests in the Barcelona Games, at the local level it seems clear that the city of Barcelona was the big success story of the Games. This was reflected in the international press coverage, as journalists generally reported very positively on the city and its people, for instance in the *New York Times*.

> The athletes never had a chance. No matter how well they jumped and ran and rowed, they could never dominate these Summer Games. The city won the Games. The people of Catalonia won the Games. (Vecsey 1992)

The combination of investment in urban change that facilitated the staging of the Games, along with the rich cultural ambience of the city and the festival atmosphere created by the local people and visitors, provided the background for the sporting events. The organizational activity was characterized by clarity of ideas, strong leadership, consensus, stability, and what Maragall (1995, 9–10) called the "enormous patience and cold blood" of COOB '92. This enabled the effective resolution of problems and meant that the organization did not lose sight of the bigger picture, which was the creation of long-term legacies for the city of Barcelona.

The main political legacy of the Barcelona Games was the consensus achieved between the different levels of public administration and rival political parties described earlier, which was maintained in pursuit of shared strategic objectives. The same combination of political actors was involved in the organization of the Universal Forum of Cultures 2004 (discussed later), although relations between the local and national levels of government have become increasingly strained. The Socialist Party has remained in power both in Barcelona City Hall (under Mayor Joan Clos since 1997) and in the Provincial Council, as has the Convergence and Union Party under Jordi Pujol as president of the Generalitat, providing political continuity.[1] At the city level, the political legacies of the Barcelona Games have been characterized by the continued city marketing efforts of the Barcelona City Hall through public- and private-sector partnership and the formation and implementation of what could be identified as an event strategy to promote and develop Barcelona's image internationally.

As for the World Fair in 1888 and the International Exhibition in 1929, the Barcelona Games marked the city physically, leaving a legacy of sporting but, above all, urban infrastructure. Between 1986 and 1992, Barcelona underwent one of the most extensive urban renewal processes ever seen in a European city. These urban projects were both directly and indirectly related to the staging of the Olympic Games.

The overall aim to be achieved through these urban planning objectives was to provide Barcelona with the basic infrastructure necessary to establish it as a competitive global city. Millet stated that

> the Olympic project translated the indications and ambitions expressed by the city of Barcelona to strengthen the metropolitan area by giving the city conditions to compete with the most important cities in the world. (1995, 195)

Barcelona City Hall's objectives to modernize the city in infrastructural terms and open it up to the sea had been achieved, and investment continued in both the physical, urban "product" and promotion of Barcelona as an international destination for tourism and business.

In terms of continued urban planning and development, between 1992 and 2004 a total of 11.8 billion euros had been invested, 2 billion euros more in preparation for the Olympic Games (Brunet 2002, 245–74). Moreover, Barcelona City Hall took the opportunity to make further urban improvements through the staging of another large-scale event, the Universal Forum of Cultures 2004. As for the Games, a new neighborhood was created, Diagonal Mar, involving the construction of a mix of high-price housing, hotels, leisure facilities, and commercial outlets where the diagonal street meets the sea. The total cost of urban investment was estimated to be 2 billion euros (one-fifth of the costs of the Olympics).

While comment on the legacies of the Barcelona Games focuses on the benefits that have made hosting the Games a success for the city, there has been little research that enables us to establish more precisely for whom they were a success. It appears that many of the benefits of hosting the Games were not distributed evenly among social groups in the city, which is highlighted by the example of the Olympic Village.

The Olympic Village project was managed through a public-private partnership agreement called Nova Icaria S.A., and involved an investment of $1.9 billion. The village was planned and built to be sold as commercial property and private housing for use after the Games, regenerating the highly industrialized coastal part of the Poble Nou district. The sale of the properties created controversy and was met with criticism by the Convergance and Union Party, the Barcelona Federation of Associations of Neighbors (FAVB), and commentators such as renowned journalist and novelist Vázquez Montalbán. The controversy centered on the "positive discrimination" in the form of tax relief that was provided to companies interested in buying property in the area. Claims were made that this was purely speculative, enabling an instant profit to be made on the resale of properties at the market price or higher. This criticism was compounded by the FAVB's calls for 40 percent of the properties to be subsidized by the local government to enable people on a low income and young couples to live in the area. Fears were expressed that the neighborhood would be transformed from its historical working-class base to an exclusive, upper-middle-class area. Indeed, Vázquez Montalbán (1989) predicted that the Olympic Village would be populated exclusively by the upper middle class, ages twenty-five to forty, becoming a "pure post-modern bourgeoisie neighborhood." Montalbán highlighted the irony of the use of Icaria, the utopian socialist community (Cabet 1848), for the public-private partnership, particularly by the socialist local and central governments.

Tejero (1992) highlighted the fact that the Olympic Village constituted planned gentrification, involving the social substitution or displacement of the lower and middle classes by the upper-middle and upper-class groups. This was combined with the development of consumer-oriented leisure spaces and service-sector activities. Indeed, the Olympic Village could be regarded as the antithesis of Icaria, and by 2002 Montalbán's and Tejero's predictions had come true. Carbonell (2002, 309–20) highlighted the fact that the inhabitants of the Olympic Village were young, well educated, and well off—33.3 percent of residents were ages twenty-five to thirty-nine (compared to 21.7% in Barcelona in general), and 41.5 percent were university educated (17.2% in Barcelona). The area also had become the most expensive in the city in terms of property prices, increasing by 233 percent between 1993 and 2001. Compared to the Sant Martí district, where it is located, properties in the village were 35.3 percent more expensive in 2001 compared to 18.5 percent in 1993.

Therefore, while the residents of Barcelona could enjoy the vastly improved public spaces in the regenerated area around the Olympic Village, the real beneficiaries have been the companies involved in the construction and sale of the properties and the "new" social elite that has moved into them.

The total estimated impact of the games was £34.6 billion, including direct and indirect investment. From the direct investment made, Brunet (2002, 245–74) discounted the costs associated with organizing the Games themselves to arrive at a direct longer-term legacy of £10.7 billion, which comprised physical urban improvements to the city. The construction industry benefited most before the Games, and economic benefits for tourism-related businesses were most marked during the Games and in the immediate post-games period (Grup d'Estudis Sociològics sobre la Vida Quotidiana i el Treball, 1997).

Apart from the increase in economic activity, Barcelona has also undergone a change in the mix of economic activities undertaken in the city (Brunet 1993). The objectives of the Barcelona City Hall in terms of modernizing the city and increasing service-sector activities have also been achieved. As part of this process, the Barcelona City Council is actively encouraging the development of the scientific and new technology companies in the city, principally through the establishment of *Plan 22@BCN* in the Poble Nou district that was partly regenerated through the construction of the Olympic Village. At the time of writing, the project had already attracted to the area international companies, including Deutsche Telekom, Nokia, Lycos, and IBM.

Indeed, the opening of Barcelona to the global economy can be highlighted by the selection of the city as a base for a variety of multinational organizations (Truño 2002, 77–103). Barcelona continued to attract foreign investment, which totaled £4.8 billion in 1998 (28% of the total for Spain). By 2002, Barcelona maintained its position as the sixth best European city in which to locate a business, according to the Cushman and Wakefield, Healey and Barker (2002) survey of 506 companies from fifty countries.

These examples of the improved international positioning of Barcelona highlight not only the success in developing the necessary infrastructure but also in the promotion of the city. In 1993, Turisme de Barcelona was created through a public-private partnership between the Barcelona City Hall, Industry and Shipping of Barcelona, Barcelona Promoció, and the Chamber of Commerce. This organization's primary responsibility is the promotion of the city to attract leisure and business tourism.

The growth of tourism in Barcelona can be highlighted as one of the most important legacies of the investment in urban infrastructure and the publicity that the Olympic Games provided. However, this legacy was not inevitable; it was achieved through the continued investment in Barcelona's tourist destination product and its promotion. On the supply side, the city's hotel offer continued to grow after the initial impetus of the hotel plan established for the Olympic Games, increasing from 118 in 1990 to 215 in 2002. In 2003, Barcelona boasted nine five-star hotels and more than twice the number of four-star hotels in 2002 compared to 1990. The city's tourism figures for the 1990s speak for themselves. The total number of tourists increased from 1.7 million in 1990 to 3.6 million in 2002. As part of this growth, the motivation for visiting Barcelona shifted from business (69% in 1990) to leisure (52% in 2001), although more of a balance between leisure (49%) and business (47%) was evident in 2002. Tourists visiting Barcelona have also become more international; in 1990 49 percent came from abroad; in 2002, this had increased to 64 percent. An average stay of 2.4 nights and the fact that 49 percent of international tourists came from Europe highlight the position of Barcelona as a European city-break destination (Turisme de Barcelona 2003).

Duran (2002, 275–93) highlighted the importance of tourism to the local economy, estimating that tourism had a direct impact of £1.4 billion annually on the economy of the city (14% of the total GDP), double the impact the industry had in 1995. If the multiplier effect of indirect impacts on other industries in the city is taken into consideration, then total economic impacts of tourism could reach £2.6 billion (ibid.).

While the direct and indirect economic investment in the city brought about growth and modernization, there have been some important side effects for the local population, including important price increases.

Moreover, while employment may have increased in the service sector, many of the jobs have been created in the tourism industry. While Garcia (1993) stated that these jobs benefited women and young people, they are often characterized by their low pay, poor work conditions, lack of development opportunities, and their temporary or seasonal nature. The Grup d'Estudis Sociològics sobre la Vida Quotidiana i el Treball (1997) summarized the impacts of the Olympic Games on employment as contributing to post-Taylorist changes, including increased flexibility, mobility and polyvalence, less regulation, the introduction of quality cycles, and increased competitiveness among workers, implemented through performance-related human resource policies. Indeed, although tourism can bring significant economic benefits, it can also bring social and cultural conflict between hosts and tourists, as well as negative impacts on the environment. Questions can be raised as to the extent to which the city has come to cater to the high-spending tourists as opposed to its residents.

Brunet (2002, 245–74) was careful to highlight the importance of indirect and intangible factors that have contributed to the economic growth and development of Barcelona. The experience of hosting the Games increased "know-how" among the organizations and individuals involved in COOB '92 but also confidence and a "culture of excellence." This knowledge, confidence, and quest for excellence have been transferred to the organization of other events in the city and to the management and operation of sports facilities, including the Olympic venues.

The Barcelona "model" of organizing the Olympic Games was characterized by public-private partnership. This management strategy continued after the Games in the operation of the Olympic venues, involving outsourcing to private companies, but with close public partnership. The Barcelona Promoció organization was created in 1988 to manage the Olympic Stadium, Palau St. Jordi, the velodrome, and the Palau dels Esports. These venues, particularly the Olympic Stadium and Palau St. Jordi, continue to host local, national, and international cultural and sporting events, such as major music concerts and the World Swimming Championships in 2003. Other venues, such as the Pircornell Swimming Pool, were opened to the public and were managed by outsourcing to private companies (Segura et al. 2002, 183–96). An important part of the public-private management model involves the implementation of social objectives such as price discount schemes for young and elderly people.

Segura and others (ibid.) stated that membership of public sports facilities in Barcelona exploded during the 1990s, with 20,000 members in 1992 growing more than sevenfold to 149,000 in 2001. This was combined with an increase in provision from the private sector, resulting in a total of 15 million square meters of sports facilities in the city. It is difficult, however, to attribute this growth in demand and supply directly to the Olympic Games, although they must have been a catalyst.

Considering more intangible factors, sport has become a defining part of Barcelona's image: "Undoubtedly, Barcelona belongs to the premier league of European sports cities" (van den Berg et al. 2000, 17).The Olympic Games built on Barcelona's rich sporting heritage, which includes FC Barcelona, producing a sport event strategy for the city. Barcelona Sports, which forms part of Turisme de Barcelona, was a product of the Olympic Games and promotes fifteen permanent sports events in the Barcelona metropolitan area, including the Spanish F1 Grand Prix and the Conde de Godó ATP tennis championship. In addition, 2003 saw Barcelona host four international events: the World Swimming Championships, the Euroleague Final Four (basketball), the World Police and Fireman Games, and the European Nations Hockey Cup.

Indeed, the 2003 Strategic Sports Plan for the city consisted of three main action points that reflect the attempts that have been made to build on the international image of Barcelona as a sports city, the expertise in event management, and the promotion of sport in social integration (Ajuntament de Barcelona 2003).

Sports facility and event managers were not the only beneficiaries of the intangible impacts of the successful organization of the games. As described earlier, the local political consensus had broadly been maintained around the continued efforts to develop the city through urban investment and promotion, particularly through the organization of events. Various authors have also referred to the increase in civic pride that occurred within the city (Moragas and Botella 1995). As stated earlier, the involvement and support of the public played a vital role in the success of the Barcelona Games. The widespread recognition that the city received on a national and an international scale for hosting "the best Games ever" improved the self-image of the community. The organizational expertise displayed served to dispel many of the tourist-based stereotypes of Spanish identity, and the cultural symbols and activities displayed in the ceremonies succeeded in communicating the distinctiveness of Catalan identity to global television audiences (Moragas et al. 1995).

Moreover, the Olympic Games marked more than the urban landscape. They have become part of the cultural heritage of Barcelona. While the Olympic Ring, the Olympic Village, and the Olympic Port have been integrated into the city and form part of the tourist destination product, the Games also marked the history of Barcelona and have gradually become part of the memories, individual and collective, of the people. Moragas and others (2003,

279–88) suggest that the reaction of the host population changes over time, passing through different phases:

- Expectation (six to four years before)
- Mistrust and criticism in the local press, or skepticism in the case of Barcelona (four to two years before)
- Agreement (one year before)
- Euphoria, local solidarity, and limited criticism (year of the Games)
- Forgetting (the first few years after the Games)
- Recovery and nostalgia: emblematic anniversaries (first, tenth, twenty-fifth, and fiftieth).

Public opinion and reaction in Barcelona passed through all of these phases, eventually recovering the nostalgia for the Games, a process that was aided by more than favorable comparisons with Atlanta in 1996 and the staging of a public party and fireworks display attended by 180,000 people to commemorate the tenth anniversary of the nomination of the city to host the Games. In 2002, the tenth anniversary of the Games themselves was celebrated which, according to Moragas and others, had to be put into its proper political context:

> The institutions of Barcelona and Catalonia were paying homage to Juan Antonio Samaranch, and the organizers used these commemorative acts to publicly launch a large-scale campaign to promote the Universal Forum of Cultures 2004, demonstrating the need to refer to the past in terms of new projects for the future. (2003, 287)

Twenty years after the seeds were sown for Barcelona, the Games were still being used as a tool by political actors, this time for the promotion of another major event in the city.

The most recent legacy of the Olympic Games was the Universal Forum of Cultures, held in Barcelona in 2004 (Botella 2002, 165–81). The Forum consisted of a combination of exhibitions, debates, and cultural displays over 141 days. The project comprised a mix of public and private developments, improvements in communication infrastructure, and investment in environmental infrastructure, to improve sustainability.

CONCLUSIONS

Much of the success attached to the Barcelona Games has been connected to the achievement of the objectives of the political elite and the companies that formed the public-private partnership. There can be little doubt that Barcelona

City Hall achieved the most successful leverage of the Games, receiving over $9 billion in investment in urban infrastructure as well as longer-term revenues from tourism and wider increases in economic activity in the city. For the other political actors, their return on investment came in the form of political representation and image enhancement, particularly through the Opening and Closing Ceremonies. According to public opinion surveys, at the international level the "Catalanization" of the Games was achieved, improving the image of the region (Hargreaves 2000). Internationally and locally the Spanish state benefited through the representation of a democratic Spain, led by King Juan Carlos I and Felipe Gonzalez, taking an important step in the reconciliation process with Catalonia. Similarly, Juan Antonio Samaranch benefited immeasurably from the successful image of the Games in Barcelona, Catalonia, but also within the IOC, the world of sport in general, and at the level of international diplomacy.

The Olympic Games therefore left their mark on the city and its citizens, producing the desired fifty years of development in only six years. The Games served as a catalyst for urban and economic change in the city, positioning Barcelona internationally and communicating its constructed image to a global audience. Barcelona City Hall maintained the momentum, continuing to invest in the city's product and image, transforming Barcelona into a thriving tourism destination and place to do business. The continued use of the Olympic facilities at both elite and popular levels for sporting and cultural events as well as the popularity of the Olympic Port and maintenance of the name Olympic Village have contributed to the integration of the Olympic Games into the city. Memory of the Olympic festival also has assured its place as a turning point in the city's history.

However, the success of the Games could not automatically be interpreted as success for all of Barcelona's citizens. In situations such as the Olympic Village, the public-private partnerships that underpinned the organization of the Games benefited certain social groups over others. While the Games may have temporarily united the city in an unforgettable festival, important social divisions remained. In the post-Olympic period, however, the issue of social inequality has focused on the integration of a growing number of immigrants from diverse cultural backgrounds, especially North and Sub-Saharan Africa, Latin America, and Eastern Europe.

The Universal Forum 2004 continued Barcelona's historical use of large-scale events to bring about urban change and development in the city. However, despite the fact that both local and global circumstances have changed in the twelve-year period since the Olympics, the strategy of regeneration and gentrification is being repeated. This suggests that it will again be the companies involved in the public-private partnership and the upper-middle-class groups that can afford to live in the regenerated area that will be the primary beneficiaries of the project. Indeed, while globalizing processes have continued to accelerate, Barcelona is now a city with an international standing, seeking to consolidate its position and achieve sustainable growth. The legacy of the 1992 Olympic Games is an enhanced international profile for the city, and the accelerated regeneration that was achieved within the Olympic project. Challenges facing the city can be faced with a confidence that the success of the 1992 event did much to instill.

NOTE

1. In 2003, Jordi Pujol stepped down, and Pasqual Maragall presented his candidacy for the presidency of the Generalitat, representing the Catálan Socialist Party.

REFERENCES

Abad, Josep Miquel. 1995. Introduction: A summary of the activities of the COOB '92. In *The keys to success: The social, sporting, economic and communication impact of Barcelona '92*, Miquel de Moragas and Miquel Botella. Barcelona: Centre d'Estudis Olímpics i de L'Esport-UAB, and Olympic Museum, Lausanne.

Ajuntament de Barcelona. 2003. *Pla estratègic de l'esport*. Barcelona: Ajuntament de Barcelona, http://www.bcn.es/esports/plaestrategic (accessed September 3, 2003).

Botella, Joan. 1995. The political Games: Agents and strategies in the 1992 Barcelona Olympic Games. In *The keys to success: The social, sporting, economic, and communications impact of Barcelona'92*, ed. Miquel de Moragas and Miquel Botella. Barcelona: Centre d'Estudis Olímpics i de l'Esport-UAB and Olympic Museum, Lausanne.

———. 2002. Els Jocs polítics: Actors i estratègies entorn dels Jocs Olímpics de Barcelona 1992. In *Barcelona: L'herència dels Jocs (1992–2002)*, ed. Miquel de Moragas and Miquel Botella. Barcelona: Centre d'Estudis Olímpics-UAB, Ajuntament de Barcelona, Editorial Planeta.

Botella, Miquel. 1995. The keys to success of the Barcelona Games. In *The keys to success: The social, sporting, economic, and communication impact of Barcelona'92*, ed. Miquel de Moragas and Miquel Botella. Barcelona: Centre d'Estudis Olímpics i de l'Esport-UAB and Olympic Museum, Lausanne.

———. 2002. El Fòrum Universal de les Cultures, la darrera herència del Jocs. In *Barcelona: L'herència dels Jocs (1992–2002)*, ed. Miquel de Moragas and Miquel Botella. Barcelona: Centre d'Estudis Olímpics-UAB, Ajuntament de Barcelona, Editorial Planeta.

Brunet, Ferran. 1993. *Economy of the 1992 Barcelona Olympic Games*. Lausanne: International Olympic Committee.

———. 1995. An economic analysis of the Barcelona '92 Olympic Games: Resources, financing, and impact. In *The keys to success: The social, sporting, economic and communica-*

tions impact of Barcelona'92, ed. Miquel de Moragas and Miquel Botella. Barcelona: Centre d'Estudis Olímpics i de l'Esport-UAB, and Olympic Museum, Lausanne.

———. 2002. Anàlisi de l'impacte econòmic dels Jocs Olímpics de Barcelona, 1986–2004. In *Barcelona: L'herència dels Jocs (1992–2002)*, ed. Miquel de Moragas and Miquel Botella. Barcelona: Centre d'Estudis Olímpics-UAB, Ajuntament de Barcelona, Editorial Planeta.

Cabet, Étienne. 1848. *Voyage en Icarie*. Paris: Félix Malteste.

Carbonell, Jordi. 2002. La Vila Olímpica, deu anys després. In *Barcelona: L'herència dels Jocs (1992–2002)*, ed. Miquel de Moragas and Miquel Botella. Barcelona: Centre d'Estudis Olímpics-UAB, Ajuntament de Barcelona, Editorial Planeta.

Cashman, Richard, and Anthony Hughes, eds. 1999. *Staging the Games: The event and its impact* Sydney: University of New South Wales Press.

COOB '92. 1992. *Official report of the Games of the XXV Olympiad: Barcelona 1992*. Barcelona: COOB '92.

Crexell, Joan. 1994. *Nacionalisme i Jocs Olímpics del 1992*. Barcelona: Columna.

Cushman and Wakefield, Healey and Baker. 2002. *European cities monitor 2002*. London: Cushman & Wakefield Healey & Baker, http://www.cushmanwakefieldeurope.com/global/en/ECM2002forweb.pdf (accessed: September 5, 2003).

Duran, Pere. 2002. Turisme: Els impactes dels Jocs i de la seva imatge sobre el turisme. In *Barcelona: l'herència dels Jocs (1992-2002)*, ed. Miquel de Moragas and Miquel Botella. Barcelona: Centre d'Estudis Olímpics-UAB, Ajuntament de Barcelona, Editorial Planeta.

Felli, Gilbert. 2002. El model organitzatiu dels Jocs després de Barcelona '92. In *Barcelona: L'herència dels Jocs (1992–2002)*, ed. Miquel de Moragas and Miquel Botella. Barcelona: Centre d'Estudis Olímpics-UAB, Ajuntament de Barcelona, Editorial Planeta.

Garcia, S. 1993. Barcelona und die Olympische Spiele. In *Festivalisierung der Stadtpolitik*, ed. Hartmut Hauberman and Walter Siebel. Stuttgart: Leiathan-Westdeutcher Verlag.

Giddens, Anthony. 1998. *The third way: The renewal of social democracy*. Cambridge: Polity Press.

Grup d'Estudis Sociològics sobre la Vida Quotidiana i el Treball. 1997. *Economía, trabajo y empresa: Sobre el impacto económico y laboral de los Juegos Olímpicos de 1992*. Madrid: Consejo Económico y Social.

Hargreaves, John. 2000. *Freedom for Catalonia: Catalan nationalism, Spanish identity, and the Barcelona Olympic Games*. Cambridge: Cambridge University Press.

Maragall, Pasqual. 1995. Presentation. In *The keys to success: The social, sporting, economic, and communication impact of Barcelona '92*, ed. Miquel de Moragas and Miquel Botella. Barcelona: Centre d'Estudis Olímpics i de l'Esport-UAB, and Olympic Museum, Lausanne.

Millet, Lluís. 1995. The Games of the city. In *The keys to success: The social, sporting, economic, and communication impact of Barcelona '92*, ed. Miquel de Moragas and Miquel Botella. Barcelona: Centre d'Estudis Olímpics i de l'Esport-UAB, and Olympic Museum, Lausanne.

Molas, Isidre. 1991. Barcelona'92 political framework. In *Olympic Games, media, and cultural exchange: The experience of the last four summer Olympic Games: International symposium, Palau de Pedralbes, Barcelona, April 3–5 1991*, ed. Muriel Ladróude Guevara. Bellaterra: Centre d'Estudis Olímpics i de l'Esport-UAB.

Moragas, Miquel de, Ana Belen Moreno, and Christopher Kennett. 2003. The legacy of the symbols: Communication and the Olympic Games. In *The legacy of the Olympic Games 1984–2000: International symposium, Lausanne, 14th, 15th, and 16th, November 2002*, ed. Miquel de Moragas, Ana Belen Moreno, Christopher Kennett, and Nuria Puig. Lausanne: International Olympic Committee.

Moragas, Miquel de, and Miquel Botella, eds. 1995. *The keys to success: The social, sporting, economic, and communication impact of Barcelona '92*. Barcelona: Centre d'Estudis Olímpics i de l'Esport-UAB, and Olympic Museum, Lausanne.

———. 2002. *Barcelona: L'herència dels Jocs (1992–2002)*. Barcelona: Centre d'Estudis Olímpics–UAB, Ajuntament de Barcelona, Editorial Planeta.

Moragas, Miquel de, Nancy Rivenburgh, and James Larson. 1995. *Television in the Olympics*. London: John Libbey.

Moragas, Miquel de, Nancy Rivenburgh, and Núria García. 1995. Television and construction of identity: Barcelona, Olympic host. In *The keys to success: The social, sporting, economic, and communication impact of Barcelona'92*, ed. Miquel de Moragas and Miquel Botella. Barcelona: Centre d'Estudis Olímpics i de l'Esport-UAB, and Olympic Museum, Lausanne.

Roche, Maurice. 2000. *Mega-events and modernity: Olympics and expos in the growth of global culture*. London: Routledge.

Samaranch, Juan Antonio. 2002. *Memorias Olímpicas*. Barcelona: Planeta.

Segura, Xavier, Àndor Serra, and Ramon Pallejà. 2002. L'ús de les installacions olímpiques. In *Barcelona: L'herència dels Jocs (1992–2002)*, ed. Miquel de Moragas and Miquel Botella. Barcelona: Centre d'Estudis Olímpics-UAB, Ajuntament de Barcelona, Editorial Planeta.

Tejero Gil, Elisabeth. 1992. Poblenou: El canvi urbanístic i la transformació social. *Papers: revista de sociologia* 38: 91–107.

Truño, Enric. 1995. Barcelona, city of sport. In *The keys to success: The social, sporting, economic, and communication impact of Barcelona '92*, ed. Miquel de Moragas and Miquel Botella. Barcelona: Centre d'Estudis Olímpics i de l'Esport-UAB, and Olympic Museum, Lausanne.

———. 2002. Barcelona'92 i la seva influència internacional. In *Barcelona: L'herència dels Jocs (1992–2002)*, ed. Miquel de Moragas and Miquel Botella. Barcelona: Centre d'Estudis Olímpics-UAB, Ajuntament de Barcelona, Editorial Planeta.

Turisme de Barcelona. 2003. *Estadistiques de turisme 2002*. Barcelona: Patronat de Turisme de Barcelona, http://www.barcelonaturisme.com (accessed September 3, 2003).

van den Berg, Leo, Erik Braun, and Alexander H. J. Otgaar. 2000. *Sports and city marketing in European cities*. Rotterdam: Euricur, European Institute for Comparative Urban Research.

Vázquez Montalbán, Manuel.1989. Icaria,Icaria.La Crónica, *El País*, October 14, p.27.

Vecsey, George. 1992. Heartfelt adéu, adéu: Barcelona won gold. *New York Times*, August 10, Section C, p. 4.

Chapter 12

Sydney 2000

Sociality and Spatiality in Global Media Events

David Rowe and Deborah Stevenson

INTRODUCTION

The Olympic Games are one of (post)modernity's most powerful media spectacles (Roche 2000), and hosting them provides the Olympic city and nation with an extraordinary opportunity both to take its own temperature and be subjected to intensive diagnosis by the media of other nations. There are now as many different, technologically enhanced contexts for watching the Olympics as there are social subjectivities of Olympic viewers. This relationship between space and sociality is important in analyzing the collective cultural significance of the Games and the mythologies and ideologies that they can promote and disseminate. In the heavily charged atmosphere of the millennial Games in a postcolonial, Southern Hemisphere nation about to celebrate its centenary, yet still struggling to reconcile with its indigenous peoples (Godwell 2000), the Olympics provided a probably unprecedented forum for appraising and assessing contemporary "Australianness."[1]

At the Summer 2000 Olympics in Sydney—hailed at the closing ceremony by outgoing IOC President Juan Antonio Samaranch as the "best Games ever"—the positioning of Aboriginal champion Cathy Freeman at the opening ceremony and her gold medal-winning performance on the track were symbolic highlights for the host city and nation. The opening ceremony emphasized the theme of reconciliation related to the history of first the colony's and then the nation's treatment of Aboriginal peoples. The choice of Freeman, a participating athlete, to light the Olympic flame was a climax to the theme of reconciliation (Rowe 2000a). She also had run the stadium lap of the torch relay with other celebrated Australian women athletes, thus representing the inclusiveness of the contemporary Olympic ideal on several levels. The Aboriginal theme had been prominent in the Sydney Olympic bid and in the arts and cultural festivals held during the Sydney Olympiad (Stevenson 1997,

1998).[2] It remained prominent throughout the Olympic event itself, especially in Freeman's two starring moments, lighting the Olympic flame and taking the gold medal in the women's 400-meters athletics event.

In this chapter, these Olympic Games are analyzed from the hermeneutical vantage points of the spectators in the stadium and in various sites across the Australian nation. Our case study, the "Freeman Final," as we shall describe it, provided a key link between these dispersed viewing sites, thus symbolically uniting a rather less-than-united nation. The analysis will show how the media relay and transform events that can be reduced to neither embodied experience nor their representation. This study will highlight the complex relationship between audience, text, and context, questioning the still-dominant binary analytical model of "being there"/"viewing from a distance." Despite the rather porous nature of this binary framework, it will nonetheless be shown that physical co-presence remains a key form of scarce cultural capital for those attending mega-media sports events, the stadium's combination of society and space providing authority over collective memory.

SPECTATORSHIP AND THE HOSTING OF THE OLYMPICS

Hosting the Olympics[3] is an activity that is much more than a technical exercise in mega-event sport management. The investment by the host goes well beyond the billions of dollars of private and public capital required to stage the Games. It is a prime opportunity for an external and internal dialogue about "the state of the nation." The feeling that the eyes of the world are on not just the field of athletic competition but also its spatial context is powerful and, to no small extent, anxiety provoking. A nation stands to be celebrated or humiliated, showcased or exposed, according to how it is seen through the eyes of the formidable battery of Olympic media devoted to each Olympic Games. Despite the universalist ethic of the Games, commentary about the Olympics is never entirely placeless. Although the athletic stadia are largely standardized, there is always a strong sense that the Games are taking place somewhere specific. For this reason, successive events are routinely identified both by year and by host city. During competitive events, cameras pull back from close-up action to reveal the idiosyncratic visual elements of Olympic venues (especially of the main stadium) and its spatial context, while commentators provide aural "local color." This spatializing and "placing" of events is especially important when the Games spill out from enclosed main stadia to other sites, such as the streets of cities during the marathon and cycling, or the waterways during the sailing and rowing.

In the Sydney 2000 Olympics, for example, it was notable that the triathlon enabled Sydney Harbor and its iconic Opera House to be featured as an integral element of a sporting experience that could not be mistaken as occurring any-where else, and that powerfully reinforced popular conceptions of Australia as a country where the urban and the natural coexist in uncommonly pleasurable propinquity (Fiske, Hodge, and Turner 1987). Furthermore, the size of the press contingent and the length of its stay prior to and during the Games (though rarely, given international media attention spans, after the Olympic caravan has rolled on) create an enormous media space to be filled with both probing and su-perficial inspections and characterizations of the Olympic nation of the moment.

Irrespective of the geographical location of the Olympics and variable levels of support for hosting them, national host populations are systematically enjoined to celebrate them. This is presented as a patriotic duty, whereby internal differ-ences need to be set aside, if only for the duration, in the interests of the greater national interest. In this sense, host Olympic discourse resembles the galvaniz-ing rhetoric of war. More positively, hosting the Games is presented as a proba-ble one-off chance to both be part of and to see a major cultural phenomenon up close rather than solely through the highly mediated experience of international television. For Australians, the opportunity to view the Games in the same time zone in Sydney, 2000, was highly unusual. Apart from Seoul, 1988, the Games of the previous two decades—Moscow, Los Angeles, Barcelona, and Atlanta—could only be seen "live" at highly inconvenient times. The importance of time-zone friendliness is revealed by Grant Farred (2001, 3) in his complaint, from a U.S. vantage point, that Sydney, 2000, "will be remembered as the Olympics that weren't" because, in the key East Coast American television market, a fifteen-hour delay was required for prime-time viewing. Given this delay and the avail-ability of more instantaneous forms of Olympic information such as the Internet, the result was, according to Farred's reading of disappointing TV ratings for NBC, "turn-off television," but was also an opportunity for the Internet to come into its own.

One way of physically overcoming the time-zone problem is to be an in-ternational sport tourist (Standeven and de Knopf 1999). This is an expensive and, in light of terrorist and other threats to health and well-being (such as from SARS [Severe Acute Respiratory Syndrome]), a potentially dangerous ac-tivity. In the host country, the barriers are principally social class based (the high cost of attendance and, controversially, the relatively small number of lower-price seats at premium events for the local population) and geography-based (in Australia, the distance between the west coast and the east coast where the Games are held involves a three-hour time-zone variation). For the reward of attending the Games in real time and space, then, many sacrifices have still to be made, even in the host nation.

Yet the familiar way of conceptualizing "live" spectatorship at the Olympics—"being there" in a physical sense or "viewing at a distance" via television (Rowe

2000b)—is being challenged by various technological, operational, and cultural innovations. Large television screens offering close-up, replay, and slow-motion images and amplified post-event interviews with athletes have been imported from the lounge room and are now *de rigueur* in the stadium (Rowe 2004). In television, the technique of "as live" presentation for simultaneous and inconveniently timed events, involving the delay of the broadcast, some cleaning up of the audiovisual text, and a sharpening of its narrative, has introduced a strong element of the simulation of the "live."

As noted earlier, the Internet can provide (either through Webcasting or "live" reports and updates) an instantaneous spectatorial experience of sorts, but so too can attendance at "live sites" or the use of new technologies such as the latest generation of mobile telephones. During the 2002 Korea/Japan Football World Cup, this expansion of viewing positions was recognized by FIFA, its governing body, which measured both the "cumulative in-home audience of 28.8 billion viewers" and, for the first time, "out-of-home viewing—a key factor in understanding today's audiences—[which] has added 2.5 billion to the total" (FIFA 2002, n.p.). Although there is close policing of the spread of "live" televisual coverage of the Olympics in order to protect lucrative broadcast rights (Boyle and Haynes 2003), the diversification of platforms and diffusion of technologies are changing the dynamics of the binary structure of being there and watching from afar.

During the Sydney 2000 Games, an observational research study was carried out, with researchers sent to various in-stadia and other locations where the Games could be watched "live" (that is, in real time, or "as live"). The aim was to understand more of how the Games could be experienced in many forms and contexts. In particular, the quality of the experience was assessed against the conventional hierarchy of the superiority of co-presence in time and space. Dayan and Katz (1992) have analyzed the dynamics of taking part in the "live broadcasting of history" and have noted that despite the prestigious nature of the in-stadium experience, the television-mediated experience may be technically superior (in visual terms, for example) and also a social experience, rather than the often-conceived isolated or atomized one. Researchers were briefed to observe their viewing contexts and to ask respondents about how the Olympics were being watched, about the relationships between the watchers, and about their interpretation of the experience. The viewing sites were classified as "There" (at the stadium); "Live Site" (public space organized around a large screen showing the Games); "The City" (other spaces of the Olympic city not dedicated to the Games); "Remote—public space" (distant spaces beyond the Olympic city where the Games could be watched, such as pubs); "Remote—private home" (viewing in domestic space irrespective of its location), and "Other" (casual encounters with Olympic texts, such as in shopping malls or aircraft). The meanings and experiences of the Games for different viewers at different spectatorial sites, therefore, were analyzed in attempting a greater understanding of both sociality and spatiality at mega-media sport events. In this chapter, the specific event in focus was the main talking point for Australian viewers—the Freeman Final.

WATCHING CATHY

Unquestionably, the Freeman Final was the most significant competitive event for Australians at the Sydney 2000 Olympic Games. This was not only because it was a rare opportunity for a track-and-field gold medal for the country but also because of the dramatic narrative of the "duel" between Freeman and the French runner who had beaten her into second place at the 1996 Atlanta Games—Marie-Jose Perec. Unfortunately, Perec—the subject of intense Australian media scrutiny—disappeared prior to the Games under mysterious circumstances, allegedly fleeing her Sydney hotel room in fear of a stalker. But the loss of the narrative of the duel was outweighed by the massive national collective investment in a Freeman victory, which was deeply entwined with the indigenous theme that ran through the Games.

Anticipation surrounding Freeman was intense, with one observer noting the familiar coupling of her ceremonial and athletic roles:

> I listen in to a conversation between two white Australian males, 30ish. . . . The dress rehearsal of the opening ceremony was "wicked." Both of them look forward to tonight: "should be a bit different." They conjecture about who's going to light the torch. They talk about Cathy Freeman and how disappointing it would be if she doesn't win. (G, 15 September 2000, train to Olympic Park)

The two most in-demand events on the Olympic ticket ballot were the opening ceremony and the women's 400 meters-final (Bruce and Hallinan 2001, 262), both of which "starred" Cathy Freeman, though in the first of these her flame-lighting role was a closely guarded secret before the event. The excitement and spectacle surrounding Freeman were noted by one television viewer of the opening ceremony, who heard "lots of "ohs" and "ahs" and "oh my gods" as Cathy Freeman walked up the steps and we saw the water tumbling down and then her lighting the water" (E, 15 September 2000, lounge-room Olympic party). But most people in Sydney, Australia, and in the wider world could not share that moment with Cathy Freeman in the same time and space, or her subsequent athletic triumph, even if they so desired. Yet all could in some way, voluntarily or otherwise, be part of it. For some, the Freeman phenomenon had been a case of overkill,[4] as the following observer notes reveal:

> An elderly woman asked a middle-aged man (both Australian) who had a newspaper:
> Woman: "Any more gold medals?"
> Man: "Don't know, love, haven't looked at it yet."
> He went on to say he was "sick of reading about Cathy Freeman." (Strangely, I had just at that moment thought "no-one's got a bad word to say about Cathy Freeman.") (G, 28 September 2000, train to Olympic Park)

The focus on Cathy Freeman before the Games had been extraordinary. An image of her had already achieved "iconic status" (Gardiner 2003, 36) through her flourishing of the Aboriginal flag after winning the 400-meters at the 1998 Commonwealth Games. For visiting media, the main social issue to be explored was Aboriginal reconciliation, which Freeman came to embody. There was some pressure on her to withdraw in protest at the nation's seeming inability or unwillingness to recognize prior Aboriginal occupation of the land, to deal with the massive social problems that followed the dispossession of indigenous peoples, and to enable significant self-determination (Bruce and Hallinan 2001). Some Aboriginal leaders regarded the Olympics as a "whitewash" and sport as a way of creating a white alibi through "the construction of invader Dreaming—particularly the perceived benefits of sport in healing the wounds of Indigenous people created by ideological policies of segregation, 'protection,' and assimilation" (Rigney 2003, 52). Others, though, saw a rare opportunity to foreground Aboriginality in a positive way, to connect symbolically Aboriginality and national pride, and to draw global attention to Australian Aboriginal cultures and peoples in a manner that did more than present the depressingly familiar list of indices of poverty, morbidity, and cultural besiegement. Roy Hay has argued that the Freeman phenomenon was not only the keynote of the millennial Games but had a profound impact on the wider political sphere:

> Cathy Freeman's triumph in the four hundred metres at the Sydney Olympic Games in 2000 and her lighting of the Olympic flame at the opening ceremony may have been symbolic and possibly ephemeral, but the resonance of both events in Australian indigenous and non-indigenous societies was palpable. For those not directly involved in the minutiae of the debates over reconciliation between these groups in Australia the influence of Freeman's two moments in the spotlight probably did more to influence the attitudes of people than any other single episode in recent Australian history. (2003, 23)

As the world's media captured the spectacular image of Cathy Freeman lighting the Olympic flame standing in a ring of tumbling water, she enhanced even her own iconicity in representing Aboriginal identity and the legacy of white appropriation of indigenous land (Gardiner 2003, 35). This chapter explores involvements with some of the dynamics of such involvements with the greatest popular political moment of millennial Australia, on the basis of the options and views available to and expressed by Olympic spectators.

VIEWING POSITIONS

There

Cathy Freeman's role in Sydney 2000, provided one of its principal narrative elements, with her lighting of the Olympic flame in the opening ceremony setting the stage for her own 400-meter race but, much more extensively, for a meditation on the condition of the Australian nation and its accommodation (or lack thereof) with its first peoples (Bruce and Hallinan 2001). Physical attendance at the Freeman Final—for many the competitive highlight of the Games—would conventionally be regarded as the superior viewing position. The principal reason for this judgment is scarcity—as opposed to the case of free-to-air television, there is a viewing capacity limitation. But viewing conditions in the stadium are no more uniform than outside. The hierarchy of in-stadium positions is, obviously yet controversially, linked to affluence and rank. Observers located in the "nosebleed" seats high above the stadium were dependent on the large screen:

> Cathy Freeman's so far away and looks tiny—like an insect. I spend all my time watching the big screen. I could do that much more comfortably at home! But the atmosphere is electric, and I'm already preparing my reminiscences of tonight. (A, 25 September 2000, Stadium Australia)

> After a bit of a wander 'round, we set off for Stadium Australia. Got inside OK—but a long way up. There are 47 tiers up here, and we're in Row 42! So high up that during the opening ceremony the only way we could have seen the lighting of the cauldron would have been on the two TV screens at either end. Young child (5–6 years) next to me said, "Look at the screen, dad, it's better!" (B, 25 September 2000, Stadium Australia)

> The ground announcer steers things but is obviously less in control than the TV announcer. The Australian crowd is more noticeable

here—they are noisily supportive of Aussies [and that's] not apparent on TV. (C, 25 September 2000, Stadium Australia)

Two forms of cultural capital are at work in this viewing position. Within the stadium, position is determined by organizational rank or material circumstances, though mediated in some cases by the luck of the ticket ballot and the capacity to pay. The second is directed outside of the stadium and derives from the possession of the scarce resource of physical attendance and so the claim of witness, irrespective of the actual quality of the viewing position:

Cathy Freeman came out to a very vocal reception. She was in her Nike suit, which she had not worn the night before. Following her win she sat seemingly stunned for what seemed a couple of minutes, but may not have been that long. She was "on screen" most of that time, seemingly emotionless. . . . She then stood, ran down to a section in front of our stand, and had the two flags thrown to her—obviously a rehearsed move. The crowd stood, cheering and waving flags from the time the race commenced until well after her lap of honor. Music played throughout and, as I understand it, some of the other events in the stadium were halted. (D, 25 September 2000, Stadium Australia)

The in-stadium spectators constantly shift between plain sight and screen image, spatially claiming their part of the venue ("our stand") and acutely aware of both the crowd's response of which they were a part and of the orchestration of that response through musical cues and adjustments to the schedules of other events. It is apparent, though, that conventional access to television has schooled the spectator to expect the kind of visual text that only it can supply, while other media, especially newspapers, offer authoritative ways of reflecting on the experience. The outcome for one observer was an acute awareness of being part of the "live broadcasting of history" but also a certain ambivalence about the personal costs and benefits of "being there":

Well, I was there—for the women's 400m final—when it was won by Australia's Cathy Freeman. What was it like? It was a fantastic race, and the crowd—partisan, hysterical, was unbelievable. All that pressure on one woman. There was cheering, clapping, chanting. If you are going to be at any event this was the one to go to. . . . There is only one news story in town—Cathy Freeman—the relief and gratitude of the nation is palpable. We are now reassured that everything is OK. A colleague who was also at the Games last night described it as "the best night of his life." There's no doubt that having been there gives one a degree of status with others. Everyone watched the race, and all said it must have been fabulous to be there and experience the crowd. On reflection today though I feel as if I've missed yesterday. On the television (or radio) you know what is happening when medals in other sports have been won, etc. You don't get this at a session of a sport such as athletics or swimming. This I feel as a loss. (B, 25 September 2000, Stadium Australia)

As another observer noted the day after attending the Cathy Freeman race, being there was in itself not enough to locate and secure it in the memory:

Funny feeling that I haven't caught up with all the post-mortem Cathy Freeman coverage. I have an uneasy feeling that I need to know and see more—and I was there! But still a strange sense of lack, from not being fully "briefed" by the media . . . sacrificed a greater grasp of the Games in the interests of a more direct connection with a small part of it. (A, 25 September 2000, Stadium Australia)

The hybridic viewing experience of being there but watching on television suggests the co-existence of two distinct types of spectatorship—one that is predominantly visual and technical in nature and another that is broadly sensual and more attuned to the embodied pleasure of being in a crowd at an historic (inter)national moment. Even some spectators who could have the best in-stadium viewing position chose to watch it on television:

The only thing worth remarking on today was Athlete's Manager and Aussie legend Herb Elliott saying that he chose to watch the Cathy Freeman Final on TV in the [athlete's] village and not at the stadium because he wanted to see Cathy's face! Despite the bad reputation of TV, he suggested . . . that it does some things better than being there. (B, 26 September 2000, living room)

Not mentioned here too is the alternative sociality of watching the Freeman Final in a space available only to athletes and officials. As will be discussed later, there are now various spectatorial options that offer permutations of this pleasure, but none yet with the authority of the enclosed stadium spectator. The socio-spatial dimension of "being there" enables the in-stadium spectator to "represent" the nation and national culture in microcosm, and so to record and disseminate the experience for socio-cultural posterity. As one observer noted:

I find myself checking the screens constantly—one for results and one for action. Lights are on, and we are in gathering darkness. Hard plastic seats, no comforts of home—it better be worth it. Saw a "blimp" shot of us—but it was pointed out to me that it's a standard shot, not in real time!

It's just gone 8 P.M. and the camera flashes are popping—it's time. . . . Crowd going bananas for Cathy Freeman. A huge noise, and she did it. A shiver up the spine—maybe being there was worth it after all!

Overheard (father to 13–14-year-old son): "There you are. You can say you seen it, you can say you were here." (B, 25 September 2000, Stadium Australia)

Comments about posterity such as those by this father were frequently heard and seemed to be the major reward for being there (Rowe 2000a). As one observer who attended the Freeman Final stated:

Numerous people have asked "what it was like" to be part of the audience in Cathy Freeman's win. There is certainly a feeling that being there was somehow more "meaningful" than watching the events on TV—although the latter provided a much-enhanced view of the events! (B, 25 September 2000, Sydney hotel)

Comments and observations also point to the fact that the big-screen coverage at the stadium is not the same as domestic television coverage. Television seeks to construct and package the entire Olympics for the viewer, while the task of the stadium screen images and associated announcements is to package a single session of the Olympics only. At the stadium, there were no references to events happening outside of the arena—no results of other competitions given, no medal tallies, and no indication that this suite of events was part of a much bigger phenomenon. There also was no race commentary, no discussion of athletes' form, and no analysis of the results—in short, no broader context. Indeed, "gaps" between activities at Sydney, 2000, were filled with pop videos. In other words, these are qualitatively different experiences—where the first (being there) seeks to contain the "viewer" within a delineated space and time and to amplify that concentrated moment, the latter (watching TV at home) attempts to take the viewer out of the "privatized" spatial and temporal location to make him or her feel part of a much larger public phenomenon.

The embodied pleasure and pain of seeing Cathy Freeman's historic win was, ironically, always directed beyond the moment, and to the future recounting of it. But it was, by definition, not possible for everyone to "be there" with Cathy, and for some her race was but one of many simultaneous Olympic events that could be monitored. It was, though, not always necessary to retreat to the private home to watch the Freeman Final, as public spaces now offer alternative, rich possibilities for sharing the mediated moment.

Somewhere Else

It is possible, using portable and miniaturized media technologies, to tune constantly in and out of events, switching from the in-stadium experience to others of spectatorial priority. For example, while at another Olympic venue close to the main stadium, one observer noted:

> During half time Cathy Freeman was running her 400m at Stadium Australia, and a huge cheer at the hockey center went up when she won, as people had been listening to their own radios and one couple even had a mini TV. About 10 seconds after she had won, it was announced over the loudspeaker which, of course, brought another cheer. . . . A couple in front of us were watching the athletics on their mini TV, oblivious to the hockey, and you could see Cathy Freeman being presented with her gold medal. As I looked up, you could also see all the flash cameras going off at Stadium Australia. (D, 25 September 2000, State Hockey Centre)

Here the Cathy Freeman moment could be experienced simultaneously and with only a slight time delay. Personal audiovisual technologies are supplemented by official announcements, with the event even marked by the visual "noise" of mass camera flashes from another stadium. It also is possible for those present in the stadium to be absorbed in the action elsewhere. This simultaneous "absorption" and "distraction" (as Rose and Friedman [1997], following Kracauer, describe the dynamic of watching TV sport), also could be typified as a kind of postmodern overstimulation, with one's gaze unable to linger for long on an object before being seduced by another. The responses at the hockey signify potentially competing socialities, with the in-stadium crowd devoted to one sport also interpellated by TV, radio, and ground announcers as followers of sporting events elsewhere. Contemporary sports spectators are, then, voluntarily or otherwise required to multi-task and to assume membership of different or overlapping temporary communities. These cultural processes take place in a wide range of contexts.

One dedicated Olympic watcher interviewed for the study experienced the Olympics through attendance and multiple media use. He privileged "being there," saying, "I can't understand people who say 'I'd rather watch it on TV because you can see much better' in this age of video recording when you can experience it live and *then* see it on TV as well" (K, male, interviewed, 4 October 2000, Sydney lounge room). Aspects of in-stadium events were felt to be uniquely contextual: "You couldn't have really got [it] on TV . . . being there live is not the same as watching it on TV 'cause even though you can't see as much, it's seeing the other people around you and their reactions. And it's hearing what can't be heard on TV—the sheer noise of it all." (K, ibid.)

Yet he could not acquire or indeed afford tickets for the Freeman Final and so experienced it at the Circular Quay Live Site:

> I was pretty tired that night. I was thinking "I could just do with sitting on the couch watching this here." . . . [But] I did want that crowd experience again, and if I couldn't see it at Homebush Bay (the main stadium), obviously, I wanted to see it at Circular Quay, so I went down and had the big crowd experience again and it was again really good to see it because, well, obviously, you got a close-up view, you got to see every detail, because it was on TV, unlike at the Stadium where you would have had to have your binoculars, and I'm sure the atmosphere at the Stadium that night would have been good, but at Circular Quay it was pretty good as well. (K, ibid.)

Having described the option of watching at home on television as "wet blankety," this Olympic spectator had an enjoyable experience of Cathy Freeman's win as part of a large Live Site crowd. Though seeing this as a second-best experience, it was visually superior and sociable (his flatmate "wasn't particularly into it," and so viewing at home would have been unsociable).

Not all spectators live in the Olympic city. Nonetheless, they too could "share the spirit," as the 2000 Olympic slogan declared, in many different ways. One researcher watched the Sydney 2000 Olympics from a distance in Darwin on the north of the continent, many time-zone hours removed from New South Wales, and it is useful to provide some excerpts from her observations:

> Two large screens are permanent fixtures at this pub. There is one located in the bar and the other outside in the beer garden. . . . There is, however, limited seating around the inside screen, and people tend to pay little attention to it. For the period of the Olympics, however, the pub was giving away a free glass of beer to anyone who went to the bar after an Australian won a gold medal in any event! . . . The TV screen in the beer garden area had not yet been turned on, and everyone was happily chatting, but the Olympics was *not* the focus. I was very excited to watch the 400m and would be cheering Cathy Freeman on. I hoped that she'd win, and we discussed that she also deserved it due to all the media focus that was on her at the time.
>
> As the start of the 400m event came closer and the commentary started to focus on the event, the foreign backpackers at our table began to comment on the extent that Australian sportspeople are built up and talked about, this discussion again began to focus on Cathy

Freeman and how difficult it would be to focus when the media was so "in her face." The beer garden area filled up very quickly from about 5: 30 P.M. onwards, and by the time the race started at about 6:35 P.M. the beer garden was full, all tables were taken, and there were many people standing (this crowd, however, could not be solely attributed to the Olympic event; free food vouchers start getting handed out at 6:30 P.M.). The volume on the outdoor TV screen was turned up very loud, and the majority of conversation ceased. The talk around our table focused solely on Cathy Freeman and then silence as the race began. Cheers arose from the crowd, "Go Cathy, Go Cathy," with a few English people trying to compete by cheering on the Brits (two in the race). Many people around jumped up and down with excitement when Cathy won the final, and in particular one Aboriginal woman in the crowd cheered and clapped, looking very elated after the race. As Cathy was interviewed, she continued to grin and looked very close to tears as she kept shouting "Good on ya Cath." (H, 25 September 2000, Darwin Bar)

The relationships between sport, space, media, nation, commerce, cultural identity, and social exchange are revealed in their deep complexity in this snapshot. To some degree, the Olympics are merely a pretext for social pleasure, a background, a "cultural wallpaper" element of a social environment, and a marketing lure for a commercial leisure facility. The nation comes to the fore, as does indigenousness in the context of international discussions about the place of Cathy Freeman and the condition of Aboriginal people in Australian society. The person who most deeply identifies with her as a fellow Aboriginal woman has a correspondingly high affective investment in her victory. The mediated event has a particular rhythm, with a strong crowd atmosphere among casual spectators who made few of the sacrifices of those who were "there," and, indeed, who were rewarded with free food and beer! There would, especially for international visitors, be a strong sense of place and memory in such a social environment, as the context of viewing is marked and recalled (in a beer garden in Darwin, far from the Games). Provision of viewing sites was plentiful, but limited space existed in social venues, thereby creating a crowd dynamic. It is by no means self-evident that this way of seeing the Freeman Final was inferior to attending the stadium itself, although its associated cultural capital is much less. It also is clear that the quality of the experience is as much a product of the social and cultural baggage brought to the viewing site by human subjects as of the structural and situational properties of the site itself.

The mega-media event of the Olympics pervades public and private spaces, such as shopping malls, making it impossible to miss, even if this outcome was desired. One observer was visiting a different city, Canberra, during the day of the Freeman Final but nonetheless was attuned to the buildup through television in her hotel and in shops and in chance encounters with other consumers. The national importance of the race was later reflected in the rare occurrence of the result being announced on the plane:

> Mixed a day's shopping with Olympics viewing. Lots of hype about Cathy Freeman's race tonight. People asking each other in shops whether they'd be watching it or not. TV on at the head of the Commonwealth bank queue while I waited for service. Lots of shops had TVs on the counter. The inside of the shopping center had a big screen over the food hall area where I stopped for lunch. Missed the Freeman race during the flight home, but the captain announced the result. Listened to the radio commentary on the award ceremony and lap of honor as I drove home. Arrived in time to see Cathy receive her gold medal. Must have been an incredible atmosphere there tonight. The crowd seemed to be going wild. (F, 25 September 2000, Canberra)

This sense of "must have been" was frequently expressed among those who were not there. Many created their own quasi-Olympic environments, especially the holding of Olympic parties with families and friends for the opening ceremony and major athletic events:

> Man (40s) in another shop buying a swag of Olympic flags for his "opening ceremony party." Getting together with some mates and their wives and kids to mark the occasion. Not actually attending any of the events, but taking holidays from work to cheer on the Aussie team from home. (F, 11 September 2000, Newcastle)

Many reported high levels of excitement and enjoyment at such Olympic parties:

> Atmosphere very "high," everyone buoyant and excited about the event to come. Everyone dressed up for the occasion, J in a brand new outfit made especially for tonight. We all retired to the formal lounge for drinks once everything was organized and made a toast to the Australian team. (F, 15 September 2000, Newcastle)

But whatever the joys of domestic celebrations of Olympic events such as the opening ceremony and the Freeman Final, being there retains its prime cultural position, and even the precise experience of the moment creates additional hi-erarchies and anxieties. As one interviewee noted:

> But yeah, with things like Cathy's event, people will say, "Where were you when Cathy crossed the line?" And there have been funny things in Column 8 [a satirical newspaper column] about how people were sitting in the stadium for an hour and decided they wanted, you know, McDonald's and were in a queue, or the toilet queue, or something, when she crossed the line. It's like "der." (K, male, interviewed 4 Octo-ber 2000, Sydney lounge room)

A toilet queue was not the place to be caught when "Cathy crossed the line." Even if you were "there."

CONCLUSION

This chapter has not attempted a comprehensive interrogation of the Sydney 2000 Olympics and its impact on the development of the Australian nation, es-pecially of its effect on the history, present and future of its Indigenous people. Rather, it has sought to demonstrate the ways in which major sport and media events create a range of positions from which to glimpse and experience social relations, cultural identities, and political conflicts. Almost everyone in Aus-tralia participated in the Cathy Freeman moment in some way, and virtually all of those who observed and were interviewed believed it to be of importance well beyond the sporting arena. When she announced her retirement from competitive running in July 2003, television and newspapers around the world took every opportunity to show images of the Freeman Final once more. The "media sport cultural complex" (Rowe 2004) produces diverse spatial and social configurations that compel most people in a country to concentrate on a lim-ited range of subjects for a time and that trigger strong, and often competing, forms of identification. As K, the "self-confessed international event enthusi-ast," put it:

> To be with your compatriots is really important. . . . And it was good to see a really big cross-section of people get behind those victories as well, because athletes are the only people we do get proud of these days. Like yesterday those scientists did have that gene break-through—you know, scientists found the gene that causes plants to flower, which is amazing really—[which will] really radically change the way we have agriculture, but it didn't draw a big crowd to cheer it

on. I mean people have Oscar parties if there's an Aussie nominated. I suppose from time to time there are things, but nothing really like sport—nothing like the Olympics . . . I mean even if you're not really sporty you would be interested in it, but there does seem to be a fair whack of people, and the TV ratings can vouch for that, who are still so curious. Particularly about people like Cathy Freeman, where 90 something percent—that was Australian TV history created by the ratings, whereby people will come together to watch them. Yeah, and I think they feel proud, yeah. In a way that we can't really express our pride. (male, interviewed 4 October 2000, Sydney lounge room)

There is no doubt that the Olympics energized a sense of Australian identity and foregrounded Indigenous issues. The legacy of Sydney 2000, is still a matter of contention, not least the long-term impact of the Freeman moment (as a breakthrough in white-Indigenous relations, or as a comforting cover for ongoing racial oppression; see Bruce and Hallinan 2001). Olympic spectatorship in its many guises, nonetheless issues a paramount invitation to reflect on the state of the host society and provides a framework for the positioning of those who watched, from their different vantage points, as bearers of collective memory.

NOTES

1. The research on which this chapter is based was funded by a 1999–2001 Australian Research Council Large Grant, "Globalization and Local Impacts." The fieldwork involved members of the research team recording their personal observations, conversations with fellow participants at the site, and caught "snatches" of dialogue and a small number of interviews. The research protocol required that neither observer nor observee/interviewee should be personally identified, and only schematic information is provided here, with individuals identified only by a letter and source characteristics.

2. The Indigenous theme was also strongly represented in the following Athens Cultural Olympiad, with Australian Aboriginal cultural artifacts from the Art Gallery of New South Wales sent to Greece in exchange for the Classical Greek items previously sent to Sydney for its Cultural Olympiad.

3. This chapter is concerned primarily with the Summer Olympics. This event has a specific character and history but of course has many features in common with the Winter Olympics, the soccer, rugby, and athletics world cups, and so on. It is important then to appreciate simultaneously both the specificity of the Summer Olympics and the ways in which it resembles and interacts with other mega-media sports events.

4. It should be noted that although media endorsement of Freeman lighting the flame was overwhelming, this view was not universally held. Apart from some, like the Olympic attendee who was quoted as feeling "sick of reading about Cathy Freeman"

because of the blanket coverage of her, there were anecdotally discerned racist undertones pertaining to Freeman's Indigenousness; some also believed it inappropriate for a competing athlete to take this key ceremonial role.

REFERENCES

Boyle, Raymond, and Richard Haynes. 2003. New media sport. In *Sport, media, culture: Global and local dimensions*, ed. Alina Bernstein and Neil Blain. London: Frank Cass.

Bruce, Toni, and Chris Hallinan. 2001. Cathy Freeman: The quest for Australian identity. In *Sport stars: The cultural politics of sporting celebrity*, ed. David L. Andrews and Steven J. Jackson. London and New York: Routledge.

Dayan, Daniel, and Elihu Katz. 1992. *Media events: The live broadcasting of history*. Cambridge, MA: Harvard University Press.

Farred, Grant. 2001. TV time's up: The forgotten Games. *Journal of Sport & Social Issues* 25 (1): 3–5.

Fédération Internationale de Football Association (FIFA). 2002. 41,100 hours of 2002 FIFA World Cup TV coverage in 213 countries. Press Release, November 21.

Fiske, John, Bob Hodge, and Graeme Turner. 1987. *Myths of Oz*. Sydney: Allen & Unwin.

Gardiner, Greg. 2003. "Black" bodies—"White" codes: Indigenous footballers, racism, and the Australian Football League's racial and religious vilification code. In *Sport and postcolonialism*, ed. John Bale and Mike Cronin. Oxford: Berg.

Godwell, Darren J. 2000. The Olympic branding of Aborigines: The 2000 Olympic Games and Australia's indigenous peoples. In *The Olympics at the millennium: Power, politics, and the Games*, ed. Kay Schaffer and Sidonie Smith. New Brunswick, NJ: Rutgers University Press.

Hay, Roy. 2003. The last night of the poms: Australia as a postcolonial sporting society? In *Sport and postcolonialism*, ed. John Bale and Mike Cronin. Oxford: Berg.

Rigney, Daryle. 2003. Sport, indigenous Australians, and invader dreaming: A critique. In *Sport and postcolonialism*, ed. John Bale and Mike Cronin. Oxford: Berg.

Roche, Maurice. 2000. *Mega-events and modernity: Olympics and expos in the growth of global culture*. London and New York: Routledge.

Rose, Ava, and James Friedman. 1997. Television sports as mas(s)culine cult of distraction. In *Out of bounds*, ed. Aaron Baker and Todd Boyd. Bloomington: Indiana University Press.

Rowe, David. 2000a. Cathy Freeman: Live at Stadium Australia, 25 September 2000. *M/C Reviews Feature Issue on the Olympics* 10 (18) October, http://www.api-network.com/mc/ (accessed May 9, 2005), n.p.

———. 2000b. Global media events and the positioning of presence. *Media International Australia incorporating Culture and Policy* 97: 11–21.

———. 2004. *Sport, culture, and the media: The unruly trinity.* 2nd ed. Maidenhead, UK: Open University Press.

Standeven, Joy, and Paul de Knopf. 1999. *Sport tourism.* Champaign, IL: Human Kinetics.

Stevenson, Deborah. 1997. Olympic arts: Sydney 2000 and the Cultural Olympiad. *International Review for the Sociology of Sport* 32(3): 227–38.

———. 1998. The art of the Games: Leisure, tourism, and the Cultural Olympiad. In *Tourism, leisure, sport: Critical perspectives,* ed. David Rowe and Geoffrey Lawrence. Melbourne: Cambridge University Press.

Chapter 13

Korea and Japan 2002

Public Space and Popular Celebration

Soon-Hee Whang

INTRODUCTION

"Football is a serious business. We need to reorientate our thinking to treat Asian soccer as a product which needs to be researched, produced, and marketed on a planned and sustained basis through every available means throughout the continent." These were the words of Peter Velappan (Tomlinson 2005, 132), general secretary of the Asian Football Confederation in December 1996. At that time, Japan and South Korea ranked first and third, respectively, in FIFA/Coca-Cola's rankings, with Saudi Arabia sandwiched in between. The awarding of the 2002 World Cup to Japan and Korea—the first both to be hosted in Asia and, indeed, co-hosted—was a suitable boost to the profile and ambition of those footballing nations. Accordingly, much work has now been carried out on the potential economic and cultural impact of the World Cup upon those national sports cultures (see Horne and Manzenreiter 2002). This has naturally included commentaries on the endemic rivalries between Japan and its former colony, Korea, the corporate base of the sporting culture in both countries, and the demographic and generational shifts represented in the rise in popularity of the Western influence on sport. In this latter context, this chapter focuses on young people's response to Asia's staging of the World Cup finals.

PUBLIC VIEWING—WHY AND HOW

For this chapter, I conducted observations and studies on the World Cup in both Korea and Japan. The research on Korea has been accumulated since the

2001 FIFA Confederations Cup, the so-called World Cup "rehearsal." The research covers the following questions: How did hosting cities prepare for and organize the event? How did citizens participate in and enjoy the preparations? And, how have local communities changed as a consequence of the event?

In Korea, three interviews were held with committee members of the "Red Devils," the national team supporters' organization, before, during, and after the World Cup. Field study also was conducted in stadiums and on the streets of cities such as Seoul, Taegu, and Incheon. After filming the fans in the stadiums and on the streets, interviews were conducted with selected supporters. In Japan, public viewing in sports bars also was researched. This, along with interviews with the KOWOC (Korean World Cup Organizing Committee) and host city World Cup organizing committee officials, provided a variety of viewpoints on the macro system of street support.

As can be seen in Table 13.1, for a variety of reasons street support was far more prevalent in Korea. Moreover, as Table 13.2 demonstrates, viewing of any sort was far more prevalent in Korea, with Koreans watching more of Korea's and other countries' games. From here, this chapter will concentrate on the phenomenon of public viewing in Korea.

FEATURES OF PUBLIC VIEWING IN KOREA

During the games, hundreds of thousands of supporters on the streets and in the stadiums were shouting "Tae! Han! Min! Kuk!" (Republic of Korea!) and "Chacha, cha, cha, cha!" while dancing and stretching their arms upward in a co-ordinated manner to show their encouragement. When the fans yelled "Tae" and "Min," they raised their volume to a deafening level. Then they would hold their arms in front of their chests and clap their hands with the same rhythm. The supporters repeated the same performance over and over again.

These fans were described in the Japanese newspaper, *Asahi Shimbun*, on June 23, 2002, as follows: "Korean supporters had been shouting 'Tae Han Min Kuk' hundreds of times. However, when the penalty shoot-out started just after 6 P.M., they became silent and held their breath for the moment of truth. When the fourth player on the Spanish team missed his penalty kick, the Korean supporters came to life again. As Hong Meong Bo scored to win the game for South Korea, supporters began chanting the 'Tae Han Min Kuk' theme. . . . Around the Kwang Hwa Mun intersection, which became the landmark for Koreans to come and watch the games, some 800,000 street supporters (figure provided by the police agency) had Seoul awash in red. The instant the Korean team secured victory, a drop curtain was pulled down, saying 'Let's Go to Yokohama!' . . . Nearly five million people were reported to have participated in street supporting throughout the country."

TABLE 13.1
World Cup, Korea and Japan, 2002: Viewing and Support Comparison

	Korea	Japan
Match Broadcasts	All 64 matches shown between three terrestrial broadcasters To allow public viewing, FIFA demanded rights fees of 2 to 5 million won (14,800–37,800 Euro) per game over and above those already paid by terrestrial, statellite, and cable broadcasters.	National broadcaster NHK and five private broadcasters showed 40 of the 64 games on terrestrial relay.
Media Attitudes	Focused on public order and kindness to foreigners, as well as cohosting competition with Japan	Anti-hooligan measures information, the Beckham phenomenon
Average Spectator Numbers per Match	39,592 people (32 matches) The total figure for the 64 matches in Korea and Japan waas 2,705,566 people, 2.5% lower than the 2,774,891 of France, 1998.	44,957 people (32 matches)
National Team Result	Reached the semifinals (7 matches)	Reached the last 16 (4 matches)
Professional League	Professional K-League started in 1982 Currently 10 teams	Professional J-League in 1993 Currently 28 teams
National Team Supporter Organization	Name: Red Devils Previous incarnation established in 1995, changed name in 1997	Name: Ultras Nippon Established in 1993 for the U.S. 1994 qualifying rounds

(continued)

TABLE 13.1 (*continued*)

World Cup, Korea and Japan, 2002: Viewing and Support Comparison

	Korea	Japan
Street Support	Scenes of street support broadcast on TV. Central government and host cities actively supported public viewing on the streets and in stadiums other than the match grounds. At 1,868 places nationwide, 2,021 large screens were set up. Aggregate Spectator Numbers over seven matches were 22,400,000(47.7% of the national population of 47,000,000). At the landmark Kwang Hwa Mun intersection, a total of 3,500,000 spectators watched the seven matches.	Public broadcasts mostly banned on public safety grounds; broadcasts at stadiums others than the match grounds partially restricted and street broadcasts prohibited.
Social Phenomena	The emergence of proud young people of the "R (Red Devils) Generation"/"W (World Cup) Generation"—open-minded people in a self-motivated community with dynamic energy The Hiddink syndrome, a phenomenon that temporarily overcame social class, regional, sex, age, and "OB (outside broadcast) network" discrimination More so than the game itself, because of interest in players' images and sexual appeal, both Korea and Japan saw a dramatic increase in female spectators. In Korea, interest in players concentrated on Korean players, whereas young Japanese, influenced by the media, spread their interest among various teams' players.	Symbolic consumption of the idolized "Beckham brand" in Japanese, "Beckham-sama" ("Sir Beckham"); the differentiated consumption of the "dashing" "Prince Ilhan," in Japanese, "Ilhan-ohji" The uniforms of each country worn as "costume play" support, for example, today in England, tomorrow Argentina The feverish competition to attract team bases—84 communities vied for 28 camps

Source: compiled by author

TABLE 13.2
Proportion of People Who Watched Their Own/Other Countries' Matches at the Stadium/on TV

	Watched other Countries' matches	Mostly watched only own country's matches	Watched few matches	Other/No response	Total
Korea	73.0%	25.0%	2.0%	0.0%	100.0%
Japan	66.0%	17.0%	12.0%	5.0%	100.0%

Source: Korea-Japan Cohosting Public Survey Choson Ilbo Mainichi Shimbun, carried out July 6–7, 2002 (*Choson Ilbo,* July 10, 2002)

Note: Survey method: Nationwide telephone survey of 1,011 people (Korea) and 1,043 (Japan) over twenty years of age, random cluster sample proportional by region

On June 26, the *Asahi* gave this description of the South Korea-Germany game the previous day: "This was the first time for the Seoul stadium to stage a match featuring the home team. When the game was over, 60,000 'Red Devils' gave encouraging applause to the players who were squatting down on the ground. Immediately after a signal from a supporter gong, the Red Devils rediscovered their voice and kept shouting 'Tae! Han! Min! Kuk!' . . . The center of Seoul, from the city hall to the Kwang Hwa Mun intersection, was transformed into a soccer stadium on June 25 and was brimming with over one million supporters. After the game, they continued to chorus 'Arirang' and the national anthem. . . . Their applause and voices echoed throughout the downtown, which was quite a spectacular view. Entranced supporters shouted at the highest possible volume, with innumerable hands rising upward." (see figures 13.1 and 13.4) As South Korea advanced to the second round, and then from the quarter-finals to the semi-finals, the drama inched closer to a crescendo.

Figure 13.1 As an example of the sheer scale of Korean street support, for the Korea-U.S. match on June 10, 200,000 people gathered in the square in front of City Hall (near the Kwang Hwa Mun, a larger street support site).
Source: Chosun Ilbo, June 11 2002.

On June 25, more than 7 million people reportedly participated in street supporting for the game against Germany. This was the largest public gathering of this scale since the pro-democracy demonstrations of the 1980s.

Where does this public passion and intoxication come from? What kind of pleasure do fans seek to gain from supporting on the streets? By so doing, how is such a transformation of body cultures initiated? Does street supporting change the meanings of space and time, thereby producing a new culture? This chapter aims to analyze the mechanism of the interactive transformation of body cultures of football supporters. The structures as well as practices that make a transformation possible also will be examined.

STREET VIEWING AS "SPORTS TOURISM"

Supporting on the Streets

A notable phenomenon was seen in Japan during the FIFA 2002 World Cup. A number of male soccer fans began to imitate the hairstyle of England's captain, David Beckham, who had gained enormous popularity among the Japanese people.

It was even reported by the *Asahi Shimbun* on June 23, 2002, that at a private school in Tokyo, "on the day the Japanese national team plays, a traditional greeting for the end of class was arranged as 'Stand up! Attention! Nippon (Japan) cha cha cha'." Japanese supporters shout "Nippon cha cha cha" to cheer their national team, thus the rhythm has been unconsciously imprinted on their minds and applied freely on different occasions. For example, when supporting foreign football teams, they say "Brazil cha cha cha" or "Espanior [Spain] cha cha cha." When it comes to the Korean national team, they shout "Nippon! Korea!" This could be thought of as a "habitus of supporters' calls," following Bourdieu's (1977) theory.

At the alma maters of members of the Japan national team, fans were even more enthusiastic. For example, the *Asahi* reported on June 10, 2002, that at the elementary school that Takayuki Suzuki attended as a child, approximately 300 children and parents of the school's junior football team watched the game on a screen set up in the school gymnasium. In addition, about 100 alumnae of the Hitachi Technical High School Football Club, the school from which Suzuki had graduated, gathered at the local chamber of commerce to watch the game. At the University of Tsukuba, from which Masashi Nakayama (a center forward in Japan's national team) had graduated, the *Asahi* recounted on June 5, 2002, that "students enjoyed the game through a relay broadcast, which was being projected on screens in the cafeterias of the schools of physical education and art."

These kinds of events were experienced throughout the country. Because the school from which a representative player graduated has a wide range of supporters' networks, junior students of those schools, children of football club teams to which national players had once belonged, and their parents became wrapped up in the World Cup. Producing space for the specific purpose of enjoying public viewing became a crucial form of participation in the global event. Japanese fans attempted to foster intimacy with individual players not only by supporting the national team but also by taking advantage of places the player associated with as a youth. Furthermore, they tried to nurture and enjoy the solidarity of this intimate relationship.

Even if fans had no personal or institutional relationship with national team players, many of them enjoyed being keen supporters. During the World Cup, municipal and prefectural governments set up numerous places for public viewing so that people who could not buy match tickets could watch the games with many fellow supporters. The public viewing stations that were established in public gyms, cultural centers, and the chambers of commerce became an important place to watch live broadcasts of the games.

TRAVELING THROUGH TIME AND SPACE

In Japan, public viewing was partly restricted; specifically, street viewing was banned. It was reported in the *Asahi Shimbun* on June 11, 2002, that "the municipal administrators of Aichi and Saitama suspended public viewing," and "they were fed up with uncontrolled public viewers," since "the over-zealous fans crowded into the stadium after the Japan-Russia game made it difficult to maintain public safety." Another newspaper, the *Nikkan Sports*, of June 11 was more scathing about the fans, stating "enthusiastic young supporters cause disturbance," "people went astray," and "the police tried to deter them." That the Japanese media attributed the suspension of several public viewing activities to deviant behavior, especially by young fans, has to do with an emerging antagonism between "young supporters making a disturbance" and "the police trying to control them." The Japanese media occasionally labeled excited young Japanese supporters as "Japanese hooligans." To avoid conflict between the two sides, and any uncontrollable situation in a public space, the authorities decided to suspend public viewing.

In Korea, on the contrary, the scale of public viewing snowballed during the World Cup. In addition to existing electronic bulletin boards on buildings and screens set up by local authorities, which totaled 2,021, dump trucks carrying large viewing screens were mobilized. These screens, provided by companies eager for advertising exposure, added an unknown number to the already large arsenal of public viewing spaces.

Korean fans, just like their Japanese counterparts, were excited to the extent that they climbed up on public transportation vehicles and shouted support for the national team. However, the police and security guards generally tolerated people who were in this state of extreme excitement. The security personnel preferred to wait for the supporters to climb down and even hugged them while they guided them away. The media broadcast such behavior, but there was no mention of it being a "disturbance" or "being deviant." In fact, they portrayed street supporters in a positive light.

What made the two countries' newspaper discourses so different? In Japan, the guidelines for one's public behavior are found in daily social life, and excitement that goes beyond a certain level is considered in a negative light. World Cup matches were considered "stand-alone," with the emphasis on the football, on individual national team matches, followed by a quick return to normal behavior. Following the example of Japanese hero Hidetoshi Nakata, a cool appearance was considered desirable.

In Korea, excitement right after the game is not deemed "deviant." Rather, it is merely part of the larger international football festival, with the emphasis on the mega-event. Freeing oneself of the shackles of normal social behavior was tolerated and in fact encouraged, creating a fun, "hot" atmosphere, compared to the "cool" of Japan.

Therefore, the same type of behavior is labeled differently in Korea and Japan. While "Japanese hooligan" was used to refer to the excited Japanese young supporters, none of the Korean media contemplated describing their local fans as being "Korean hooligans."

As the Korean team continued to progress through the tournament, the number of supporters mushroomed (see figure 13.2). Japanese newspapers described them as young people, supporters, and civilians and inserted pictures of the rapturous crowds. Although the young, energetic crowds that dominated public places might have caught the eye of most readers, virtually all social demographics from the young to the old were cheering the team on the streets. Moreover, between one-half and two-thirds of the street supporters were women, and 40 percent of the Red Devils' members are women (Kim 2002).

They purchased team uniforms, painted their faces and bodies, and prepared various supporting goods. Street supporters, as though they were going on a day trip, brought picnic blankets, hats, sunglasses, snacks, and drinks and headed for the public viewing location. The space for public viewing became something of a tourist attraction.

This behavior of boisterous merrymaking meant two things to them: watching a game, and enjoying a short trip, or, in other words, "sport tourism"

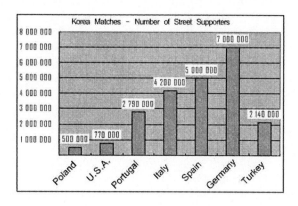

Figure 13.2   Korea Matches—Numbers of Street Supporters
Source: Sege Ilbo, July 2, 2002

(Standeven and De Knop 1998). That street supporting enables people to enjoy sport entertainment and sightseeing makes the fans' performance more meaningful. Street fans find a special space far removed, if not always physically, from where they live and work in the predictable rhythms of everyday life.

This special trip, unlike an ordinary trip that is a temporary movement of relatively long distance to seek something new, takes probably only ten minutes by public transportation. However, the experience during the journey is quite different from their daily lives. The time and space associated with street supporting can provide people with an extraordinary experience of excitement.

During the World Cup, street supporters threw themselves into the special settings of this global sporting event, seeking an extraordinary experience available only for a fixed period, and then they returned to their daily lives. As the fans changed back to regular commuters, the symbolic space of public viewing became just a street for public transport.

THE TRANSFORMATION OF SYMBOLIC MEANINGS: STRUCTURE OF THE STREET SUPPORTERS' BODY CULTURES IN KOREAN STREET SUPPORTING

To understand the body cultures of street supporters, it is necessary to examine the structures and practices of individuals that constitute these particular cultures:

the content of the street supporting; the way the meanings attached to space changed as time passed; and the differentiation strategy of street supporters' body cultures. Then, taking the practices of individual supporters into account, this analysis will apply Goffman's (1959) dramaturgical perspective and Bourdieu's (1977) notion of habitus, which can be considered suitable analytical tools for the purpose of this study.

By analyzing the way fans communicate and interact with one another among the staged gathering of individuals on the streets, the techniques of bodies can be unveiled. Rather than verbal communications and "expressions given," "expressions given off" (Goffman 1959, 4), which include broader types of behavior in nature that others can interpret symbolically, are the more appropriate conceptual emphases for this research. Assessing the changes of "the definition of the situation" (Goffman 1959, 3–4) as time goes by and "the arts of impression management" (Goffman 1959, 208–37) in certain situations contributes to understanding the strategy of street supporters who create and share the meanings of the symbolic space.

The changing meanings over time can be categorized into the following four stages: "symbolic transformation," "supporting," "recurrence," and "symbolic reformation."

First Stage: Symbolic Transformation of Space

The first stage appears during the preparation period. Street supporters arrived in town at around 10 A.M. to wait for the games that began at 3:30 or 8:30 P.M. Prior to the kickoff, the streets were packed with fans. To avoid traffic jams and congestion, public traffic access was temporarily suspended in some areas so that people could travel more smoothly. Police and security guards were mobilized to control the traffic, and ambulances were carefully deployed.

Public screens and relay broadcasting systems were set up, official sponsors of the World Cup prepared stages for their advertisements, and singers and cheerleaders got ready to give performances. Street vendors started selling items such as national flags, horns, and uniforms (see figure 13.3). People who had gathered on the streets rushed to buy food, drinks, and products to support their team, repeatedly practiced their chants and cheering, and took part in various entertainment. The event was a carefully stage-managed affair involving many different actors.

The way in which supporters define the public space and "main involvement," as well as "side involvement" (Goffman 1963, 43), of the street supporters varies. As time goes by, they begin to exchange "expressions given off" with one another with the intention to show that they are ready to support their team. Both the macrostructural and microindividual factors establish a basis for the second stage, "the space of supporting."

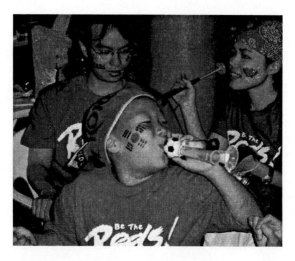

Figure 13.3   A boy dressed in supporter's items.
Source: Author's photograph.

Second Stage: Space of Supporting

When the game is broadcast on a public screen, the streets begin to function just like a soccer stadium. In this process, the way in which street supporters participate in the event and interact with each other is transformed from a "main involvement" to a "side involvement." The former tends to monopolize the attention of street supporters, leading them to became absorbed deeply into the game. The latter helps keep in order the supporters' behaviors that the main involvement previously induced (Goffman 1963).

For example, the initial role (the main involvement) of the police and security guards in the first stage is to maintain public order. However, in the second stage, their main occupation involves observing the game. Law enforcement becomes no longer necessary, since the spectators are so engrossed in the game. Maintaining public order thus becomes the secondary concern for security personnel. There also is a change in priorities for street vendors. Their main involvement was initially selling merchandise. In the second stage, however, watching the game replaces their primary objective.

The change for street supporters is rather obvious. During the first stage, they behave differently, such as dining, joining in amusement activities, and asking other fans to write their wishes and names on the national flag. In the next stage, their primary objective consists solely of watching the soccer game.

Supporters on the streets form and then share a common "definition of the situation." This space, which has been carefully produced, imposes rules as a "dominant involvement" (Goffman 1963, 44), under which everyone must watch the game. Directed by the Red Devils' commanders, street supporters begin to sing "Arirang" and repeatedly shout "Tae! Han! Min! Kuk!" In this sense, street supporting is voluntary as well as involuntary. Enforcement exists to the extent that people tend to regard being quiet or supporting in their own way as inappropriate in this particular setting.

It must be emphasized that people are involved in this setting to a very high degree. If they do not express strong support, they may suffer Bourdieu's "symbolic violence." Symbolic violence is differentiated from actual violence in that depending on the state of one's symbols, such as language, values, way of thinking, school grades, and so on, one may be socially sanctioned. For example, one may be made to be ashamed of or to develop a complex over one's differences from arbitrary culture (Bourdieu 1977; Bourdieu and Passeron 1977).

In the environment of Korean street support, there are examples of social sanction arising from people not cheering. During the Korea-Spain match of June 22, 2002, Mr. and Mrs. K. were street supporters at the Kwang Wha Mun intersection. They wanted to chant "Tae! Han! Min! Kuk!" and sing "Victory to Korea" and the rock arrangement of the national anthem along with everyone else. But, as Mr. K. explained, "I desperately wanted to cheer for the team. However, I was embarrassed, and simply couldn't. On that, the people around us looked down us as if to say 'why aren't you cheering?' Their attitude was 'why won't you cheer together?' Those glances and attitudes were truly horrible, and hurt us" (Cho 2002, 210). In such a place, the insults, humiliation, and unpleasant feelings that they suffered by not cheering are a form of symbolic violence.

However, the reasons for Mr. K. not cheering ran much deeper than mere surface shame. In the same place in 1987, Mr. K. was a commanding officer in the military police arrayed against the pro-democracy demonstrators. During the demonstrations, the students defying the police were constantly singing the national anthem and other songs. Five years later, when thousands of students outnumbered the police, the national anthem was again sung with gusto, making the police break out in a cold sweat. Thus, for Mr. K., the national anthem became an object of fear.

Recalling those painful memories, and despite the ebullient mood around him, Mr. K. felt a deep sadness, and he was simply unable to sing the national anthem joyously and lightheartedly. But after Korea's victory, when the street was enveloped in excitement, he was at last able to do so. Alongside the young people who he had once feared, with his daughter on his shoulders and with tears rolling down his cheeks, he sang the national anthem and conquered his demons.

Different Pleasures in
Street Support and Stadium Support

Street supporting gives a different type of pleasure than supporting in the stadium. Street fans are unlikely to maintain a normal physical distance between other fans, since the restricted public spaces for street supporting attract millions of people. As the Korean team continued to win, the density of supporters per viewing space soared. However, for fans watching in the stadium, the physical distance remained consistent throughout the tournament due to the predetermined seating arrangements.

The physical distance between individuals is socially and culturally determined. This is not the case for street supporters, because they are obliged to accept an abnormally close distance to other people. Under such circumstances, one's personal territory is regularly intruded upon. In this sense, street supporters have no choice but to expose themselves to the surveillance of others, which compels them to act as fanatical enthusiasts. Abandoning the normal and then awakening and articulating the new body culture is a transformative process hugely attractive to the eager supporters who gather on the streets.

Figure 13.4   Korean Supporters Shouting "Tae! Han! Min! Kuk!"
Source: Author's photograph.

THE RE-FORMATION OF SYMBOLIC SPACES AND
ITS ACCUMULATION: DIFFERENTIATION STRATEGY OF
STREET SUPPORTERS

The body cultures of street supporters and those in the stadiums are different not only in their physical distance but also in their performance. Supporters in the stadium regard themselves as "the twelfth player" and believe that their support can affect the result of the game. Therefore, they try to boost the morale of their team and jeer the opposing team. On the other hand, street fans acknowledge that they cannot directly influence the game. Instead, they seek to maximize their enjoyment and excitement. A quasi-stadium is produced in the public space through the effort of those street supporters, in which they attempt to reach their own climax away from the stadium.

Street fans bring a greater variety of supporting goods to the game than those spectators in the stadium. They carry gongs, bugles, bottles, and balloons, with the simple objective of making louder noise. Street supporters know that in the stadium cheers and applause echo effectively around the grounds, while on the streets such noise can have no effect on the outcome of the contest. Street supporters generate a collective enthusiasm, which is likely to enhance a sense of solidarity as well as national identity.

Third Stage: Space of Recurrence

After the end of the game, the supporting space is normalized to a place of regular transportation of people. This period occurs when street fans return to their daily lives (Whang 2002). Public screens and stages are withdrawn, underpasses that were closed during the match are reopened, and police and security personnel return to their normal duties. Vendors wind down their businesses, and the spectators, some of whom enjoy the atmosphere of the festive occasion for a while, gather their belongings and go home. Many street fans then voluntarily participate in cleaning the streets. For example, cleaning the Kwang Hwa Mun Square usually takes seven to eight hours. At the start of the World Cup, cleaning took a similar amount of time, but as street support numbers ballooned, the time needed to clean up fell! For the Korea-Spain quarterfinal of June 22, 2002, 800,000 people packed the square. After the game, 260 cleaners and 35 trucks converged and collected 240 tons of garbage, forty times the amount of a regular day. But with the help of the Red Devils, the whole job was finished in one and a half hours. They certainly earned the nickname "the human vacuum cleaners" (Cho 2002).

Figure 13.5   Korean supporters cleaning up after the match.
Source: Author's photograph.

However, cleaning the streets also has ceremonial implications. From the outside, cleaning can be seen as a highly functional activity, but to the participants, pursuing this kind of pleasure is highly symbolic in nature. First, it represents the closing of the day's event and, second, moving forward to the next stage. The fans can enjoy acting as initiators of a new stage and ending the previous one. The game itself is finished by the players, but the broader spectacle of support and celebration is finished off by those cleaning up—on their own terms (see figure 13.5).

Fourth Stage: Symbolic Re-formation of a Multistructural Space

After the game has ended, the streets return to normal, as though nothing out of the ordinary had occurred. However, for street supporters, this familiar public space after the carnival is not exactly the same as it was, both culturally and symbolically. Through the experience of having enthusiastically supported the national team, people formed meanings and collective memories attached to this specific time and space. The reformation of such public space has taken place periodically throughout Korean history.

For example, South Korea experienced large-scale pro-democracy demonstrations in the 1980s on the same streets. This provided Koreans gathering on the streets with a special significance associated with democratization, a time of strife, solidarity, and national identity (Whang 2002). After the 2002 FIFA

World Cup, enthusiastic street supporting has given two additional meanings to the streets: the scene of a global event and the pleasure of supporting. Consequently, this familiar public space, which is essentially the place that reinforced a sense of solidarity and national identity, has awakened multiple meanings for the Korean people, and it is defined in this study as a "space of a symbolic re-formation" in a cultural as well as a symbolic sense.

The people who led this re-formation by public viewing were those between the ages of ten and twenty-nine—those who did not participate in the pro-democracy demonstrations in the 1980s. After the 2002 FIFA World Cup ended, the symbolic status of these young people became high in Korea. This is the birth of "the proud young generations." They are called the "W generation" or the "R generation." The letters refer to the World Cup generations and the Red Devil generations, respectively. Major characteristics of those generations are found in "self-motivated community," "dynamic energy," and "open mind." They act voluntarily, organize a community, and engage themselves in it with much enthusiasm, and in doing so, they have rediscovered their national flag and the "red complex" of their national identity.

In this sense, the birth of "proud young generations" coincides with the birth of "farsighted, old generations," people over thirty who have been liberated from frustrating contemporary history. Instead of endlessly labeling youth as the "computer generation," the "closed-room generation," and the "generation of irresponsibility," these older people have come to see youth in a more positive light, rechristening them as the "W generation" and so on. Largely due to the World Cup, they have widened their perspectives and opened their minds beyond closed, nationalistic worldviews.

When they look back on the World Cup, all those who participated in public viewing happily recollect that precious time of the victory as a brilliant experience. They then imagine slipping out of their daily lives and reverting to that special time and space to watch the game. This destination of pleasure is unforgettable for Korean street supporters. The organizers of the finals had their political motives. The corporate sponsors may well have been very satisfied at the worldwide exposure of their products. Asian sport was profiled well in the honorable performance of the Japanese side and the outstanding progress to the semifinals of their Korean counterparts. But as this chapter has demonstrated, perhaps the most significant impact of the event in Korea at least was the popular celebration on the streets. Too often, Bourdieu's (1977) notion of habitus is used to describe a rigid, oversocialized framework in which human agents have little room to maneuver. Yet part of the definition of habitus is its constant remaking. The supporters on the streets in Seoul and at other Korean sites have shown how the habitus of the public culture of Korea can be challenged and reconstituted on the basis of the sports event.

REFERENCES

Bourdieu, Pierre. 1977. *Outline of a theory of practice.* Cambridge: Cambridge University Press.

Bourdieu, Pierre, and Jean-Claude Passeron. 1977. *Reproduction in education, society, and culture.* London: Sage.

Cho, Shin Jae, ed. 2002. *Woldukap—uridure iyagi: Yuwolu bulgun hyokmyoung* (The World Cup—Our stories. June's Red Revolution). Seoul: Wolgantyosunsa.

Goffman, Erving. 1959. *The presentation of self in everyday life.* New York:Doubleday Anchor.

———. 1963. *Behavior in public places: Notes on the social organization of gatherings.* New York: The Free Press.

Horne, John, and Wolfram Manzenreiter, eds. 2002. *Japan, Korea, and the 2002 World Cup.* London: Routledge.

Kim, Hyun Mee,. 2002. 2002 nen warudokappu no "joseika" to josei "fandamu" (2002 World Cup "feminization" and "female fandom"). *2002 inside out: Korea-Japan symposium: Beyond the FIFA World Cup shared event, different experiences—Globalization state gender media and cultural studies.* Seoul: Yonsei Youth and Cultural Studies Center.

Standeven, Joy, and Paul De Knop. 1998. *Sport tourism.* Champaign, IL: Human Kinetics.

Tomlinson, Alan. 2005. *Sport and leisure cultures.* Minneapolis: University of Minnesota Press.

Whang, Soon-Hee. 2002. Warudokappu sakka koria japan ni hikareru shintai—ouen suru kotono kairaku (Bodies attracted to the 2002 FIFA World Cup Korea–Japan—The pleasure in supporting). In *Ajia shinseiki 4. Kofuku: Hen'yo suru raifusatairu.* (Asian New Century Vol. 4: Happiness: Changing lifestyles), ed. Aoki Tamotsu et al. Iwanami Shoten, 167–80.

ACKNOWLEDGMENT

This chapter draws on fieldwork and projects that are also featured in Whang, Soon-Hee (2004), "Football, fashion, and fandom: Sociological reflections on the 2002 World Cup and collective memories in Korea," in John Horne and Wolfran Manzanreiter eds., *Football goes East: Business,culture, and the people's game in China, Japan, and South Korea.* London: Routledge, 2004.

Contributors

Eduardo P. Archetti, who died in June 2005, was Professor of Social Anthropology at the University of Oslo, Norway. An Argentinean, he brought a powerful analytical intellect to bear upon numerous everyday and popular cultural forms. His main publications were *Guinea Pigs: Food, Symbol and Conflict of Knowledge in Ecuador* (1997), *Masculinities: Football, Polo and the Tango in Argentina* (1999), and *El potrero, la pista y el ring: las patrias del deporte argentino* (2001). His interests embraced numerous cultural forms and practices; one of his last publications, edited jointly with Noel Dyck, was *Sport, Dance and Embodied Identities* (2003).

Claire Brewster is a part-time lecturer in American history at the University of Newcastle, and has a research post at the University of Nottingham. Her research interests are in twentieth century Mexico, especially the social and political work of Mexican intellectuals (1968–1995). She has published a book on the Mexican Student Movement and its aftermath, *Responding to Crisis in Contemporary Mexico*. She is currently working on the salient features of sport in twentieth-century Mexico, and the use of sport in State cultural projects, leading up to the staging of the 1968 Olympic Games.

Keith Brewster is Lecturer in Latin American History at the University of Newcastle, UK. He leads undergraduate and postgraduate modules on Latin American history and co-convenes the university's Americas Research Group. His research interests are varied, and include a monograph and articles on the political history of twentieth-century Mexico. More recently he has focused on the political manipulation of sport by the post-revolutionary State in Mexico and his publications in this area include articles in special editions of *The International Journal of the History of Sport and Patterns of Prejudice*.

Robert Edelman is Professor of Russian History and the History of Sport at the University of California, San Diego. A former sportswriter and radio commentator, Edelman published two books and numerous articles on Imperial Russian history before the appearance of *Serious Fun: A History of Spectator Sports in the USSR* (Oxford UP, 1993) which won the annual book awards of the Amateur Athletic Foundation of Los Angeles and the North American Society of Sports Historians. He is presently writing a history of the Spartak Moscow football team before, during and after Soviet power. He lives in Solana Beach California with three children, two dogs and one wife.

Robert Gordon is Senior Lecturer in Italian at the University of Cambridge and a Fellow of Gonville and Caius College. His recent publications include *Culture, Censorship and the State in 20th-Centurty Italy* (co-editor, Oxford, 2005) and A Difficult Modernity. *An Introduction to 20th-Century Italian Literature* (London, 2005).

Allen Guttmann began publishing as an Americanist but shifted to sports studies in 1973. His first sports-related book was *From Ritual to Record* (1978, 2004). In addition to the Olympic studies cited in the text, his other books include *Sport Spectators* (1986), *A Whole New Ball Game* (1988), *Women's Sports* (1991), *Games and Empires* (1994), *The Erotic in Sports* (1996), *Japanese Sports* (with Lee Thompson, 2001), and the three-volume *International Encyclopedia of Women and Sports* (with Karen Christensen and Gertrud Pfister, 2001). His most recent book is *Sports: The First Five Millennia* (2004), a social history of the world's sports.

Chris Kennett obtained his doctorate from Loughborough University in the field of sport and leisure policy. He is head of research and training at the Olympic Studies Centre (CEO-UAB) and associate lecturer in the Department of Sociology at the Universitat Autònoma de Barcelona (UAB). He also lectures on the International Programme at La Salle University, Barcelona. His research interests have focused on the impacts of the Olympic Games and he has been published in the areas of sports management and Olympic studies. Currently he is undertaking research into social integration and sport.

John London is Reader in the Drama Department of Goldsmiths College, University of London. His books include *Reception and Renewal in Modern Spanish Theatre* (MHRA, 1997), an anthology of performance texts entitled *The Unknown Federico García Lorca* (Atlas, 1996) and *Theatre under the Nazis* (Manchester University Press, 2000) which he edited. He has also co-edited two books on Catalan theatre and is the author of studies on fascist literature, art and public spectacle.

Tony Mason, until his retirement, was Professor at de Montfort University. His books include *Association Football and English Society 1863-1915* (Harvester Press 1980), *Sport in Britain* (Faber 1988), *Passion of the People? Football in South America* (Verso 1995) and his edited volume *Sport in Britain: A Social History* (Cambridge University Press 1989). His recent publications include *100 Years of Football—The FIFA Centennial Book* (2004, with Pierre Lanfranchi, Christiane Eisenberg and Alfred Wahl), and an article on the England versus Hungary football match in 1953, in *Sport in History* (Winter 2003/4).

Miquel de Moragas Spà is Professor of Communication at the Universitat Autònoma de Barcelona (UAB) and Director of the Olympic Studies Centre (CEO-UAB) and the Institute of Communication (InCom-UAB). Since 1995, he has coordinated the International Chair in Olympism (IOC-UAB). He has published on the cultural and media coverage of the Olympic Games, the impacts of the Games, and the development of Olympic Studies. He is author of the books *Los Juegos de la Comunicación* (Fundesco, 1992); *The Keys to Success* (Servei de Publicacions de la UAB, 1995); *Television in the Olympics* (Libbey, 1995); and *Barcelona: l'herència dels Jocs* (Planeta, 2002).

John J. MacAloon is Professor and Academic Associate Dean, Social Sciences Graduate Division at the University of Chicago. An anthropologist and historian, he has conducted fieldwork on the Olympic Games and Olympic Movement for nearly forty years. He is author of the celebrated *This Great Symbol: Pierre de Coubertin and the Origins of the Modern Olympic Games*, a new edition of which will appear in 2006, as well as of dozens of other scholarly papers and edited books on the cultural politics of international sport. An executive committee member of the IOC 2000 Reform Commission and a founding member of the Olympic Museum Research Council, he has advised Olympic bid committees, Olympic Games organizing committees, and National Olympic Committees around the globe.

David Rowe is Director of the Cultural Industries and Practices Research Centre (CIPS) at The University of Newcastle, Australia. He is widely published in academic contexts, and a regular commentator on social and cultural issues in print, broadcast and online media. His books include *Globalization and Sport: Playing the World* (co-authored, 2001, Sage), *Sport, Culture and the Media: The Unruly Trinity,* and an accompanying edited collection *Critical Readings: Sport, Culture and the Media* (both 2004, Open University Press). His main research interests concern culture and social relations, including the tabloid press and its construction of popular ideologies and identities.

Deborah Stevenson has researched and published extensively in the areas of urban sociology and cultural policy studies. Her sole authored research books are: *Cities and Urban Cultures* (2003); *Agendas in Place: Cultural Planning for Cities and Regions* (1998); and *Art and Organisation: Making Australian Cultural Policy* (2000). In 2004 she co-edited a special issue of the *International Journal of Cultural Policy* on urban space and the uses of culture and is currently completing *Tourist Cultures* (with Stephen Wearing) for Sage, UK. She is Deputy Head of the School of Social Sciences at The University of Newcastle, Australia.

Alan Tomlinson is Professor of Leisure Studies at the University of Brighton, UK, where he leads the Sport and Leisure Cultures area, is Head of the Chelsea School Research Centre, and deputy chair of the university's Research Degrees Committee. He has published many articles and book chapters, and has edited and/or authored more than 20 works on sport, leisure and consumption. From 2000–2003/4 Professor Tomlinson edited the *International Review for the Sociology of Sport*. His book *Sport and Leisure Cultures* (University of Minnesota Press) was published in 2005. His current research interests focus upon the construction of the sporting spectacle.

Soon-Hee Whang is Associate Professor of Sociology in the Institute of Social Sciences, University of Tsukuba, Japan. She is a board member of the Japan Society of Sociology Association (2005–2007). As a specialist in the sociology of sports, culture and education, she has published many articles and book chapters. She received the academic award of the Korean Association of Japanology for her book, *Japanese Elite High Schools—A Social History of School Culture and the Alumni Association*—(Sekaisisousha, 1998, in Japanese). Her current research interests focus upon the reconstruction of the sporting body, understood from the perspective of a reflexive sociology.

Christopher Young is Senior Lecturer in German in the Faculty of Modern Languages, University of Cambridge, and a Fellow of Pembroke College. He has authored/edited seven books on German language, literature and culture, and is currently engaged on a monograph on the 1972 Munich Olympics. He has been a Fellow of the Alexander von Humboldt Foundation (in Cologne, Germany). With Alan Tomlinson, and Andrei Markovits (University of Michigan), he edited a special issue of *American Behavioral Scientist* (2003), on the theme of sport and cultural space.

Index

SUNY series on Sport, Culture, and Social Relations
CL Cole and Michael A. Messner, editors